Taking the long view
A study of
longitudinal documentary

Richard Kilborn

Manchester University Press

Manchester and New York

*distributed in the United States exclusively
by Palgrave Macmillan*

Published by Manchester University Press
Oxford Road, Manchester M13 9NR, UK
and Room 400, 175 Fifth Avenue, New York, NY 10010, USA
www.manchesteruniversitypress.co.uk

Distributed in the United States exclusively by
Palgrave Macmillan, 175 Fifth Avenue, New York,
NY 10010, USA

Distributed in Canada exclusively by
UBC Press, University of British Columbia, 2029 West Mall,
Vancouver, BC, Canada V6T 1Z2

British Library Cataloguing-in-Publication Data
A catalogue record for this book is available from the British Library

Library of Congress Cataloging-in-Publication Data applied for

PN
1992.8
.D6
K55
2010

ISBN   978 0 7190 7864 4 hardback
ISBN   978 0 7190 7865 1 paperback

First published 2010

Typeset by Special Edition Pre-press Services
www.special-edition.co.uk
Printed in Great Britain
by MPG Books Group, UK

For my granddaughters
Isobella Mary
and
Alexandra Grace

Contents

Acknowledgements

I would like to thank all those who have helped in the preparation of this book. First and foremost I would like to thank the long doc filmmakers themselves for taking time out from busy production schedules to talk to me about the experience of producing these works. My particular thanks go to Michael Apted, to Barbara and Winfried Junge, and last but not least to Rainer Hartleb, who was kind enough to escort me round some of the locations where *The Children of Jordbrö* series was filmed.

As ever I have benefited from discussing some of the wider issues involved in long doc production with other academics working in the documentary field. I am particularly grateful to John Corner and Brian Winston for the encouragement they have given me. I am also indebted to the organisers of the 2008 *Visible Evidence* documentary studies conference held at the University of Lincoln for having had the courage to devote one 'strand' of the event to discussing the long doc phenomenon.

I would also like to acknowledge the support given by friends and colleagues at the University of Stirling during the writing of this book. I would like in particular to thank John Izod for some valuable comments on the original manuscript and Oron Joffe for help in the formatting of the work. I am also grateful to the AHRC for providing the funds that enabled me to carry out some of the initial research on the project.

My thanks to Manchester University Press and to Matthew Frost and his team for seeing this project through to its conclusion.

Note on availability of recordings and online material

DVD or VHS recordings of all the documentaries covered in this book can currently be obtained from the sources listed below. Film distribution companies and broadcasting organisations are constantly seeking to maximise the commercial potential of their products, so readers may discover that they can now access the films in question via additional outlets and in alternative forms. The information provided below provides a rough guide to what is available at present, and readers are advised to conduct their own Internet searches to check whether more recordings have become available since this book went to print.

The *Seven Up* series is currently available in the following versions:

- The *Up* series (*7 Up*; *7 plus 7*; *21 Up*; *28 Up*; *35 Up*; *42 Up*): Distributed by First Run Features. Format: 6-DVD box set (Region 1). DVD release date: September 2007. Run time: 710 minutes.
- *7–49 Up* (*7 Up*; *7 plus 7*; *21 Up*; *28 Up*; *35 Up*; *42 Up*; *49 Up*): Distributed by Network. Format: 6-DVD box set (Region 2). DVD release date: February 2009. Run time: 500 minutes.
- *The Children of Golzow* (*Die Kinder von Golzow*) is available in a three-box DVD set (made up of 18 DVDs), which contains the work in its entirety. It is also available in a VHS version (10 cassettes) covering the films made in the period 1961–2002. Further details on availability of recordings can be obtained from: absolut Medien (Berlin) (www.absolutmedien.de).
- *The Children of Jordbrö* (*Barnen från Jordbrö*) is available in a DVD

version distributed under the title *Pizzorna frân Jordbrö*. This is a 4-DVD box set comprising all the Jordbrö films. For more information on where to obtain these discs contact: Olympia Filmproduktion HB, 11825 Stockholm (olympiafilm@telia.com).

- *Born in the USSR* (*7 Up, 14 Up and 21 Up*) and *Born in South Africa* (*7 Up, 14 Up and 21 Up*) are available as DVD recordings from Granada Media (www.granadamedia.com/international).

In addition to the recordings of the works themselves, long docs – especially Michael Apted's *Seven Up* series – have frequently been the subject of debate in online forums and discussion groups. Just insert the title of one of the better-known long docs in your web search engine and see how many results you come up with.

Introduction

The origins of this book go back to the autumn of 2005 when I attended a joint presentation given by Michael Apted and Granada Television producer Jemma Jupp at the Sheffield International Documentary Film Festival. Apted had recently completed the seventh film (*49 Up*) in his well-known *Seven Up* series and used the occasion to reflect back on more than 40 years' involvement in a project that is perhaps the best-known example of a 'longitudinal documentary' (which for the sake of brevity I shall from now on refer to as 'long doc(s)'). In the course of this presentation Apted was at pains to emphasise his special commitment to the *Seven Up* project ('It's the centre of my working life. It gives a continuity to my life'). Despite his now having lived for several decades in the United States, he was also keen to underline what he perceived to be the complementarity between his career as a well-known maker of feature films and his documentary work. As he put it: 'The blending of documentary and fiction became in a sense my calling card. It's how I got jobs.' The other point that Apted sought to emphasise at Sheffield was the role played by Granada Television in developing and nurturing the project. By the time that the fourth programme in the series (*28 Up*) had been made, it was clear that the formula that Apted and Granada had developed for *Seven Up* was proving highly successful, so – like any commercially minded television company – Granada began to consider ways in which the format could be extended. This led eventually to the making of the Russian and South African versions of *Seven Up*.[1] Both these series, begun respectively in 1989 and 1992, adhere to the same basic *Seven Up* formula, but have required the injection of more commentary than the original series on which they are modelled, given domestic audiences' presumed unfamiliarity with the socio-political situations in those countries.

In the course of the Sheffield festival event I also conducted an extended interview with Michael Apted about his work on the *Seven Up* series. This encouraged me to go looking for other long doc works structured along similar lines to *Seven Up*; in other words, documentaries which had begun tracking subjects when they were still very young and which had followed them, as had *Seven Up*, through adolescence and into adulthood. I also began to consider a number of other factors relating to the production and reception of these works. What features do individual long docs have in common with each other in addition to their longevity? What are the principal challenges that filmmakers face when working in this mode? What explains the widespread popularity of such work? My quest for other examples of long doc works quickly resulted in the discovery that *Seven Up*'s two best-known international 'competitors' were the German series *The Children of Golzow*[2] and the Swedish series *The Children of Jordbrö*. Both series had already been in production for several decades. *The Children of Golzow* had been running since 1961 (though there were some reports that the directors Winfried and Barbara Junge were thinking of calling it a day soon).[3] I also learned that the Swedish director Rainer Hartleb, having worked on *The Children of Jordbrö* for more than three decades, was also planning to bring the curtain down on the project in 2006.

As I pursued my research into how these projects had originated and developed, I was intrigued to discover that both 'continental' long docs had strong East German connections. *The Children of Golzow* had its beginnings in the former German Democratic Republic (GDR) where it was produced under the auspices of DEFA, the East German state-owned film company.[4] Having spent time during the early 1960s living and working in Berlin (including frequent visits to the East), I knew something about the filmmaking environment out of which the Golzow chronicle (as it is generally called) originated and was well aware of the special challenges faced by East German documentarists. In the case of *The Children of Jordbrö* the East German connection has to do with the fact that the work's director Rainer Hartleb originally hails from East Germany (Thuringia). Even though he has been living in Sweden since 1952 and has become a Swedish citizen, Hartleb still retains links with

Germany and has also latterly become acquainted with Winfried and Barbara Junge.

I am very grateful to both the Junges and to Rainer Hartleb, as indeed I am to Michael Apted, for having taken the time to discuss with me at some length the pitfalls and delights of long doc film-making. When I first met the Junges, for instance, in May 2006 in the modest surroundings of their East Berlin flat, I began to recognise just how much stamina, commitment and sheer gutsy determination is required for such projects. On that occasion I was also made aware of what such a long-term involvement signifies in purely human terms. On the day I met them, the Junges had just returned from Golzow, a small town some 80 kilometres to the east of Berlin, where they had been visiting Jürgen, one of the leading protagonists in the Golzow saga. Jürgen, whom the Junges had known since he was a child of seven, was terminally ill with cancer and indeed died a few weeks later, still only in his early fifties. This had clearly been a difficult visit for the Junges, but hearing them talk so movingly about Jürgen and his contribution to the Golzow films was a poignant reminder of the very special relationship that can develop between filmmakers and their subjects in this type of work. Participants in such long-stay projects become in a very real sense members of the filmmaker's extended family.

The present study also seeks to throw light on the role played by particular broadcasting institutions or film companies in the production of these works and on the possible reasons for long docs' remarkable popularity with successive generations of viewers. Whether viewers have accompanied the long doc in question through all the phases of its development, whether they have joined it at some intermediate stage along the way or whether, indeed, they have begun to engage with it as a completed artefact with its own life history, long docs encourage particular forms of audience engagement and involvement. Not the least of these pleasures is the opportunity that a long doc provides for reflecting on one's own life-journey. Typically, viewers will be first introduced to long doc subjects when the latter are still of tender years, generally when they are about to enter their first year of primary school. Maintaining contact with these subjects as they move through the various stages of their formal education and beyond, viewers begin to develop the kind of relationship with the real-life protagonists that is, arguably, of a comparable order to the one they enter into with characters in soap opera. As I shall be returning later in this work (Chapter 5) to the topic of long docs' affinity with soaps, I will content myself here with simply emphasising the importance of long docs' episodic mode of presentation. One of the defining features of the long doc sub-genre is their use of what I term an 'incremental' form of narrative. With each successive instalment or episode of the work, the slowly unfolding text is subject to a characteristic process of expansion and consolidation. When working on new long doc instalments, there-fore, filmmakers confront the difficult challenge of having to recon-cile the need to complete the updating process (covering the latest stage of a subject's life journey) with the need to carry out what is, in effect, a reversioning exercise (carefully re-editing the 'back-story' footage included in previous films).

Revisitations

Insofar as they represent an attempt to chronicle a series of events in, and experiences of, the socio-historical world from the point of view of a chronicling observer, long docs can justifiably be categorised as mainstream documentary texts. As far as their other defining feature is concerned, that of longitudinality, this is something that long docs have in common with a number of other media texts which seek to secure the interest of an audience or readership by extending their coverage over an extended period of time. Pivotal to such longitu-dinal accounts is some kind of revisitation. This concept, it should be noted, includes the idea of reworking material already collected, as well as generating new textual material by revisiting people and places that have already featured in earlier programmes.[5] In a media world in which there is increasing concern to gain maximum mileage for a successful programme concept, the idea of the 'revisi-tation' is one that is being employed to an increasing extent. It is part of the much-vaunted recycling imperative as broadcasters struggle to survive in ever more competitive times (see also Chapter 1, p. 12). The major appeal of such programmes for audiences is that viewers feel that they are being reacquainted with already familiar locations or that they are receiving updated information on devel-oping situations.[6]

With long docs, the idea of the revisitation acquires absolute centrality, insofar as it is a major expectation of viewers, when they tune in to the latest episode or instalment, that they will be appropriately updated about how the lives of the featured subjects have developed in the period since the last visit. A significant component of this expectation – especially when there is a long interval between updates – is the curiosity about what physical changes will have occurred. Witnessing, for instance, the physical impact that the ageing process has upon the individual, especially on the subject's face, constitutes one of the special – and some might argue dubious – pleasures of long doc watching.[7] Each new update brings with it, therefore, a heightened *frisson* of pleasurable expectation as to how much facial weathering one can register and what can be read into such changes.

Time management

Another aspect of long docs I will be exploring in this book is how time is handled. Whereas producers of traditional biographical accounts will be able, when planning the structure of the work, to calculate how much time and space to allocate to each phase of the subject's life, the long doc filmmaker is confronted by a completely different form of challenge. In each new film, the filmmaker is not only committed to updating viewers about the more recent developments in the community or in the lives of subjects but also required to (re)-introduce scenes or images from yesteryear. Individual filmmakers have devised different strategies for structuring this retrospective material into accounts where the primary focus will always be on the present vantage point. The fact remains, however, that audiences associate long doc viewing with a regular switching of focus as the filmmaker moves backwards and forwards along the axes of individual life journeys.

Chronicling function

As with most other forms of documentary, one of the claims made for long docs is that they communicate significant information about the socio-historical world. An associated claim is that, because one of their primary concerns is to tell us about longer-term developments, long docs have an important chronicling function. This claim should, however, be treated with some caution, since individual filmmakers have different views on how strongly the chronicling impulse is embedded in their work. Some filmmakers, such as Winfried and

Barbara Junge, claim that what they have produced represents a piece of 'longitudinal film observation' (*Langzeitfilmbeobachtung*). According to the Junges, one of the primary motives of their work has been to track the lives of a group of East Germans (all originally from the same village) against the background of what was happening in the wider world. The aim was to produce the 'chronicle of a generation' (Junge, 2008: 11). Other filmmakers, however, have been far more far more circumspect regarding the social-political significance of their work. Michael Apted, for instance, whose *Seven Up* series has sometimes been regarded as offering some illuminating insights into the changing social fabric of Britain during the last four or more decades, has always been quick to assert that he has never consciously sought to draw any explicit connections between the lives of his subjects as depicted in the *Seven Up* series and wider developments in the public sphere. He even goes so far as to suggest that any such attempt would be counter-productive in that it would introduce an unnecessary additional strand into an already quite overloaded narrative. As he remarked to me:

> I've never tried to put it [*Seven Up*] in a self-consciously wider context … I once tried to produce a sequence [in *42 Up*] in which subjects gave their responses on the death of Princess Diana, but I decided to ditch this. What's important is *their* lives. They dramatise the politics rather than expand on the politics. (Interview, 2007)

Structure of chapters

Chapter 1 (*Reflections on longitudinal documentary: form and function*) examines some of the principal generic features of long docs and considers the highly significant role that particular institutions have had on their production, promotion and dissemination. Other questions covered in this chapter are: First, how are long docs related to the broader documentary project and to other types of factual/documentary programming (including the various forms of Reality Television)? Second, to what extent could long docs be considered to be fulfilling a chronicling function? Can they, for instance, be classified as a kind of 'oral history'? Third, how are these works constructed with respect to their formal design?

Chapter 2 (*Short histories*) provides brief overviews of the works that are treated in far greater detail in subsequent chapters. The main purpose of these overviews is: first, to draw attention to the particular sets of circumstances out of which the long docs arose; second, to provide a brief indication of the factors that led them to acquiring a longitudinal dimension; and third, to alert readers to the significance the works in question have acquired within the national documentary traditions of which they form a part. In producing these overviews I am aware that, whilst the majority of readers may have heard of, or seen, films in the *Seven Up* series, not all that many will have the same familiarity with the German and Swedish long docs. I have therefore included more detailed information on the production contexts out of which the Swedish and German works arose in order that readers have at least some basis for comparing them with their British counterpart.

Chapter 3 (*Getting started*) is a study of how the individual works originated, with a special emphasis on the nurturing role of particular institutions. As with the vast majority of media products, it was primarily the programming requirements of institutions that led to these works coming into being. Moreover, without the continuing support of these institutions long docs could never have aspired to the longevity that has become their most striking feature. A further issue relating to the role of institutions concerns the point at which the decision is taken to make the work longitudinal. No small number of long docs, including Apted's *Seven Up,* began life as single, stand-alone productions before being 'upgraded'. Explanations have therefore to be sought as to what circumstances led to this upgrading.

Chapter 4 (*Gaining and maintaining momentum*) traces the history of these works once they have acquired sufficient momentum to ensure their further progress. As one might imagine, many different factors combine to determine the developmental path of these projects. In certain cases (especially with *The Children of Golzow)* the very fact that they have been so long-lived has provided valuable case-study material for exploring wider media developments in the countries or regions where they have been produced.

Chapter 5 (*Never-ending stories?*) Though long docs will, sooner or later, come to an end, they can also be regarded as classically 'open' forms of narrative. The chapter explores the affinities that long docs have with soap opera texts, which have similar aspirations to never-endingness. Both long docs and soaps rely on an episodic mode of delivery and both seek to persuade their audience that they are attempting to chronicle real-time developments.

Chapter 6 (*Towards an ending*) is concerned to explore the variety of ways in which long doc filmmakers contrive to bring their work to a satisfactory conclusion. The chapter also addresses more general questions relating to the narrative organisation of these works whose success crucially depends on filmmakers' ability to produce a satisfactory balance between the parts of the text which trace subjects' past histories and those that encourage audience speculation about possible future developments.

Notes

1 The *Seven Up in the USSR* series (alternatively entitled *Born in the USSR: 7 Up; 14 Up; 21 Up in the USSR*, etc.) was first screened in 1991 (with subsequent updates in 1998 and 2005. The *Seven Up in South Africa* series had its first airing in 1992 (with subsequent updates in 1999 and 2006).

2 For many years *The Children of Golzow* was listed in the Guinness Book of Records as having the longest production schedule in the history of film.

3 Barbara Junge has been the editor of the Golzow series from 1978, and co-writer and director from 1988.

4 Non-German speaking readers will find some useful background material on DEFA in Allan & Sandford's *DEFA: East German Cinema, 1946–1992* (Berghahn Books, 1999).

5 As often as not, the revisitation idea was not part of the original programme concept but occurred to broadcasters after a programme had scored higher ratings than anticipated.

6 There are some tangible cost benefits with the types of revisitation programme in which significant excerpts from the original programme can be included, with a concomitant reduction in the amount of new footage that needs to be generated.

7 It might even be appropriate in this context to use the German term *Schadenfreude*, the dubious pleasure taken in witnessing another's discomfiture or, more literally, the joy caused by the 'damage' (*Schaden*) they have sustained.

1

Reflections on longitudinal documentary: form and function

Most documentaries, it might be claimed, have a longitudinal component. In contrast to news and current affairs programmes that will concentrate on providing brief updates or snapshot accounts of the contemporary scene, documentary productions are generally more concerned with longer-term developments and with the wider ramifications of a subject.[1] Sometimes, perhaps most memorably in the case of a documentary such as Ross McElwee's *Sherman's March*, the very process of painstaking investigation and quest for evidence will become part of the textual fabric of the documentary (see Cuevas & García, 2007: 153–79). The very fact that, with documentaries, the subject will normally have been extensively researched and material will have been gathered over a longish period might be seen to reinforce the claims that the work makes on our attention. Moreover, whilst a documentary may be proposing a particular argument about a specific set of events, it does so not only by inviting viewers to form a judgment on the basis of evidence supplied but also by encouraging them to go beyond the text in order to access other sources of information (Nichols, 1991: 142–3, 162–4).

Long docs are generally counted amongst the more serious types of documentary work insofar as they tend to encourage a considered, reflective response from their audiences. As with every other media work, however, the nature of this response will be partly determined by the medium for which the long doc in question was originally conceived.[2] In the last couple of decades or so, some long doc producers and a number of critics have begun to voice certain misgivings that reality television might be having on the attitudes of long doc subjects towards their participation in these projects. The fear is that, given the proliferation of the various brands of reality programming and the celebrity status accorded to reality show performers, this might encourage long doc subjects to start thinking of themselves primarily as performers rather than as participants in a more serious documentary project. According to Michael Apted, the popularity of the new reality television formats has indeed had an impact on the way his long doc subjects now view their involvement. In one interview he has even observed that he is fearful lest some of his subjects seek to exploit what they see as their commodity value by demanding much more 'performance' money than he currently pays them[3] (see Freedland, 2005b). When I asked Apted, however, whether he felt that the *Seven Up* series in any way pre-empted or foreshadowed the reality shows that began to dominate television schedules in the late 1990s, he was – understandably enough – keen to deny the existence of a link between a type of television programming that was primarily entertainment-oriented and a programme such as *Seven Up* that was designed to elicit a more thoughtful response.[4] What he did suggest, however, was that the high profile that reality programming had achieved might well have had some impact on the way that audiences might be disposed to interpret a series such as *Seven Up*. According to Apted, it might actually help sharpen viewers' awareness of the gulf between a more serious type of documentary enterprise (*Seven Up*) and a category of lightweight entertainment that relied on contrivance and manipulation. As Apted put it when I interviewed him: 'People have become far more savvy as a result of watching this stuff … they see that it's *transparently manipulative*' (Apted, 2005, my emphasis). It might also, in his opinion, help to create an additional frame of reference for audiences when assessing the performative contributions of long doc subjects.

For all the attempts to establish generic affinities between long docs and some of the new reality formats, there remain, then, some significant differences. There is, as Apted suggests, a world of difference between the constant manipulation being practised in a reality show and the occasional contrived situation that occurs in a long doc. For sure, filmmakers will sometimes arrange a special reunion at which long doc subjects are reassembled solely for the purposes of the film, but even this type of constructive intervention pales into insignificance when compared with all the staging that goes on as the latest group of celebrity-hungry contestants are herded into the specially constructed *Big Brother* house in order that they may loudly and histrionically emote. Producers of long docs are more concerned with quietly tracing and chronicling the lives of others in a way calculated to elicit a more reflective and even at times philosophical response from the audience.

Documentary work with a longitudinal dimension

There has, over the years, been a relatively large number of works that have a longitudinal dimension. In the case of Germany one can almost speak of a longitudinal tradition. In addition to *The Children of Golzow* there has been *Berlin – Ecke Bundesplatz* (directed by Hans-Georg Ullrich and Detlef Gumm, 1985–2004), a series of films chronicling the everyday life of residents in a district of (West) Berlin, and Volker Koepp's Wittstock films (1975–97) that trace the lives of a number of women in a small town in East Germany. The Wittstock films (there are seven in all) form an interesting point of comparison with Junge's Golzow cycle, though there are some significant differences. Koepp begins his longitudinal account not when his subjects are children but when they have begun working together in a Wittstock textile factory. The films thus throw light on working conditions in East Germany as well as giving more general insights into everyday life under socialism. Just as Winfried Junge had done, Koepp continued to track the lives of three of his subjects after the *Wende*[5] (*Neues in Wittstock*, 1992, and *Wittstock, Wittstock,* 1997), before deciding to move on to other types of documentary work.

There are many more examples of documentary film work like that of Junge and Koepp that chronicle developments in a specific local (or national) context by returning to people and places on a more or less regular basis. Equally interesting, however, are those instances where filmmakers revisit material that had been shot many years previously and produce a new film that contains a critical re-evaluation of the earlier footage as well as an update on how the participants have fared in the twenty years since the initial work had been put together. The film *Twenty Years Later* (1985) by the Brazilian filmmaker Eduardo Coutinho exemplifies this kind of revisitation. The earlier material – in this case footage from a 1964 docudrama focusing on the murder of a peasant organiser – is shown to those who had participated in the making of that film, but *Twenty Years*

Later also contains some extensive reflections on the nature of documentary evidence and the privileged role of the filmmaker as (re)interpreter of events.[6]

Revisitations

Within the field of television programming the practice of revisitation is motivated not only by a desire to throw new light on a developing situation but also by the economically driven need of broadcasters to ensure that maximum mileage is derived from material that has already been generated.[7] In an era where the search for new programming ideas has become ever more intense, the ability to recycle existing material is proving to be especially attractive. The BBC series *What Happened Next?* (BBC, 2008) provides a good example of how the revisitation idea can be productively exploited. The essential idea is that each programme in the series will provide an update on what has happened to individuals featured in past BBC documentaries. In 1978, for instance, the BBC produced a programme *Living in the Past* which, incidentally, some have seen as a prototype for reality shows in the *Big Brother* mould. The programme traced how, over a period of one year, 15 volunteers coped with living in a specially contrived Iron Age settlement. The *What Happened Next?* episode of 21 May 2008 caught up with what had happened to some of the volunteers in the intervening years and invited them to reflect back on what their involvement in the original programme had meant for them.

From small acorns mighty oaks ...

Whilst the idea of revisitation is key generic component of long docs, the works under consideration in this study also share other features worth commenting on. Most of these long docs had relatively inauspicious beginnings and in some instances were not even planned as long doc projects. Apted's *Seven Up* series began life as a stand-alone *World in Action* special. Winfried Junge's *Children of Golzow* started as a single short (13-minute) documentary with no guarantee of having its life extended, whilst Rainer Hartleb's *Children of Jordbrö* could easily have been restricted to being a one-off current affairs programme reporting on schoolchildren's first day at school in a Jordbrö primary.

A number of factors are involved in any decision by a broadcaster or a film production company to convert what might have initially been envisaged as a one-off programme or stand-alone work into a longitudinal series, and I will be considering some of these factors in greater detail in Chapter 3. I would like at this point, however, to make two general observations about the processes by which such works spring into life, both of which have important consequences for the further development of the project. First, in cases such as the *Seven Up* series where longitudinal status is conferred on what was conceived as a one-off current affairs programme, decisions taken by the production team at the outset (especially ones relating to selection of subjects) will have far-reaching implications for the series over the longer term.[8] The second observation relates more specifically to the longitudinality of these works. Because long docs are, by definition, works that are produced over extensive periods of time, they are subject to a number of determining influences, many of which could not have been foreseen at the time when the projects were first launched. To this extent, long docs bear some resemblance to a living organism. Their future prospects will be determined partly by their genetic structure and partly by the environmental conditions to which they are exposed. This will require filmmakers to make certain 'course corrections' as a long doc develops, including compensating for the loss of one or more participating subjects or having to adjust to new situations brought about by changes occurring within the media environment.

Operating in the long doc mode

It goes without saying that, as well as requiring the ongoing support of a broadcaster or film funding agent, every successful long doc represents a huge personal commitment on the part of the film or programme maker. Without their drive, enthusiasm and dedication, none of these projects would have gained the momentum that has ensured their longevity. Makers of long docs will also need to have developed a number of specific skills required to be a successful long-haul operator. Some of these relate to how one goes about acquiring and retaining the co-operation of subjects over a considerable period of time. Others concern the development of appropriate storytelling and chronicling techniques when working with an ever-expanding volume of material.

One of the major challenges that long doc filmmakers have had to address concerns the ethical issues raised by this form of documentary (Rosenthal, 2002: 363–5). All documentarists are (or should be) aware of what they owe their subjects, but it could be argued that makers of long docs carry even greater responsibility towards those trusting souls who allow the camera to intrude upon their lives when it is impossible to predict what the consequences of such long-term exposure will be. With long docs the participants' giving of consent is complicated by the fact that it will be normally someone other than the subject (often a parent, guardian or teacher) who will have consented on that person's behalf. By the time he or she becomes fully aware of the implications of longer-term involvement, they may well feel under an obligation to remain with the project, even though they may experience it as an unwelcome intrusion.

Relations between filmmakers and their subjects are also ones in which issues of power are involved. There have, for instance, been a number of documented cases where a long doc participant has decided to withdraw from a project because they felt they were able to effect so little control over how they were represented. On the other hand, the odds are not entirely stacked in favour of the film or programme maker. From the filmmaker's point of view, the decision by a long doc participant to withdraw from the project is potentially far more damaging than a subject's withdrawal from virtually any other form of documentary. There, a substitute informant or interviewee can usually be found, whereas in long docs long-serving subjects are literally irreplaceable.

All this means that long doc filmmakers feel specially obligated towards their subjects.[9] For this reason they will spend considerable time, including dormant periods when filming is not taking place, in maintaining good working relations with their participants and attempting to ward off any (additional) media intrusions into subjects' lives. Nevertheless, because they are so dependent on subjects' continuing co-operation, long doc filmmakers will often be prepared to be more accommodating to their subjects than in other forms of documentary. Not only will they make a point of showing subjects rough-cut versions of the scenes in which they appear, but they will also generally accede to requests for certain offending material to be excised. Though this inevitably results in a certain loss of editorial control, it is a price that most filmmakers feel worth paying in exchange for retaining the good will of their subjects. It is also the case that, as time goes by, subjects begin to recognise that, in exchange for their continuing participation, they can extract certain favours and concessions from those who have engaged their services (including, if they are living abroad, being flown back home, at the filmmakers' expense, to visit family and friends).

A kind of ethnography?

Making a longitudinal documentary has certain points in common with ethnographic filmmaking. Both will frequently involve working within a bounded community and attempting to chronicle the lived experience of those residing there (Nichols, 1991: 41–2). Both require a sharp eye for the significant detail and a highly developed capacity for attentive listening (Loizos, 1993: 16–44). Long docs also take on an ethnographic dimension insofar as they frequently involve the incoming filmmaker in a form of participant observation. Both Winfried Junge and Rainer Hartleb adopted what some would regard as an ethnographic approach in the early phases of their work. This enabled them to gain the trust of the respective communities and to develop good working relationships with their chosen subjects.[10] As time went by, however, and the focus of Junge's and Hartleb's attention switched to the tracking of individual life-journeys, so the ethnographic orientation of these works becomes much less discernible.

Whilst none of the works in this study can lay claim to being a fully fledged ethnographic study, some of the issues raised in ethnographic debates are still of relevance when assessing the production of long doc texts. The filmmakers' responsibility to those whose lives are being documented is one such issue. Ethnographers have always been aware of the ethical responsibility towards the communities they choose to study, especially when their 'findings' are to form part of a televisual or filmic account produced for a wider public. Those whose lives and cultural practices have been documented and reported on in this way will often complain about the distortions that have crept into such accounts and will sometimes feel that the community has been seriously misrepresented. Long doc productions have been occasionally beset by similar problems when subjects who have agreed to be part of a long doc study have responded with some hostility to how they and their community have been portrayed (see Chapter 3, pp. 66–7).

Modes of filming: the fixed interval and the arrhythmic approach

Operating in the longitudinal mode allows for several different approaches to filming, dependent among other things on the medium (film or television) in which the filmmaker is working, on the wishes or policies of the funding agent and on particular design features incorporated into the original project. The type of contractual arrangement the filmmaker has entered into will always, of course, have implications for the number of films produced and the regularity with which they appear. Take, for example, the long doc series *Growing Up in Australia*, the first instalment of which was screened on the Australian ABC TV network in October 2006. The series is a television spin-off from a government-sponsored longitudinal study of Australian children being conducted by the Australian Institute of Family Studies. This study, which was launched in 2004, sets out to explore the lives of 10,000 Australian children over a seven-year period.

Growing Up in Australia exemplifies what I refer to as the 'fixed interval' approach to long doc filmmaking in that the series, produced by Film Australia, is based upon selected children being visited and interviewed at eighteen-month intervals.[11] Making a long doc according to a fixed timetable brings a number of benefits for the filmmaker. Michael Apted, for instance, having fallen into a seven-year rhythm of filming, quickly realised there were distinct advantages of operating in this way. First and foremost, it allowed his subjects a certain amount of downtime during which they could pursue their lives away from the glare of publicity. Furthermore, during the longish periods of absence, not only would subjects' outward appearance have changed, but also it was more likely that their lives would have been marked by one or more significant events since we last encountered them.[12] The one potential disadvantage of the fixed interval method is that, if filmmakers remain totally faithful to these 'rules of engagement', they may not be present to record especially noteworthy events in the lives of subjects and communities.[13]

As an alternative to the fixed interval approach, filmmakers may choose to follow a less regular pattern of visitations. The employment of this 'arrhythmic' mode may be considered a more appropriate way of working in the case of those long docs where the declared intention is to chronicle events over a long period and to highlight what are seen to be significant changes and transitions. The advantages of this approach, from the filmmakers' point of view, are that it allows them to be present at certain events (a wedding, a funeral, a class reunion) where it is known that most of the participants will be attending and where some interesting interactions between subjects can be anticipated. It also gives filmmakers greater flexibility when it comes to following up developing situations.

Any discussion about the rival merits of fixed interval and arrhythmic approaches also has to take into account the role of the respective sponsoring institution. With those long docs that fall in to the fixed interval category, programme commissioners and producers will normally have reached a contractual agreement about delivery times and the length of individual instalments. With long docs of the arrhythmic variety matters will be necessarily more complicated, since work on the film will be prefaced by a series of negotiations between filmmaker and sponsor concerning every aspect of the commissioned work. In the case of *The Children of Golzow*, for instance, the making of each film was accompanied by sometimes-tense discussions between the filmmakers and their superiors within the DEFA hierarchy. Much of the wrangling would centre on whether the production of the next Golzow film could be timed to coincide with some public event or some special anniversary in the GDR calendar. Getting the go-ahead for the next film in the Golzow cycle was therefore dependent not only on persuading those with commissioning responsibility at DEFA that a further episode in the cycle was justified in purely filmic terms but also on making the case that the film could seen to be raising audience awareness of GDR achievements.

The times they are a-changin': long docs as chronicles

It has sometimes been suggested that long docs have a special claim on our attention in that they allow viewers to witness the impact that wider developments in society are having on a particular group of individuals (Rosenthal, 2002: 64–5) By tracing the manner in which subjects, over an extended period, respond to the demands of the changing times, long docs supposedly not only give us insight into how adept individuals are at adjusting to new situations; they also provide a socio-political record of the times themselves. One does well, however, to treat these claims with some circumspection. As already suggested, projects which start life with a distinct sociological orientation have a habit of slowly transmuting into works with a far more biographical inclination.

Take *Seven Up*, for instance, which began life as a *World in Action* special. The programme was transmitted in 1964 at a time when Britain was slowly moving out of the period of post-war austerity. One of the primary remits of this programme was to consider whether, as some claimed, Britain was still an essentially a class-ridden society. (The choice of *Seven Up* subjects was partly determined by a desire to show that it was!) As soon as *Seven Up* acquired longitudinal status, however, the series became far less explicitly sociological in its orientation. The focus of attention switches to the tracing of individual life-journeys, though it is still possible to regard the larger *Seven Up* text as representing a chronicle-like account of the transformations that have occurred in British society over the last few decades. As Brian Winston has commented: 'Without doubt, the *Up* films provide the best insights into life in Britain in the last half century' (Winston, 2007). With Rainer Hartleb's *Children of Jordbrö* one detects a similar developmental pattern. The original intention was to produce a longitudinal study of a newly established community on the outskirts of Stockholm by homing in on the lives and experiences of some of the younger citizens. Yet just as with *Seven Up* – though to a lesser degree – the initial chronicling intentions of the author are slowly subsumed into a more person-centred documentary account.

If most long doc filmmakers attempt in some way to show how individual lives are shaped and influenced by a number of external or environmental factors, in other cases the specific reason for initiating a long doc was to examine the consequences of epoch-making political transformations. In the case of the *Born in the USSR* and *Born in South Africa* it was the knowledge that both countries were about to enter a period of far-reaching political and economic change that persuaded Granada to provide the funding for such long doc enterprises. There was, in other words, a calculation that a Russian and a South African long doc based on the *Up* films' concept would be a powerful means of chronicling the dramatic changes occurring at such a critical juncture in these nations' history. *Born in the USSR* and *Born in South Africa* were literally timed to start at a point where a carefully selected group of seven-year olds were having their first experience of life in a post-communist and post-apartheid state.

With *The Children of Golzow*, on the other hand, the key moment of historic change, the fall of the Berlin Wall, came at a much later point in the development of the project. Nevertheless, viewed in its entirety, the series has an even stronger claim than any of its counterparts to have performed a chronicling function. Starting at a time (August 1961) when the Berlin Wall had just been built and carrying on, as it did, well into the new millennium, *The Children of Golzow* not only documents the lives of subjects under a communist regime; it also follows their fortunes as they adjust to living under the conditions of a market economy – with all the joys and sorrows which that has entailed. Viewed from the present, post-communist perspective, *The Children of Golzow* has proved to have an additional chronicling function. It provides, namely, some revealing insights into the media environment in which it was produced, especially the difficulties that filmmakers face when working under conditions of quite strict state censorship.[14] Because the Junges continued to work on the Golzow chronicle after the fall of the Wall, it enabled them to present a series of trenchant critical reflections on the conditions under which earlier films were made and on the compromises the filmmakers had to enter into. As such, *The Children of Golzow* acquires additional historical value, both as a chronicle of filmmaking in the GDR and as an account of the experiences of erstwhile GDR documentarists as they struggled to adjust to the new political realities (see Chapter 6, pp. 172–3).

The cumulative quality of long docs

If long docs are seen to have special value on account of their chronicling capacity, it is worth examining in what ways they differ from the many other types of programming that seek to engage with historical topics. Standard television histories, such as those that attempt to re-examine the contributions made by well-known historical figures or the rise and fall of particular civilisations, will all tend to use a number of conventional techniques. These histories claim to be authoritative insofar as they are seen to be drawing on a body of documentary evidence culled from a wide range of sources: film and video archives, libraries and collections of official documents and (last but not least) interviews with witnesses of events and with other testimony providers. The production of such histories involves a reconstructive or interpretative process, one in which the programme makers can clearly be seen to have 'taken a view' on how and why events may have occurred. With long docs, on the other hand, the view of history that they project is communicated somewhat more obliquely. It is a view that emerges when members of the audience themselves begin to reflect on the implications of what has been shown rather than one that is explicitly articulated in any accompanying commentary. Viewed in epistemological terms, long docs communicate with their audiences by means that can be described as 'cumulative' or even 'accretive'. They are cumulative in the sense that, over time, each new film or programme instalment adds to, or complements, the picture that viewers have formed hitherto. No final judgment or verdict can be offered, since the concern is as much with future possibilities as it is with past achievements. It is this incremental quality of long docs, which, arguably, provides a clue to their popularity, since it corresponds to the way in which we ourselves process events and experiences in our everyday lives. Confronting the screen image of a known individual, in this case a long doc subject, after a period of time has elapsed since we last encountered them, and receiving an update on that person's 'news', is very reminiscent of that real-life experience of meeting up with someone we only see very occasionally. Just as, when we meet our long-lost friend, one of our instinctive reactions will be to register what toll the passing years have taken, so too when we tune into the latest episode of a long doc there will be some pleasurable anticipation attached to ascertaining the extent to which faces or behavioural attitudes have changed.

Long docs can, however, play on this incremental quality in one further respect. This has to do with what I will call the 'dual perspective' discernible in each new episode of the constantly evolving story. Just as with the latest episode of a soap opera, so with the most recent instalment of a long doc, the primary narrative requirement is to bring us up to date with events in the lives of foregrounded characters. Yet at the same time – and this is what accounts for the dual perspective – the long doc in question will always be seeking to situate these more recent events against the backcloth of subjects' lives hitherto. Thus, one of the primary requirements of a long doc narrative from the viewer's point of view is that it should be regularly punctuated with reminders of the past. Such reminders can take several forms, and I shall be returning to this topic in later chapters. For the time being I would just like to point out that one of the implications of this constant juxtaposition of past and present is that it actively encourages viewers to apply particular terms or frames of reference in seeking to interpret these works. In Apted's case, for instance, the way in which the images of childhood are constantly fed into the biographical accounts of *Seven Up* subjects is always inviting viewers to consider the extent to which the experiences of those early years have a determining influence on the people they have become.

A kind of oral history?

If one of the primary ambitions of long docs is to chronicle the life histories of individuals, it could be legitimately claimed that they represent a kind of oral history. Both oral historians and long doc filmmakers focus on the lives of those who have been often conspicuous by their absence in other forms of historical chronicling. As Perks & Thomson have noted: 'The most distinctive contribution of oral history has been to include within the historical record the experiences and perspectives of groups of people who might otherwise have been hidden from history' (1998: ix). In the same way that oral histories might be thought to fill some of the gaps left by conventional forms of historicising, so it could be claimed that long docs are able to complement historical representations provided by more traditional forms of expository documentary (see Kilborn & Izod, 1997: 58–64, 94–8; Nichols, 1991: 32–8).

Just as oral historians coax from volunteer informants their personal memories and recollections of past events, so do long doc filmmakers encourage their subjects to embark on a similar memory flow. Oral historians may also, just like long doc filmmakers, stay with their informants for considerable lengths of time in order that the full story can emerge. The emphasis in both cases is on making connections between what has been experienced at a very personal level and events and developments occurring within the wider public sphere (Portelli, 1997: 6).[15] The result is that both oral history and long doc projects are concerned with producing what is sometimes referred to as a 'history from below'.[16]

Whilst there are some strong links between oral history and long docs, it is worth noting that there are also some marked differences, though these may not always be as significant as they might at first appear. Oral historians will generally be more concerned to allow informants the greatest possible freedom in recollecting events and articulating their memories. However, sometimes such historians will feel the need to provide their subjects with certain prompts in order to trigger the memory flow. Some subjects may regard such prompts as indicative of a more active or purposive intervention on the part of the historian, suggesting that the latter may be exercising more control over the informant's responses than the historian may fondly imagine. As Ronald Grele has noted: 'Oral history interviews are constructed, for better or for worse, by the active intervention of the historian. They are a collective creation and inevitably carry within themselves a pre-existent historical ordering, selection and interpretation' (Grele, 1998: 42). With long doc filmmaking on the other hand, the situation is often more transparent in that the subject's remarks will normally be identifiable as part of a conversational exchange.[17] This exchange still contains a purposive element, however, in that both interlocutors recognise that parts of what is conversationally disclosed will be used in future long doc instalments.

Mindful of this distinction, it should probably come as no surprise to learn that oral history and long docs resemble each other most strongly when the former is subject to the mediating influence of an authoring agent. Take, for instance, the case of *Akenfield* by Ronald Blythe, one of the best-known examples of oral history work to have been published in the last half century. The book, published in 1969, is an attempt to trace the development of the English village of Akenfield in Suffolk through the memories of those who have lived there. To these ends Blythe interviewed fifty village inhabitants at some length. The twenty chapters of the book are built around the villagers' memories of erstwhile village life, but they also contain extensive explanatory material in order to provide readers with the requisite amount of contextualising information. Though the emphasis is always on the stories recounted by the subjects themselves, Blythe's shaping influence is everywhere apparent. In terms of how speech and dialogue are rendered, all the rough edges – hesitations, mumblings and repetitions – have been smoothed away in the interests of producing a readable text. The result is a book that combines biographical appeal with that of a sociologically informed chronicle.

If one compares Blythe's historical account with a putative longitudinal documentary focused on Akenfield lives, some significant differences would emerge.[18] In the written chronicling mode the presence of an authoring, mediating agent is everywhere apparent. Each biographical account is prefaced by a lengthy introduction and by sometimes extensive authorial reflections on changes that have occurred in village life during the period under review. The reader quickly gets used, however, to being switched between these third-person introductions and the first-person accounts in which individual villagers recount their personal stories. The relationship that readers enter into with Akenfield villagers is, nevertheless, markedly different from the one viewers would forge with subjects in a longitudinal documentary. In *Akenfield,* in spite of Blythe's attempts to reproduce in written form the dialectal coloration and other idiosyncratic markers of the individual voice, the work still requires an act of imagination on the part of readers to recreate in their mind's eye those uniquely personal qualities of voice, physiognomy and personality that would be more viscerally conveyed in the long doc.[19]

Performativity

Viewers' recognition that the utterances of a subject form part of a communicative exchange also prompts further questions concerning whether subjects in oral history projects have been pressed into producing the kind of performance that falls in line with the historian's expectations. With long doc subjects, however, it might be contended that there is an even greater pressure on subjects to perform, especially given the status they will often acquire as media personalities (Kilborn, 2003: 13–14). When they first become involved in the project, participants may be quite oblivious to any role-playing requirements, but with each successive update many of them become keenly aware that what the film or programme maker seeks is for them to deliver a suitably tailored performance.[20]

Subjects' knowledge that they have been thrust into a relationship in which there is a demand for them to deliver a performance (on terms largely determined by the filmmakers), can put considerable strain on the relationship between the two involved parties. It is one of the aspects of long doc filmmaking that requires very sensitive handling on the filmmaker's part. Mismanagement of subjects in any way increases the likelihood that they will wish to distance themselves from the project – either temporarily or permanently. If, on the other hand, both parties are able to acknowledge that they are locked into a special kind of relationship (one in which each is expected to perform a particular role), then this can provide the basis for a productive association that can extend over many years.

From the audience's point of view there is some evidence to suggest that one of the special pleasures of long doc viewing is being able to key into that often quite knowing relationship that has developed between subject and filmmaker over the course of many years of filming. Viewers are well aware that subjects are, in a sense, cast as participants in a long-running real-life soap opera, one in which their appointed task is to give regular updates on the most recent stage of their life-journey, to talk about family and career concerns and to reflect on what they think the future holds for them. Audiences also recognise that, when it comes to the conversational exchanges that feature so prominently in long doc texts, the filmmaker will always take up a background position in order that the subject can dominate the stage. This is part of the accepted 'script' where each actor is performing their allotted role according to a particular set of expectations. Yet in the same way, however, that the performances of certain reality television subjects are sometimes marked by what some critics have called 'moments of authenticity' (Hill, 2007: 141), so the exchanges between interlocutors in long docs are also occasionally marked by similar revealing moments where subjects drop their performance masks and appear in what some would see as a more authentic guise (i.e. one where signs of the personal bonding that has developed between a filmmaker and their subjects will begin to intrude upon the more performative aspects of the exchange).

There is a good example of such mask dropping early on in *Everyone's Fine*, the final film of the *Children of Jordbrö* cycle. Thérèse, one of the central female protagonists, is responding to the filmmakers' enquiry as to how she goes about balancing work and family commitments. She continues her reflections for quite some time before pausing to gather her thoughts. Here, in a normal conversational exchange, one would expect some kind of rejoinder from the other party, but Hartleb is clearly intent to coax some more confessional utterances out of Thérèse and remains silent, in the hope that she will start talking again. At this point, however, she gives him an impish grin and exclaims 'Hey Ho!' as if to indicate that she now wishes to step out of her allocated role as interviewee and resume a less contrived form of exchange. There are no small number of occasions – most of them occurring when a long doc has been running for quite some time – when a subject seeks to convey to the film-maker that they are not entirely comfortable with what is being required of them.[21] It might be seen as part of subjects' growing recognition that they have become involved in a project whose ground-rules have been devised by others and where they have only limited control over how they are being represented.

Personal biographies

Long docs have proved to have a strong appeal not only for their national audiences but also for a much more widely diffused, international constituency of viewers who probably have little or no experience of the micro worlds that respective subjects inhabit. This is further proof, if any were needed, that one of the elements of long docs' more universal appeal lies in the possibilities they offer for engaging with personal or family biographies.[22] Biographies have always been popular artefacts, whether they take the form of a written biography or a filmic account of a life-journey such as Apted's *Coal Miner's Daughter* (1980) a biopic that portrays the life of country and western singer Loretta Lynn's rise to fame from very humble beginnings.[23] Much of the appeal of these texts has to do with their ability to encourage various levels of viewer or reader empathy with the biographical subject.

The majority of biographical works will organise their narratives according to the chronological principle, though biopics and some literary biographies will sometimes adopt the extended 'flash-back' approach. Long docs on the other hand will, for the most part, be more complex in their narrative structure. Whilst their primary narrative trajectory may be to propel us forward to discover all that has happened to subjects since last we encountered them, there is an equally strong impulse to juxtapose past and present events. As a consequence of this, long docs inculcate in their viewers the expectation that interest will be switched between sequences that present the subject at different stages of their life-journey. The repetitive nature of these returns to the past arguably skews or inflects these accounts in a way that distinguishes them from all other forms of biography. For instance, given the frequency with which particular scenes from the subject's childhood are replayed in successive updates, long docs tend to encourage interpretations in which life is seen as involving a retreat from an erstwhile state of childlike innocence.[24] The regular inclusion of these interpolated childhood scenes also provides an impetus for viewers to consider the extent to which traits that seem to define the adult person may have been discernible, albeit in somewhat attenuated form, at a much earlier stage of development. These may include physical markers such as the use of certain types of body language or temperamental or attitudinal traits such as an inclination to be more introvert or extrovert in one's behaviour.

The dynamic character of long docs

In seeking to analyse the structure of long docs, one of the images that I have found useful to describe their characteristic narrative trajectory is that of the 'time shuttle'. The idea of shuttling suggests regularly traversing backwards and forwards over more or less known terrain and thus seems more applicable to the particular dynamics of a long doc text than the term 'flashback'. The latter tends to be used in filmic discourse as a means of, first, acquainting an audience with some remembered incident in a character's past or, second, providing a narrative pointer to some earlier event about which viewers need to be made aware. The evocation of past events in long docs, on the other hand, is part of a slightly different narrative exercise, in that the historical sequences in question will almost always have formed part of an earlier film with which a substantial number of viewers will already be familiar. Long doc viewers thus become accustomed to being shuttled backwards and forwards on this longitudinal time axis between sequences that depict a slowly unfolding present-day reality with others that recapitulate an already known past. In settling down to watch the latest instalment of a long doc, viewers will therefore – whether consciously or unconsciously – bring to the viewing experience a particular set of expectations, many of which concern the balancing of past and present timeframes within the overall narrative mix. Long doc filmmakers themselves, of course, will have given considerable thought to how they can best structure their texts in order to play off the various time-planes one against the other. One of the consequences of the constant adjustments that are being made to the long doc text is that viewers become involved in a constant process of re-evaluation, as they absorb information that may cause them to revise the views they may already have formed about subjects and events. It is also quite possible that they will have to dig into their personal memory banks in order to retrieve information about the subject which was included in a previous episode but which has now had to be ditched in the interests of narrative economy. As each new instalment comes on stream, there is a slight shift in narrative focus in order to give more space to the covering of events that have occurred since the last iteration. Given the constraints that are institutionally imposed on the length of episodes, there always needs to be a concomitant reduction in the time and space allotted to material evoking the less recent past. This form of accommodation, though not often remarked upon, is a striking feature of long doc works, especially as they enter their mature phase. It results in a characteristic fore-shortening of the subject's life, though, as already noted, relative prominence will still be given to scenes from childhood, especially those which, in Apted's phrase, have acquired the status of 'golden highlights'.

Whilst all long docs will be primarily concerned to provide a retrospective account of subjects' lives, they can also be seen to be encouraging all manner of speculation about how those same lives will develop in the future.[25] Insofar as they have a strong prospective element and also employ an episodic mode of presentation, long docs bear a strong structural resemblance to soap opera. I shall be examining this aspect of long docs in much greater detail in Chapter 5 of this work, so will for the time being merely comment on the way in which the prospective element is often built in to the original remit of these works. As well as encouraging conjecture about what will become of the individuals on whom the spotlight has been trained, all the long docs currently under review were also to some extent concerned – initially at least – with future developments of the respective societies to which the protagonists belonged. In the case of *Seven Up*, for instance, the 1964 *World in Action* film that laid the foundations for the later series signals in the first few minutes that one of its aims is to get viewers thinking about who will be the country's managers, politicians and trade-unionists in the year 2000 and what kind of Britain one could look forward to as the new millennium dawned. Likewise most of the early films in *The Children of Golzow* series were partly designed to encourage the belief that the country was moving towards a more assured, if not utopian, future and that connections could be drawn between the education that the Golzow youngsters were receiving and the building of a more egalitarian society founded on socialist principles. With *The Children of Jordbrö* the future-gazing element is possibly less pronounced than in the British and German examples, though it is worth remarking that one of the original aims of the work was to consider how much substance there was to politicians' claims that they were in the process of building a new Sweden.

In the mind of the beholder ...

If it is the case that most long docs, as they develop, become less sociologically orientated and more concerned with the tracing of individual journeys, this shift of focus has evident implications for the way in which audiences respond to these works. As viewers are confronted with the fragments of subject biographies in successive iterations of a long doc, they are stimulated to undertake a particular type of reflective activity. In the course of imaginatively reassembling a picture of individual subjects from all the verbal and visual information supplied, viewers will, almost inevitably, find themselves drawing comparisons between the development of protagonists' lives and the course that their own life-journeys have taken. The stimulus that long docs provide for viewers to involve themselves in what Rainer Hartleb has described as existential forms of contemplation has sometimes been seen as one of the main sources of their continuing appeal (Corner, 2009). In other words, it could be claimed that long docs have an inbuilt tendency to activate within the viewer a process of critical self-examination. As the American film critic Roger Ebert has commented on the *Seven Up* series:

> In following these journeys through life, I am reminded every seven years that although many things seem foreordained in childhood, others change. We grow, we learn, we adapt ... As more and more years pass, the segments devoted to each subject grow more crowded. Apted is probably not penetrating to their deepest secrets, but that would not be the point. This is not an exposé but a meditation. *The real work goes on in the mind of the beholder. Revisiting these now-familiar faces, seeing how they've done, I think of my own life ... Anyone watching these films goes through a similar process of self-examination, I imagine.* Why am I me and why not you? Why am I here and why not there? (Cited in Singer, 1998: 11, my emphasis)

Notes

1 Television histories will very often be concerned to trace the longer-term impact of decisions taken by governments or rulers, as well as seeking to explain the circumstances that led to actions being taken or to certain events occurring.

2 Some long docs have been designed principally for cinematic exhibition, whilst others have been commissioned for television screening. The different institutional origins of these works result in significant differences in the presentational and stylistic features that each long doc exhibits. The producers of *The Children of Golzow* had particular problems when, in the latter stages of their project, they had to produce versions that fell in line with the requirements of television broadcasters.

3 From *28 Up* onwards Apted has paid his subjects a relatively modest sum for their regular participation in the *Seven Up* series. He has also divided up any prize money that the films have won.

4 For more on recent developments in entertainment-orientated factual TV programming see Kilborn, 2003: 7–50.

5 I have decided to use the German word *Wende* (change, turning point) when referring to that period of decisive political and social change brought about by the fall of the Berlin Wall. The term *Wende* has a particular associative aura in German in that it not only refers to the series of political events that led to the collapse of the German Democratic Republic; it also evokes a more general sense of 'period of decisive change' in the wake of these events. For more on this term see Silbermann, 1994: 36.

6 For more on Coutinho's film see Perks & Thomson, 1998: 385–6.

7 Granada Television has sought to gain maximum benefit from the *Seven Up* series by effectively patenting the format. All other national versions based on this format are produced under a franchising arrangement whereby Granada maintains supervisory control. Apted, who admits to having been 'very involved in the politics of the franchise' (Apted, 2005), has acted as consultant or executive producer on some of these other series.

8 As we shall discover in Chapter 3, Apted became acutely aware that the manifestly political agenda of the original *World in Action* team had left him with a very unrepresentative group of subjects.

9 Michael Apted has conceded that he finds that the most stressful part of making the *Seven Up* films is keeping his participants on board (Apted, 1998).

10 In the early stages of the *Children of Golzow* project, there is some evidence to suggest, the filmmakers were viewed with some suspicion by members of the Golzow community. These suspicions were doubtless fuelled by the knowledge that Junge and his team were DEFA film-

makers whose activities were subject to state supervision.

11 For more information on this innovative project see: www.aifs.gov.au/growingup/new.html.

12 In Apted's case, adhering to a seven-year rhythm of filming also left him ample time to pursue other projects.

13 A further potential drawback of working in this mode is that it can sometimes lead to a more distanced relationship with subjects than would be seen where a form of participant observation is being practised.

14 For more on documentary production in the GDR, see Kilborn, 1999: 267–82; Jordan & Schenk, 1996: 14–269.

15 Historical biographies have a similar dual focus to long docs. They trace an individual's life through all the stages of development, and they also attempt to situate that life within the society or community to which that person belongs.

16 A claim that is frequently made for oral history is that it contains a strong democratising impulse (people being enabled to speak for themselves about how they see the world).

17 It is sometimes the case, however, that the markers that identify the remarks as arising out of a conversational exchange will be quietly removed in the editing process.

18 Blythe's 1969 portrait of Akenfield has acquired a longitudinal dimension in the form of Craig Taylor's *Return to Akenfield: Portrait of an English Village in the 21st Century* (2006), which contains reflections by present residents on the changes that have occurred in the last five or six decades.

19 One gains a good idea of how difficult it is to reproduce the highly individual qualities of spoken utterance if one compares the transcribed version of interviews, such as those reproduced in the book version of the *Seven Up* series (Singer, 1998) with the audio/video recording on which the transcript version is based.

20 It is also worth bearing in mind that most of the subjects in the long docs under review will have become involved in these projects in their early childhood, at an age where individuals are generally less inhibited and performance comes more naturally.

21 One of the best-known examples of a subject stepping out of their appointed performative role and taking up a different stance vis-à-vis their interlocutor comes in *49 Up* where Jackie proceeds to gives Apted a piece of her mind about how she feels the programme has (mis)represented her (see Chapter 6, pp. 156–7).

22 In recent years there has been an explosion of interest in the tracing of family trees. This has also given rise to a number of television programmes in which individuals trace their family roots. A series such as *Who Do You Think You Are?* (BBC 2, 2007) has certain resemblances with some of the long docs currently under review. In both, the focus

of interest is on the various factors (genetic, environmental, economic) that caused the ancestor's life to develop as it did.

23　There are many types of fictional work that also focus on the tracing of life-journeys. The German *Bildungsroman*, is a form of novel that traces the spiritual and intellectual development of the central character from childhood to the grave.

24　The idea is eloquently expressed in the following lines from Wordsworth's 'Immortality' ode: 'Heaven lies about us in our infancy! / Shades of the prison-house begin to close / Upon the growing Boy.' ['Ode, Intimations of Immortality from Recollections of Early Childhood']

25　Most long doc subjects can anticipate that they will be asked about their hopes and ambitions for the future, in the knowledge that these pronouncements will very likely feature in a subsequent programme where stated ambitions will be subsequently weighed against actual achievements. Not all long doc makers are equally tenacious in prob-ing subjects about future aspirations. Rainer Hartleb hardly ever asks his subjects to assess their future prospects, whereas Michael Apted is always very keen to learn about participants' future plans.

2

Short histories

This chapter provides short overviews of the long doc works that will be the subject of more extensive analysis and inquiry in subsequent chapters. I offer these potted histories in the knowledge that not all readers will be familiar with the works in question and that they might therefore welcome a brief introduction about how the films came to be made, together with some indication of the significance they have acquired. By staking out the ground in this way I also hope to be able to flag up the shaping influence of different production contexts and of different broadcasting or filmmaking traditions.

Seven Up[1]

The *Seven Up* series had its origins in May 1964 when Granada Television transmitted a one-off 'special' in their *World in Action* series. Granada was already making a reputation for itself as a company with a clear, left-leaning political agenda and *World in Action* was its flagship current affairs programme. Michael Apted, later to become director of the *Seven Up* series, had a relatively junior role to play in the making of this *World in Action* special. Having only joined Granada the previous year on a graduate training programme, he was still learning the ropes as far as programme making was concerned. For this particular programme he was given the tasks of researching and of conducting some of the interviews.

As mentioned, *World in Action* was at the time already beginning to acquire a reputation as a hard-hitting investigative programme that, in the words of one observer, 'sought to provide in-depth analysis of a single issue made around arresting visual footage without an on-screen reporter' (Finch, 2003: 19). In accordance with the general remit of the *World in Action* series, the programme was to be broadly sociological in its aim. The early 1960s were a time when Britain was emerging from a period of post-war austerity and where change was in the air. This particular *World in Action* programme, with its rather quirky *Seven Up* title, was designed to test the validity of the claim that Britain was in the grip of a social revolution by considering the prospects of a group of seven-year-olds all drawn from different social backgrounds. As Apted himself remembers:

> It occurred to Tim Hewat, [the] Australian journalist who was run-
> ning *World in Action*, that it might be a good time to have a hard look
> at England and see whether or not this social revolution was in fact
> having any genuine impact. Hewat's great idea was to take this look
> through the eyes of seven-year old children. Were the great cultural
> events changing for ever the class system that has permeated England
> for close on 800 years? Did everybody have a fair chance, or did the
> accident of birth bring power, wealth and success? Were children made
> into winners or losers by class divisions? (Cited in Singer, 1999: vii)

In order to show whether there was any substance to the claim that, in spite of all the talk about a new age dawning, class background still had a determining impact on an individual's life-chances, the *World in Action* team used the old Jesuit maxim 'Give me the child until he is seven, and I will show you the man' as a motto for the programme. The aim was, in effect, to discover which of the two forces, nature or nurture, played the more significant role in deter-mining a child's future.

Together with his fellow researcher Gordon McDougall, Apted set about finding 14 seven-year-olds to be subjects of the *World in Action* programme. The dice were loaded from the outset, however, since most of the children were chosen from opposite ends of the social spectrum. The selection of children was made, one imagines, in order that the programme be better able to substantiate the thesis it wanted to advance about Britain still being a country wracked by class divisions. The sample was also, however, chronically imbal-anced in terms of gender and ethnicity (only four girls and only one non-white child).

As a *World in Action* Special, the *Seven Up* programme was conceived as a one-off 40-minute programme, even though a concern with future developments is clearly embedded within the original design. As the programme's narrator (Douglas Keay) informs viewers: 'We've brought these children together because we wanted a glimpse of England in the year 2000.' Likewise when individual children are being interviewed by members of the *World in Action* team, all of them are encouraged to voice their thoughts on what they think the future will bring.

With a programme that was so centrally concerned with assessing the future prospects of its protagonists, it is perhaps difficult to credit that it was to be several more years before anyone at Granada gave any thought to making a follow-up programme that would check on how the *Seven Up* children were shaping up.[2] In the event, it was not until 1970, six years after the original *World in Action* programme had been transmitted, that it was suggested to Apted that he might consider revisiting the *Seven Up* children (see Chapter 4, pp. 71–2).

As a reminder to viewers that it was a sequel to a previously transmitted programme, the update was given the title *Seven Plus Seven*, although it is now more customarily referred to as *14 Up*. As virtually all long doc filmmakers have discovered, interviewing teenagers when they are going through the throes of puberty brings its particular challenges. Apted refers to the making of *14 Up* as an 'embarrassing nightmarish experience' (Apted, 2005). The programme was, however, of crucial importance to the whole longer-term series in that it clearly showed how the idea of revisitation could be incorporated into a longitudinal project of significant proportions. In Apted's words: 'You could see the beginnings of a powerful idea and from then on it was frankly down to whether Granada and I would hang in with it. And they did. And I did' (ibid.). With *14 Up* Apted had acquired the necessary momentum to pursue the *Seven Up* idea over a much longer period.[3] Having settled into the seven-year rhythm, Apted and his team have gone on to produce a volume of work which constitutes, in the words of one observer: 'a canon of individual documentaries unique in television history' (Jones, 2000).

By the time he came to make *21 Up* Apted had left Granada and relocated to the United States where he began to make a name for himself as a director of feature films.[4] This voluntary exile on Apted's part led to Granada at one point (just before *28 Up*) considering whether they might have to find a new director for the *Up* films. By this time, however, Apted had already been associated with the project for more than two decades and had also developed a reasonable working relationship with most of his *Seven Up* subjects. What also probably tipped the balance against Granada attempting to find another director was that the series was beginning to bear Apted's authorial imprint. He has continued in his role as director of these programmes and has always felt a special commitment to the *Seven Up* project. Despite the considerable acclaim he has received as a Hollywood director, he has consistently maintained: '[The *Up* films are the] bedrock of my filmmaking career. They're the centre of my working life. They give continuity to my life. They're a major antidote to the film-fiction business' (Apted, 2005).

In common with all other long doc filmmakers, Apted has discovered that his involvement in *Seven Up* has been a constant learning process. As he looks back on how the project has developed over the years, he is, for instance, aware that in each new *Up* film he has slightly adjusted his approach in the light of what he has learned from previous iterations. He also recognises that, as the series has developed, so each new instalment acquires its own particular style and tone in accordance with the kinds of issues that tend to preoccupy people at certain stages of their lives (Apted, 1998). Thus *35 Up* has a more sombre tone, as several subjects are seen coping with the experience of parental bereavement, whilst *42 Up* is marked by an altogether more reflective tone as participants begin to look back on the road that they themselves have travelled. (Singer, 1999: x)

Apted is also conscious of the fact that certain external factors have also had a bearing on the series' development. For example, the period between the making of *42 Up* and *49 Up* had coincided with the upsurge of reality television programmes, in particular high-profile shows like *Big Brother* and *Survivor*. Apted is not alone in feeling that the celebrity status acquired by numerous reality show performers had rubbed off on at least some of his own subjects and that they had begun to view their involvement in the *Up* films project through different eyes (see Chapter 1, pp. 9–10). At the same time Apted is honest enough to admit that there may have been other reasons for what he calls his subjects' 'heightened sensitivity' about being in the film (Apted, 2005). He acknowledges, for instance, that some of their discontent may have had its roots in how he had allowed some of his own prejudices to intrude when pursuing certain lines of inquiry with them.[5] A particular accusation was that he had shown a regrettable tendency to represent subjects using rather crass stereotypes. Jackie, for example, one of the East End girls who had appeared in each of the *Up* films, takes him to task in *49 Up* about how he had constantly misrepresented her in the earlier films. Her particular grouse was that he had never allowed her sufficient space to express her own views and opinions (see Chapter 6, pp. 156–7).

The resonance of *Seven Up*

By way of concluding this short survey of *Seven Up* I would like to make a few brief remarks about the resonance that the films have had at home and abroad. One explanation that is regularly cited for the films' appeal is that they are able to address their audiences on different levels. At one level they can claim to provide a unique record of British life spanning several decades of significant change. Another explanation for the programmes' success is that – rather like the subjects themselves – the *Seven Up* project has been able to adapt to changing times. Originally conceived as a one-off programme that would investigate the continuing inequities of the class system, the project, as it has evolved, has revealed a capacity to develop in altogether different ways. What we are now presented with is a series of nuanced portraits tracing the life-journeys of individuals with whom we have been able to form strong empathetic bonds. As Stephen Lambert, executive producer of *42 Up* put it:

> What's happened as the programme has evolved is that it has become social history. It is not as rigidly focused on class any more, but that's because the class system itself is not as rigid. So the programme has changed to become one about middle age and the problems of middle age which are marriage, divorce, children and death. (Cited in Brooks, 1998: 2)

However else one views the *Seven Up* series, it is now generally regarded as a landmark documentary with the kind of iconic status that has allowed it to become a reference point for many other artists and filmmakers. The prize-winning contemporary British artist Gillian Wearing, for instance, has always had a special interest in the way that the media, especially television, have reflected and documented changing social attitudes. She has, for this reason, incorporated footage from a number of 'classic' television programmes into her film installation work. Wearing claims that, together with Paul Watson's seminal documentary series *The Family*, one of the most formative influences on her sociologically oriented artwork has been the *Seven Up* series (Jeffries, 2006: 18).

For successive generations of viewers, but perhaps particularly for those who belong to the generation from which the subjects themselves are drawn, the *Seven Up* series has gained a special cultural significance. Whenever, for instance, I have mentioned to fellow Brits that I was working on a project on longitudinal documentary, a frequent reaction has been, 'You mean, stuff like the *Seven Up* series.' The popularity of these films has, as already indicated, led to various attempts to launch international versions, though the original series has also gained a relatively high global profile (see Chapter 1, pp. 18–19). Some observers (including Apted himself) have expressed surprise that the films have evidently been able to strike a chord with audiences who could not be expected to pick up on some of the more culturally specific references. Such audiences are, however, clearly able to identify with some of the more universal elements of these life-stories. Thus, somewhat belying the claim that the series is rich in socio-political insights, it would appear that the source of the films' appeal may well lie in their ability to evoke in an especially powerful way what Apted has repeatedly referred to as the 'drama of ordinary life' (Apted, 1998).

The Children of Golzow

Just like Apted's *Seven Up* series, Winfried and Barbara Junge's *The Children of Golzow* (1961–2008) can also lay some claim to being an historically significant chronicle of the times. The series traces the lives of a group of (former) citizens of the GDR who were born in the 1950s and grew up in the small town of Golzow. With the fall of the Berlin Wall, the series accompanies the Golzow subjects as each of them attempts to negotiate the difficult transition from life in a one-party state to one lived in a multi-party democracy. There are certain resemblances here with *Born in the USSR* and *Born in South Africa*, both of which also sought to chronicle similar periods of radical political transformation and the impact on individual lives. The difference, however, is that in the case of *The Children of Golzow* the filmmakers had already accompanied their 'children' for almost three decades before the decisive transition (*Wende*) occurred. Thus, whatever other merits *The Children of Golzow* may have as a long doc, its particular historical value may well prove to lie in its study of how a group of individuals, whose formative years were spent in the GDR, found themselves having effectively to rebuild their lives after their country ceased to exist.

The Children of Golzow has another affinity with *Seven Up* in that both projects began when the children had just entered the first year of primary education. There the similarities start to fade, however, since *The Children of Golzow* focuses on children belonging to one community as opposed to a specially selected group of children drawn from various parts of the country and from widely differing social backgrounds. *The Children of Golzow* therefore evokes a much stronger sense of place than *Seven Up*. Indeed it might even be claimed that the early films in the Golzow cycle are as much concerned with developments within the community as they are with tracking individual life-journeys. What also distinguishes *The Children of Golzow* from its British counterpart is that the longitudinal idea was built in to the project remit right from the outset.

The person who had the idea of tracing the lives of a generation of young GDR citizens from their early schooldays into early adulthood was Karl Gass, a seasoned documentarist in his own right and, at the time, mentor to a group of aspiring young filmmakers including Volker Koepp, Gitta Nickel and the director of *The Children of Golzow* Winfried Junge.[6] In the autumn of 1961 and as part of his filmmaking apprenticeship Junge received the following instructions from Gass:

> You are to go and film the up and coming generation from the time they enter school to the time their own children are of school age. This may take from 20 to 25 years. We'll begin with their first day at school. If this film's a success, we'll then proceed to make a series of short or medium length films. We'll still have to decide at what intervals we'll produce these films, but maybe we'll end the series with a feature-length summary. The whole cycle will provide a portrait of a generation growing up in a socialist society. (Junge, 2004: 11)

Thus it was that, shortly after the building of the Berlin Wall in August 1961, the *Children of Golzow* series began. Junge completed three short Golzow films in the course of the next five years and the experience he gained in making them enabled him to win his spurs as a long doc filmmaker.

Going longitudinal

Even though Gass had conceived *The Children of Golzow* as a long doc series, it took some time (four or five years to be precise) before its longitudinal status was confirmed. According to Junge, it was the success of the third film in the series *Eleven Years Old* (1966) that persuaded Junge that he should maintain his association with the project. Even so, when Junge looked back on the origins of the project many years later, he admitted – just like Apted – that there was an element of serendipity in how he became and stayed involved. As he once remarked: 'It certainly wasn't part of any life or career plan' (Junge, 2004: 34).

For as long as the children remained at school, Junge and his team were able to use Golzow as a focal point for their work. As soon as the youngsters had completed their school studies, however, many of them left Golzow to pursue careers elsewhere in the GDR. Their ties with Golzow became less strong, with the consequence that the town and the surrounding area become less significant as the central filming location. As the cycle develops, then, there is a discernible shift in the thematic focus of the work. Just as in *The Children of Jordbrö*, an earlier preoccupation with group-centred activities – life in the classroom, gatherings in the youth club, family get-togethers and the like – gives way to a greater concern with individual life-journeys. The spotlight is no longer on the children *of* Golzow; it now falls on the children *from* Golzow.

A major turning point in the history of the Golzow long doc came in the late 1970s and early 1980s with the production of two much longer films, the rather curiously titled *Spare No Charm and Spare No Passion* (1979) and *Biographies – The Story of The Children of Golzow* (1980–81). Both these films employ different narrative strategies from those used hitherto, and both illustrate what can be achieved if a long doc filmmaker is able to paint on a larger canvas. *Biographies* is a work of considerable importance in the history of the Golzow cycle in that it was the first film in the series which brought Junge and his team a measure of international recognition. Based on the stories of just nine out of the original cast of twenty children, *Biographies* is also the first Golzow film to make significant use of subjects' back-stories (and this almost twenty years into the project!).[7]

In spite of the largely positive reception accorded to *Biographies*, the 1980s were difficult years for GDR filmmakers, so the Junges (by this time Winfried's wife Barbara had formally joined the filmmaking team) were forced to look to other sources of financial support for their project. The consequence of this was that for their next film *The People of Golzow (Analysis of the circumstances of a place)* (1984) the Junges had to turn to GDR Television to obtain the necessary funding. The film was timed to coincide with the 35th anniversary of the GDR and the 675th anniversary of Golzow itself. In GDR times the heavy hand of state control was felt even more strongly in television than it was in film production, and this is plainly evident in *The People of Golzow*. Junge himself admits that those who had commissioned the film had a determining influence on its content. Among other things, for instance, demands were made that the director 'deselect' those Golzow subjects not considered exemplary enough for the propagandising purposes of GDR television.[8]

Undoubtedly, the decisive moment in the history of the Golzow cycle came with the fall of the Berlin Wall. Not surprisingly, this led to a radical reappraisal of all aspects of the project, and for a time it seemed possible that the demise of the GDR would also signal the end of the whole Golzow series. The Junges were, however, able to gather together sufficient funding to allow them to make *Screenplay: The Times* (1992) the film that, among other things, chronicles subjects' experience of the *Wende*. *Screenplay* is arguably the most significant of all the Golzow films. Naturally enough, it contains a strong retrospective element as subjects look back on more than three decades of living in a country that is in the process of being absorbed into its larger neighbour.[9] *Screenplay* is also the work in which Junge himself, for the first time in the whole history of the Golzow cycle, takes the opportunity to indulge in some extensive, self-critical reflections on the making of the film, especially with regard to the constraints under which GDR filmmakers were forced to operate.

Screenplay is also epoch-making in a further sense. In order not to leave us with any doubts that the filmmakers are also entering a new era, Junge himself – for the first time in the history of the project – becomes an active screen protagonist. Rather than continuing to be a disembodied voice-over presence as he had been hitherto, he now allows himself to be filmed in conversation with his subjects. They compare notes with each other on their experiences of the *Wende* and start to reflect on what they think the consequences of these unsettling events will be for all East Germans. Junge and his subjects are now able to develop a much closer relationship than in the lifetime of the GDR. Any residual doubts that the Golzower may have had about Junge's links, as a DEFA filmmaker, with the state authorities have also disappeared. In all the post-*Wende* films Junge's Golzow subjects clearly relish being able to speak their mind on a whole range of issues that had previously been off-limits.

In the decade following the production of *Screenplay* the Junges succeeded – though not without a great deal of difficulty – in securing sufficient funding from a number of sources to enable them to make eight full-length film portraits of individual Golzower. By the time they had completed the last of these films, Junge was in his late sixties, and he and his wife began to give active consideration to ways in which they might contrive a suitable ending for the Golzow series. Perhaps understandably, after so many years of active and committed involvement, the Junges were opposed to a too hasty departure, and their leave-taking took the form of a lingering fare-well that extended over a two- to three-year period. During this time they produced two very long films, each lasting more than four and a half hours, under the umbrella title *And If They Haven't Passed Away, They're Living Happily Ever After*. Parts one and two of this epic farewell were screened in 2006 and parts three and four followed in 2008. In bringing down the curtain on the Golzow series. *And If They Haven't Passed Away* largely adopts the same biography-centred approach of previous films. The farewell film not only reac-quaints us with some of the better-known Golzow protagonists but also reintroduces us to several subjects with whom the filmmakers had temporarily lost contact.

Even a short synoptic account of the Golzow series has to take into consideration the very particular conditions under which they were produced. For the first three decades the films were made under the auspices of DEFA, the state-owned East German film company.[10] As a full-time DEFA employee Winfried Junge had job security and also enjoyed relatively favourable working conditions. He could also rely on the kind of technical and logistical support that was the envy of many filmmakers in the West. All these benefits have to be set against the not inconsiderable number of constraints under which East German filmmakers were required to work. Like most of his contemporaries, Junge had to be ever mindful that making films under these conditions could always involve something of a trade-off. For one's voice to be heard at all, one always had to prac-tise self-censoring discretion, since there were clear expectations on the part of the state authorities concerning what kind of image of Golzow and its citizens should be projected. More than once in the long history of *The Children of Golzow* tensions arose out of the disjuncture between the expectations of the powers-that-be and the desire of Junge and his team to produce a more honest account of the realities they encountered. Junge has sometimes been taken to task, mostly by West German observers, for not introducing a more socio-critical element into his Golzow films. Such criticism does not, however, pay sufficient heed to what was actually possible under the conditions that prevailed in East Germany at this time. While any more open dissent would not have been tolerated, filmmakers could sometimes introduce more implicit forms of critique into the sub-texts of their work.

For German audiences, especially those who belong to the generation that lived through the Cold War period, the Golzow films will always carry a special resonance, bringing to mind, as they do, all those memories of mutual suspicion and of bitter divisions between implacably opposed states. Viewers who, on the other hand, come to these films without the burden of such memories will most likely have a very different response. Whilst acknowledging that the Golzower were subject to a large number of socio-political constraints, new generations of viewers will, arguably, be much more disposed to seeing the more universal relevance of these films. For instance, witnessing the Golzower as they seek to re-orient themselves, personally and professionally, after the traumas and challenges of the *Wende*, may put such viewers in mind of wholly different kinds of life-changing experience. The 'displacement' of the Golzower came about as a direct consequence of the collapse of communism, but this experience has its parallels in many other instances where individuals or groups are forced, out of political or economic necessity, to distance themselves – physically or emotionally – from the place they regarded as their '*Heimat*'. The future resonance of these films may well lie in the recognition that these Golzower stories have much wider applicability.

The Children of Jordbrö

The beginnings of *The Children of Jordbrö* (1972–2006) go back to the early 1970s when Rainer Hartleb was working as a television journalist for Swedish Television. His original idea was to produce a documentary that would reveal the full human impact of a new housing policy being introduced at the time by the Swedish government. For Hartleb, chronicling the lives of a group of children as they went through their first years at school would provide an excellent illustration of the gulf between government rhetoric and what ordinary people were actually experiencing. Hartleb was convinced that only a longitudinal study would do justice to what he was seeking to convey. It did take him some time, however, to convince his paymasters at Swedish Television of the merits of a prolonged investigation. Like broadcasters the world over, they were initially very resistant to the idea of supporting a project where long-term viewer interest could not be guaranteed.

Over the next eight years he completed a set of twelve one-hour films, each of which was aired on Swedish Television.[11] By this time the Jordbrö series had gained a sufficiently high profile with its Swedish audience to enable Hartleb to secure funding for further instalments in the unfolding narrative. In 1987 he produced *Back to Jordbrö*, a film that updates viewers on how the children have been faring in the period since they left full-time education. By this time the subjects were well into their twenties, and we see them confronting relationship and marital problems as well as seeking an appropriate niche in the employment market. *Back to Jordbrö* resonates with a poignant melancholy, as viewers are made aware of the often-painful gulf between subjects' erstwhile boldly stated ambitions and their present-day all-too modest achievements.

The later films in the Jordbrö cycle also follow the general pattern of other long doc series in that the emphasis is now more on the individual portrait rather than the collective study. This is best exemplified in the two films made in the course of the 1990s: *Once Upon a Time There Was a Little Girl* (1992) centres on the figure of Mona Jönsson, now in her mid-thirties, as she reflects back on her life from the time we first confronted her as a slightly rebellious eight-year-old being cajoled out of her bed by her mother to the present day when she has parental responsibilities of her own. *Once Upon a Time* is also significant in the way that it elicits an especially reflective response from the audience. The film is edited in such a way that, as we accompany Mona through the various stages of her life, we are encouraged to reflect on what aspects of personality contribute towards the unique trajectory of an individual's life-journey. *Once Upon a Time* is also to some extent a reflexive film in that, more than in some of the earlier films, the filmmaker makes viewers aware of the structuring and shaping role that he has had in the construction of the work.[12]

By the time Hartleb came to make *A Pizza in Jordbrö* (1994) he had come to the conclusion that the Jordbrö opus had probably run its course and that now was the time to move on to new projects. As one Swedish observer has commented: '*A Pizza in Jordbrö* [was] intended to be the last of the series … His major oeuvre was complete. He drew a mental line under it. Time to move on' (Weman, 2006: 5). Since *A Pizza in Jordbrö* was designed as the last film in the cycle, it contains distinct valedictory overtones. It is also a quietly nostalgic film, calculated to evoke reflections on how the passage of time impacts on all our lives. More than twenty years have now passed since the Jordbrö cycle began. As with most long docs of this vintage, *Pizza* is edited in such a way that viewers are constantly shuttled between past and present. For instance, in the time that has elapsed since our last visit, several subjects have become parents. This enables Hartleb to work in a number of scenes from yesteryear that allow us to compare the parenting that the subjects themselves received with how they are now bringing up their own children. A further theme that is foregrounded in *Pizza*, though it has been touched on in earlier films, is how the children of immigrant families have fared in the time since we first encountered them as seven- or eight-year-olds. How easily have they integrated into Swedish society? What feelings do they have for the countries that their parents left behind as they sought to build a new life in Sweden? How do their lives compare with those of their Swedish counterparts?[13]

Following *Pizza*, and true to his private resolve, Hartleb attempted – at least as far as his filmmaking career was concerned – to put Jordbrö behind him. He began to embark on new projects, including one *Wiedersehen in Hildburghausen* (1996) in which he sought to trace his family roots in Thuringia. What Hartleb had not reckoned with, however, was that a long doc such as the Jordbrö series in many ways develops an impetus and life of its own. And so, indeed, it proved. In 2004 Hartleb, approached a Swedish documentary film commissioner with a view to securing funding for a new project. The commissioner was, apparently, not overly enthusiastic about Hartleb's pitch but was curious to know how the 'folks in Jordbrö' were getting on (Weman, 2006: 5). Hartleb was seemingly not at all certain whether it would be a wise move to resurrect the Jordbrö project, but he allowed himself to be persuaded that he should give it a try. Though not at all certain about how some of his subjects would respond to the request to step on to the stage once more, Hartleb duly began work on a new film *Everyone's Fine* which premièred in 2006.

By entitling his film *Everyone's Fine* Hartleb – perhaps with tongue in cheek – was possibly seeking to reassure the members of his audience who had loyally followed the series for more than three decades that they need have no major concerns about how things would turn out for his subjects in the longer term. However much Hartleb attempts to persuade us that all will be well, the film is not without a distinct undertow of sadness. (The mood of sadness is reinforced by the plaintive piano underscoring.) Hartleb is clearly concerned, however, not to allow melancholy to become the dominant theme. He is therefore concerned to introduce several sequences into the film in which the darker and the lighter aspects of life are held in some kind of equilibrium. As Hartleb himself has observed: 'The new film [*Everyone's Fine*] has more life experience, it's more serious. It has its moments of light and dark, of pain and sorrow. It's deeper, more existential if you will' (Weman, 2006: 5).

Notes

1 Throughout this work I have generally chosen to use the term *Seven Up* when referring to Apted's series. Some critics and observers (including Apted himself) occasionally use the descriptor 'The *Up* films', but *Seven Up* remains the term most frequently employed when making synecdochic reference to the series of films produced at seven-year intervals over a period of more than four decades.

2 One has to bear in mind, however, that broadcasters were operating in very different conditions in the 1960s. When *Seven Up* was first broadcast, there were only three terrestrial channels in the United Kingdom (two BBC channels and one ITV channel). This was the time of the 'comfortable duopoly'. Programming ideas and formats had not yet become prized commodities, and terms such as 'format development' and 'programming concepts' were likewise not yet part of broadcasters' everyday vocabulary.

3 Stella Bruzzi provides some useful insights into the production history of the *Seven Up* films, especially concerning the contribution of the producer Claire Lewis who has been with the series since *28 Up* (see Bruzzi, 2007).

4   As well as working on several television series, Apted has directed many
    well-received films including *Coal Miner's Daughter, Gorky Park, Gorillas
    in the Mist, Nell* and *Amazing Grace.*

5   With the wisdom of hindsight, Apted freely admits that in some of the
    early *Up* films, he made the mistake of allowing too many of his own
    class-determined preconceptions to intrude when interviewing his
    young subjects.

6   For useful introductions on East German documentary filmmaking
    see Allan & Sandford (eds), 1999; Jordan & Schenk (eds), 1996; and
    Silbermann, 1994.

7   Junge had already produced one individual portrait of a Golzow sub-
    ject in 1975 when he made *I Spoke With a Girl,* a 30-minute biography
    focusing on the life of Marie-Luise.

8   A number of possibilities had been discussed in the course of the 1980s
    for extending the life of the project. Among other suggestions it had
    been mooted that the Junges might produce a series of individual biog-
    raphies of Golzow subjects to be screened on GDR television in the au-
    tumn of 1991. This would have coincided with the thirtieth anniversary
    of the Golzow series.

9   *Screenplay* also brings echoes of a number of German books and films
    produced in the time immediately following World War II, where writers
    and filmmakers are seen attempting to come to terms with the trau-
    mas of the recent past (the process known in German as *Vergangenheits-
    bewältigung*).

10 As was the case with all other former communist states, all forms of
    media activity in the GDR were under strict state supervision.

11 At a later date the twelve one-hour films were edited and adapted by
    Hartleb to form two single films *The Children from Jordbrö* (covering the
    period 1972–75) and *Living in Jordbrö* (1975–81).

12 Right at the outset of the film, for instance, the audience is invited to
    reflect on the manner in which this particular story is framed and pre-
    sented. As the narrator puts it in the opening sequence: 'Once upon a
    time! That's how many stories begin, even true ones.'

13 Hartleb clearly feels a special affinity with those who, like himself, came
    to Sweden when they were very young and were confronted with the
    challenge of adapting to a new way of life.

3

Getting started

The main aim of this chapter is to explore the conditions under which the long docs under review came to be produced and to consider the role played by particular organisations and institutions in the nurturing of these works. Questions that will be addressed will include: What lay behind the original decision to commission the work? What relationship was there between the film or programme maker and the sponsoring institution? What was the principal motivation for the filmmaker(s) concerned to become involved in such a project? What were the criteria for choosing a particular filming location or a particular group of subjects? In talking about how the individual projects originated, I shall be taking a close look at the role played by the institutions that produced and promoted these works. No-one would deny that works that span several decades of a director's career represent a considerable personal achievement. On the other hand, each of these long docs is closely identified with, if not deeply indebted to, a particular broadcasting or filmmaking organisation.

A couple of points should be made at the outset concerning the basic form and structure of long docs. Firstly, it is possible to draw certain parallels between the works themselves and the individual life-journeys of the participants. In both cases one can discern a number of 'given-at-birth' qualities that will continue, over the longer term, to exert a powerful if not determining influence. Secondly, long docs – just like the individuals whose lives they trace – are very susceptible to the impact of external events. These parallels are especially apparent at times of dramatic socio-political change where long doc subjects – and sometimes the filmmakers – find themselves having to adapt to radically changed circumstances. In this sense long docs not only chronicle the lives of individuals but also provide valuable insights into filmmaking and broadcasting developments.[1]

Whilst hard-headed funding or sponsoring agents may be disinclined to enter into totally open-ended arrangements in which long doc filmmakers can rely on having their project funded over an indeterminate period, broadcasters are well aware of the economic benefits that accrue from a series or serial mode of presentation.[2] In the last two or three decades, for instance, there has been a commercially driven move away from the one-off single drama towards serial and series modes that can be relied on to maintain audience attention over a number of episodes (Creeber, 2004: 7–18; Holland, 1997: 113–17). With film and television documentary products, the pressure to generate large viewing figures may not be felt quite so acutely, but this does not mean that broadcasters will not be looking to certain types of factual or documentary product to fulfil particular scheduling needs. One of the best recent illustrations of the tendency to exploit an episodic mode of presentation has been the docu-soap. This was a form of television factual entertainment, popular during the second half of the 1990s, which combined structuring features derived from soap opera with elements of observational documentary. Docu-soaps allowed viewers to tune in on a regular basis and see real-life (often larger-than-life) individuals discoursing most entertainingly on their everyday concerns (Kilborn, 2003: 57–8, 89–121).

With docu-soaps, part of the original concept involved the calculation that the programme would comprise a series of episodes presented over a period of some weeks, with the possibility of the programme returning for a further series if the first outing proved a ratings success. With long docs on the other hand, it is by no means always the case that they have seriality planned in from the outset. Some long docs started out as modest one-off documentaries before acquiring longitudinal status (see also Chapter 1, pp. 12–13). And even where it has been accepted that a topic really needs to be treated longitudinally (as was the case with Rainer Hartleb's Jordbrö series), there can still be reluctance on the part of the broadcaster or funding body to enter into a long-term contract with the film or programme maker until the series has proved its worth in audience ratings' terms.[3] All the more reason, therefore, to pay especially close attention to the precise genesis of the chosen works to consider in what ways the circumstances of the works' origination may have influenced the course of their further development.[4]

Seven Up

Whatever the conditions under which long docs originate, it goes without saying that, to be at all successful in the longer term, they require a special kind of nurturing. Not only does the film or programme maker have to make a long-term (sometimes life-long) commitment to the project; a long doc also needs the support of a broadcaster or sponsoring agent. Michael Apted, for instance, has always been keen to express his debt to Granada, not only for having been responsible for originating the series but also for having, over the years, continued to give the project its support. In his words:

> One of the reasons that the *Up* films have survived is that Granada has always been there. I've a lot to thank them for. They've always been willing to bankroll it. In an institutional sense the support of Granada has been crucial to the survival of the *Up* series. (Apted, 2007)

Granada was one of the new independent UK television companies formed in the 1950s. It was, at least in the early days of its existence, a decidedly left-leaning institution and there were expectations of its programme makers that they would adopt a politically progressive stance and vigorously contest Establishment views. As David Plowright, who joined the company in 1957 and eventually (in 1975) went on to become its managing director, put it:

> Granada Television was the most precocious of the independent [new] television companies. It was swashbuckling and successful and it was irresistible for the first generation of commercial television programme makers keen to challenge the monopoly of the BBC. (Cited in Finch, 2003: ix)

Apted had joined Granada in 1963 as a production trainee. The company was still in its pioneering phase, and even 40 years after the event Apted can still recall the excitement and exuberance of those early days:

> It was intoxicating stuff for lily-livered boys straight out of college ... There was a genuine populist drive to talk about real issues in

a language that everybody could understand – to be passionate and accessible, to care about what you were saying and not to talk down to the audience … It was dazzling to watch, for underneath there was a powerful humanity and willingness to take on a social and civic responsibility which in today's world, and not just in broadcasting, has vanished. (Ibid: 76–7)

During the first few years he spent working at Granada, Apted gained many of the skills that enabled him to develop his renowned versatility as a film director and programme maker equally at home in a wide range of genres, both fiction and non-fiction. At Granada there was no formal training as such, and much of what Apted learned – and was to stand him in good stead over the decades to come – was in his phrase simply 'picked up as he went along' (Apted, 2007). Apted himself has always been keen to emphasise that the experience he gained at Granada of working in various forms of narrative fiction has been particularly helpful when he has been editing the *Up* films (Apted, 1998).

The *Seven Up* story begins in 1964 when Apted and a fellow production trainee were assigned to work on a special *World in Action* programme. The programme was to be the last edition to be produced by the man who until then had been running *World in Action*, the charismatic Australian Tim Hewat. Hewat plays a similar role in the history of *Seven Up* as Karl Gass does in the history of *The Children of Golzow*. Just like Gass, Hewat wanted to make a programme that looked at a generation of seven-year-olds, considered their future prospects and related all this to broader socio-cultural developments.[5] Hewat's interest in the topic may well have arisen out of his fascination, as a visiting Australian, with what he doubtless saw as the continuing inequities of the British class system.[6] As he put it many years later after he had returned to Australia:

I had long been fascinated by the Jesuit claim:'give us the child until he is seven and we will give you the man.'How much, I wondered, did the class structure in Britain shape the likely lives of its children? The result was *Seven Up,* a fascinating and devastating revelation. (Cited in Finch, 2003: 199)

What distinguished the *Seven Up* film from others in the *World in Action* series was that the production team had much longer (six weeks) to complete this 'Special' programme than they would have had for a standard *World in Action* broadcast. In spite of this relative luxury of not having to put the programme together at breakneck speed, Apted and the other members of the production team were given a very strong steer by Hewat as to how the programme should be structured. According to Gordon McDougall, one of Apted's co-workers, a few off-the-cuff remarks by Hewat about the criteria for the selection of subjects were to have an important determining effect on the whole *Seven Up* series, As McDougall puts it:

> That first day Tim [Hewat] took us to the top of Golden Square [the location of Granada's London office]. 'If I'm making this show,' he said, 'I start with the camera up here and twenty children down in the square.'Voice over:'Here are twenty children, these five are going to be winners.'Zoom in.'These fifteen are going to be losers.'Zoom in.'Now we're going to show you why.' *We smiled internally at the crassness of the style and spent four months making a programme which said exactly that.* (Cited in Finch, 2003: 79, my emphasis)

Dutifully following Hewat's promptings, the *World in Action* team set about selecting a suitable cast of children who would fit the prescribed specifications and who were, in the programme makers' eyes, likely to become 'winners' and 'losers'. Choosing as they did children from what Apted has described as the 'extremes of the social spectrum' has proved to have had far-reaching and long-lasting consequences for what later became the *Seven Up* series. For instance, it has somewhat limited the claims that are sometimes made for the series that it reveals the changing face of Britain, since so many of those who were to be centrally involved in engineering these changes are conspicuous by their absence.[7]

The original *World in Action* 'Seven Up'

Though *Seven Up* has long since acquired the status of an extraordinarily successful series in its own right, its origins as a *World in Action* 'Special' are still clearly marked and have to be accounted for. The *World in Action* strand has gained almost legendary status in the history of broadcasting in the United Kingdom (see Goddard et al., 2007). In particular, it is regarded as representing a high point in the history of current affairs programming on television. Programmes produced by the *World in Action* were celebrated for combining a sharp analysis of contemporary social and political issues with an ability to get through to a mass audience. The strand also developed a well-deserved reputation for the uncompromising style of its investigative reporting and for tackling some of the more controversial issues of the day.[8]

The *World in Action* tone is, however, immediately detectable in the original *Seven Up* programme, which certainly does not pull any punches when setting out its agenda. The opening credits are played out to the kind of dramatic musical accompaniment that one associates with current affairs or factual genres. There is then a brief sequence showing children exercising in a school gym, before we switch to the key establishing scene in which we are introduced to the sample group of children gathered together at London Zoo. The commentary, spoken by an authoritative middle-class white male voice, as was customary in broadcasting of the period, informs us:

> This is no ordinary outing to the zoo. It's a very special occasion. We've brought these children together for the very first time. They're like any other children, except that they come from startlingly different backgrounds. We've brought these children together, because we wanted a glimpse of England in the year 2000. (*Seven Up*)

After a brief pause, the same voice solemnly continues: 'Give me a child until he is seven, and I will give you the man' (ibid.).

The scene having been set in this way, the narrator then briefly introduces each of the children, telling us where they are from and providing details about their family background. Careful thought has evidently been given to where these introductory scenes are shot, since they also have the function of providing additional visual clues about the social environments from which the children originate. Tony, for instance, the working-class lad from the East End of London, is filmed fighting with other boys against the background of a run-down East-End primary school. The suggestion is that this kind of environment is not one in which children will be educationally advantaged. As Douglas Keay, the narrator, informs us: 'The world of the seven-year-old can be primitive, even violent.' All this is in stark contrast to the far more ordered and disciplined worlds that other children are shown to inhabit. Charles, Andrew and John, for instance, the three plummy-voiced posh boys attending private preparatory schools, are filmed in relatively plush surroundings. Likewise when we are first introduced to demure Suzy, she is sitting deeply ensconced in the chintzy armchair in the headmistress's study. The children from these more privileged backgrounds seem to have their life trajectories mapped out for them right from the moment of birth, whilst the future lives of the others are clouded in much greater uncertainty.

Having set out its agenda in this way, the *Seven Up* programme moves forward at a relatively swift pace, switching the attention regularly between scenes featuring the 'haves' and those focusing on the 'have-nots'. It is through this constant juxtaposition of apparently irreconcilable worlds that the political message of the programme emerges. As often as not, the individual sequences are allowed to speak for themselves, but at certain key moments the narrator will intervene to provide some guidance on what conclusions we should draw from this exposition. Against shots, for instance, of young boys at a preparatory school being taught how to march, we are told: 'A few [children] from the age they are born are trained to accept discipline'. Likewise, following a sequence in which shots depicting the ordered world of Suzy's ballet class have been juxtaposed against those of scruffy East-End kids fighting with each other, the narrator quietly observes: 'The distinction between freedom and discipline is the key to their whole future.'

As the original *Seven Up* programme nears its conclusion, its makers prepare the ground for us to take our leave of this very heter-ogeneous group of subjects. At the end of their specially arranged day, which has involved a trip to the zoo and a party, the children are brought together in seeming harmony in an adventure play-ground where, as one might have expected, they seek the company of those with whom they feel socially most at ease. This provides the narrator with the cue to restate what the programme had set out to achieve and to direct one more searching question at the audience: 'If some of our children didn't get on, does it really matter? None of them are likely to meet in the same classroom.' This final quip about the children being unlikely ever to meet in a real life situation also serves to underline the programme's thesis about the rigidity of the British class system.

Whilst there is much about this original *Seven Up* programme that marks it out as a one-off 'Special' in the *World in Action* strand, it is not difficult to see why, at a later date, Granada decided to turn it into a longitudinal series. Firstly, even though the *Seven Up* chil-dren had only made relatively brief appearances in the first *Seven Up* programme, many of them had such endearing personalities that one could confidently anticipate that many viewers would welcome the opportunity of being reacquainted with them.[9] Secondly, many of the original programme's thematic concerns turned on what would become of these children in the future. A strong case could therefore be made for a follow-up programme that would update viewers on whether the children's lives were developing along the lines that they or others had predicted. Would the lives of the three upper-class boys from privileged backgrounds in fact follow their anticipated course? And by the same token, would those from poorer backgrounds be held back in the longer term by their not having had the same head start in life? In other words: was the actual course of events proving it to be the case that there was a direct correlation between family background or early environment and what the children went on to achieve?

As viewers take their leave of the children that the *World in Action* '*Seven Up*' has contrived to bring together, they are encouraged to reflect on the messages the programme has attempted to convey. Just before the closing credits, the narrator reminds us of the Jesuit claim, 'Give me a child until he is seven, and I will give you the man', and then goes on to utter the concluding words: 'This has been a glimpse of Britain's future.' With this striking, almost poetic, statement the curtain is brought down on the *World in Action* 'Special', though – looked at from another perspective and with the benefit of hindsight – this closing phrase could also be seen as holding the door open for a possible revisitation at some unspecified future date. It was, however, to be a further six years before Granada decided to take such a step and to attempt to unlock what they saw as the programme's unrealised potential.

The Children of Golzow

Just as the *Seven Up* series owes much to the backing it has received from Granada Television, so the (East) German long doc *The Children of Golzow* would not have come about without the long-term support of DEFA, the state-owned company responsible for film production in the GDR for as long as that separate German state continued to exist.[10] Since DEFA played such an important nurturing role during the first three decades of the Golzow cycle's life-span, readers are entitled to know a little more about the workings of this organisation and in particular its relationship with the state authorities.

During the 45 years of its existence DEFA produced more than 750 films, some of which attracted considerable attention outside the borders of the GDR. For a country of this size (17 million inhabitants) this represents a considerable achievement. As in most other socialist states, all forms of media activity in the GDR took place under the watchful and controlling eye of the Party. Filmmakers had to operate under quite severe constraints. Yet, whilst some filmmakers were all too willing to produce work tailored to the propagandist requirements of their political masters, there were others far less prepared to fall in line with Party dictates.[11] To put this more bluntly: Provided they did not overstep the mark and seek to express their views on a number of taboo issues, GDR documentary filmmakers had greater room for manoeuvre than one might have imagined. As one critic has noted:

> Those working for the DEFA documentary studios had considerable opportunity for free artistic expression. Compared with television, which dutifully conformed to Party wishes, DEFA gained the reputation of being a place which offered creative opportunities for self-confident, critically minded directors and production teams. (Zimmermann, 1995: 9, my translation)

Almost inevitably, the fortunes of DEFA also became tied up with power struggles within the party and with ongoing attempts to use film to project a favourable image of the GDR and its people, both internally and externally. The impact of political developments on the activities of GDR filmmakers is nowhere better illustrated than by what occurred in the years immediately following the building of the Berlin Wall in August 1961. This period, which, incidentally, coincided with the production of the first two Golzow films, was a time during which, ironically enough, writers and artists in the GDR felt that they could enjoy a greater measure of creative freedom, now that the country had allegedly secured its borders against the threat of foreign incursion. Any hopes that filmmakers may have entertained that the spirit of greater openness was there to stay and that they would be encouraged to tackle more controversial subjects, were cut short four years later when the Party intervened to halt the spread of what it considered to be dangerously liberal ideas. At the Eleventh Plenum of the Party's Central Committee in December 1965, Erich Honecker, who was later (in 1971) to become First Secretary of the Party, launched a bitter attack on a number of authors and filmmakers who were accused of undermining the carefully constructed foundations on which a new socialist society was being built and of driving a wedge between Party and people. A series of repressive measures were undertaken to curb these undesirable developments A number of recently produced films had their release or exhibition certificates withdrawn and orders were given for work on other films still in production to cease.[12] This particular instance of state intervention clearly points up the kinds of pressures that filmmakers like Winfried Junge must have felt at various times during his career as a DEFA filmmaker, but particularly during the early days when he was seeking to build a filmmaking reputation. Establishing and maintaining good working relations with his Golzow subjects was proving challenging enough. Remaining in good odour with the various state officials and members of the DEFA film commission, on the other hand, arguably required even more highly developed skills.[13]

The start of the Golzow project

Just as with Rainer Hartleb, it took some time before Winfried Junge discovered that his *forte* lay in documentary. After attending school in Berlin, Junge did a one-year teacher training course before enrolling on a four-year programme at the film school in Potsdam-Babelsberg where he trained to be a *Dramaturg* (script editor). Having successfully completed the course, Junge was sent to join a DEFA production group headed by the experienced and respected director Karl Gass. Under Gass's supervision Junge extended his repertoire of filmmaking skills and over a two-year period had a hand in the making of several short films, most of them in the factual or documentary category.

It was whilst working for Gass that Junge began to realise that his filmmaking strengths lay more in directing than in script editing. It was also during this time that Junge first developed a particular interest in documentary. Even as a student Junge had felt more drawn towards documentary than to fiction film, but it was working under Gass's mentorship that convinced him that, if he was going to make a mark as a filmmaker, then it would probably be as a documentarist. Junge was especially enthusiastic about the work of renowned filmmakers such as Joris Ivens, Richard Leacock and Chris Marker. The quality he most admired in these other filmmakers was their ability to let events speak for themselves rather than foisting their own interpretations and explanations on the audience. Central to Junge's thinking about documentary was the belief in the powers of careful observation. As he put it once in an interview:

> I began to empathise more and more with those [filmmakers] who had a social mission, who were willing to put their trust in authenticity and who took up a discreet position vis-à-vis their subjects. Above all, I had a lot of time for those who were not trying to make an artistic statement. (Cited in Junge, 2004: 22, my translation)

As already suggested, the idea for what later became the Golzow cycle of films came originally from Junge's mentor Karl Gass.[14] Like almost all good ideas, Gass's proposal has the virtue of simplicity. It involved producing an extended documentary account of the experiences of a generation of East German children from the time they start school till such time as their own children enter school more than two decades later. The proposed chronicle would focus especially on the education process but would also have to move outside the confines of the school as the youngsters moved into the next phase of their lives (further study, apprenticeships, their first jobs, the forging of possibly long-term relationships). The overall intention was thus nothing less than to produce a portrait of a generation growing up in a socialist society.

Though Junge recognised that such an idea might have considerable potential in the longer term, his more immediate concern was to get over the first hurdle: the short film depicting the children's first encounter with the school where they would be spending their next ten years. In preparing for this mission, Junge and his team soon became aware that filming a group of six- or seven-year-olds in a classroom setting would bring its fair share of challenges. Much that went on would be unpredictable and there would be a constant danger of missing what turned out to be quite significant events. Junge did derive some consolation, however, from the thought that children of this age are generally much less inhibited than older children and for this reason would possibly be less fazed by the presence of the camera.

As with any long doc project of this type (focusing on children attending the same school) one of the most crucial decisions that had to be taken concerned the choice of location. Junge rightly guessed that this would be an issue where there would be particular sensitivity on the part of the state authorities and of his superiors in the DEFA organisation. Once again he received a strong steer from his mentor Karl Gass as to where the project should be set. Gass felt that it should not be in one of the major conurbations such as Berlin, Dresden or Leipzig but 'in as remote an area as one can find' (Junge, 2004: 12). Junge accordingly narrowed his search to the Oderbruch area to the east of Berlin and close to the Polish border. With the help of a district education official, Junge inspected various schools in the area before deciding on Golzow. Junge clearly felt that, in terms of the remit he had been given, Golzow ticked most of the relevant boxes. The school was one of the recently introduced *Landschulen* (rural schools) which children would attend for their ten years of basic schooling, thus ensuring some continuity for the purposes of a longitudinal project. Golzow was also a place that had still not entirely recovered from the ravages of war and would thus presumably provide opportunities for reminding viewers of the need to continue devoting one's efforts to the building of a new, socialist society. Finally, and by no means of least concern, Golzow had some logistical advantages for a group of DEFA filmmakers. It was within striking distance (80 km) of their studio base in Berlin, thus guaranteeing them swift and easy access to their filming location and also enabling Junge and other members of his team to maintain contact with their subjects even when filming was not taking place.

Like his two fellow long doc filmmakers Apted and Hartleb, Junge was still relatively inexperienced when he started out on the Golzow project. It took him some time to develop the kind of techniques that would stand him in good stead over the coming decades. Just as Junge had anticipated, filming a group of lively seven- and eight-year-olds in a classroom setting also proved to be far from straightforward. He acknowledges, for instance, that for the very first Golzow film *When I First Go to School* (1961) he and his cameraman Hans-Eberhard Leupold employed a judicious amount of re-enactment in their attempt to capture the drama of certain classroom exchanges. The film thus presents what might be termed a dramatically enhanced account of events. At the same time, Junge and his team also made limited use of secret filming techniques. They concealed their camera in a hide-like contraption located outside the classroom and attempted to film events from this outside perspective. The results of these endeavours bore no relation to the effort that had to be invested and they soon abandoned such practices. Just like Rainer Hartleb in *The Children of Jordbrö*, Junge soon realised that, as a non-participant observer, you need to be sharing the same space as the subjects whose interactions you are recording (see Hesse, 1974: 18).

In retrospect, Junge freely admits that his first Golzow film has a number of shortcomings and that part of his motivation for making the second Golzow film just one year later was to correct some of the mistakes he had made in the first. In *One Year Later* (1962) Junge reveals much greater assurance in dealing with both his subjects and his subject matter. By situating himself this time inside the classroom, not only is the presence of the camera and the filmmaker acknowledged but also the filmed events themselves are recognised as partly resulting from the interactions of the parties involved. The other noteworthy feature of the second film is that Junge here begins to focus more on individual children rather than the activities of the whole class. Viewers are thus encouraged to reflect on how individual personalities are formed and to speculate on how they might develop in the future.

With the making of these two short films Junge had convinced his immediate DEFA superiors that he should be allowed to continue work on the Golzow project. The largely positive response to the films also enabled Karl Gass, as head of the documentary unit responsible for their production, to secure the funding and permissions necessary for further Golzow films to be made. Like all other GDR filmmakers, however, Junge was well aware that – for the project to stand any chance of gaining longer-term support – he would have to be careful not to incur the displeasure of the state authorities. This would inevitably involve the striking of certain compromises, especially with respect to the amount of contextualising information he chose to include. In the first two Golzow films, focusing as they had done on the children's first experiences of life at school, Junge had employed a broadly observational approach and had been able to justify not including any explanatory or interpretive commentary. He realised, however, that the longer he worked on the project, the greater pressure there would be for him to provide the kind of commentary that drew attention, for instance, to how the education the young Golzower were receiving was preparing them for life as active and productive members of GDR society. In other words, Junge recognised that the inclusion of any form of commentary would be bound to lead to accusations of his being ideologically complicit. On the other hand, without at least some indication of a commitment to the socialist cause, there would be difficulties in getting his work approved by the relevant authorities. As Junge once remarked when he looked back on the reception of the first Golzow films by representatives in the Ministry of Culture:

> We received a level of support and approval [from cultural officials] for our documentary approach, one based on the observation of significant events. This was in spite of the fact that the political leadership had always been suspicious of work that only sought to observe and refused to take a stand or provide a judgement. The threat of not showing sufficient degree of commitment hung over us like a sword of Damocles. (Cited in Junge, 2004: 33, my translation)

With these first two Golzow films Junge gained a reputation for himself as an emergent long doc filmmaker. It was not until he made his third film *Eleven Years Old* (1966) that the DEFA authorities were willing to give the project a little more support. There is, for instance, a reference in the opening credits of *Eleven Years Old* to the plan to follow the lives of the subjects until they were in their mid-twenties.[15] The success of the film when it was shown and the plaudits received at the 1966 Leipzig Documentary Festival also seem to have boosted Junge's confidence to the point that he could privately acknowledge that the Golzow project was, from now on, going to form an important part of his professional life. In his own words: 'I felt that, if people get something out of these films and are to keen to know what becomes of these children, I'm happy to be part of this project' (ibid.).

The Children of Jordbrö

Just like Junge and Apted with their long doc projects, Rainer Hartleb was still at an early stage in his filmmaking career when he began working on *The Children of Jordbrö*. Hartleb had joined Swedish Television in 1968 and had begun training as a television journalist. During this period he contributed to a number of current affairs programmes that covered a wide range of contemporary socio-political issues. Many of the programmes on which worked belonged to the category of investigative journalism. He remembers one programme in particular, for instance, that set out to show the extent to which Swedish consumer behaviour was largely determined by different levels of personal income. The manifest intention was, in Hartleb's words, to 'expose the underlying inequalities of Swedish society and the impact this had on people's lives' (Hartleb, 2007).

In the course of the 1960s Sweden had begun to gain the reputation of being an especially progressive society with a strong record on social welfare. However, Hartleb was not entirely persuaded by the claims of some politicians that Sweden was becoming a more egalitarian society and that some of the old inequalities had been eradicated. His suspicions were that there was a clear disjuncture between the utopian declarations of establishment politicians about the 'dawning of a new age' and the experience of those who belonged to the more disenfranchised groups in society. In Hartleb's words: 'People thought that Sweden was a welfare state. Everything was equal on the surface, but I kept wondering what was it like just below the surface' (ibid.).

Hartleb's strong desire to expose some of the less palatable, hidden realities that politicians wished to conceal may be regarded as one of the factors that led to the making of the Jordbrö series. As often is the case with works of this type, however, a number of factors were involved in Hartleb's decision to commit himself to a project that would – though he did not know it at the time – occupy him for the next thirty or more years. One quite important reason that needs to be taken into account, however, is that Hartleb was at the time looking for an escape route out of being a television journalist. He had served his apprenticeship in television and had already gathered some programme-making experience, but he was far from happy at the prospect of remaining in television journalism. In his own blunt self-assessment: 'I knew I wasn't at the right place when I started with television. I completely failed in that field. I also knew I was not talented for studio work. I couldn't do it. I did not have the skills. I only felt stressed and unhappy' (ibid.).

Accepting that he was temperamentally not suited to the cut and thrust of television journalism, Hartleb considered whether he might not be better advised to try his luck as a freelance documentary filmmaker. Casting around for documentary ideas he might be able to develop, he spotted an advertisement in a local newspaper promoting new apartments that were being built in the Stockholm suburb of Jordbrö. This was part of a new government-initiated project, the so-called 'Million Programme', that had as its goal the building of a million new homes in the course of a decade.

Immediately Hartleb began to speculate whether this might provide the subject matter for an extensive documentary investigation. What also caught his attention, however, was what he saw as the likely discrepancy between what those promoting the Jordbrö housing scheme were promising and the probable reality that the new occupants would experience. In Hartleb's words:

> What struck me in these advertisements was the use of the oak-tree motif and the implication that each child in this suburban paradise would have his/her own tree to climb in. I straightaway saw the contradiction. (Hartleb, 2007)

Hartleb quickly concluded that the best way of tackling the subject would be through a longitudinal documentary that would focus on the experience of incoming families and on how they actually adapted to living in this new environment.

When Hartleb looks back on the origins of the Jordbrö series, he has always been keen to acknowledge the inspiration given to him by the work of the North American social anthropologist Oscar Lewis. It was one of the first things he mentioned in our interview: 'Lewis's book had a huge impact on me. I wanted to do something similar.' In 1961 Lewis had produced what proved to be a highly influential book *The Children of Sánchez*. The book chronicles the experiences of members of the impoverished Sánchez family who were living at the time in Mexico City. Lewis's intention was 'to give the reader an inside view of family life and of what it means to grow up in a slum tenement in the heart of a great Latin American city which is undergoing a process of rapid social and economic change' (Lewis, 1961: xi). Lewis had got to know Mexico quite well when he was working there as US representative of the Inter-American Indian Institute. During this time he had taken a particular interest in the lives of poor Mexican families. The project that eventually resulted in *The Children of Sánchez* had begun as an attempt by Lewis to show the consequences of individual families having to move, for economic reasons, from the outlying (Aztec) area into the urban environment of Mexico City.

Lewis's account of the experiences of the Sánchez family and their move to Mexico City is a classic longitudinal study, spread over a number of years and based on a series of taped interviews with family members. Hartleb was, as suggested, very taken with Lewis's work. He was impressed not only by what he saw as the sociological value of this project but also by Lewis's whole approach. For instance, even before Lewis started the formal interviewing process, he had taken care to spend time with the family, thus establishing a trusting relationship with them. This meant that, when the time came for him to tape their conversations, members of the family were able to talk to him as they would to a trusted friend. Much of the success of *The Children of Sánchez*, in Hartleb's opinion, was attributable to the way in which Lewis combined the critical detachment of the ethnographic observer with the empathy of a more involved participant. What also appealed to Hartleb was the way in which Lewis, in his book, reproduced, with the minimum of authorial comment, what the members of the Sánchez family had told him. This was again something that Hartleb echoed in his own filmmaking practice.

Though Hartleb may have been clear in his own mind about wanting to produce a similar kind of chronicle to Lewis's, he nevertheless had a number of practical issues to address. He still needed the support of a sponsoring agent and he also needed to gain access to such members of the Jordbrö community as might be willing to participate in such a project. It was here that, as he recalls, he had a stroke of good fortune. At around this time, his own daughter was about to start school and Hartleb had been gathering the kind of information one needs, as a parent, to prepare one's child for their first encounter with the formal education system. Spurred on by thoughts about the role that the school as an institution plays in the socialising of children, it dawned on Hartleb that a school would be an ideal starting-point for a project of the type he envisaged. In Hartleb's words:

> I thought a school class would be a good thing to concentrate on. Among other things, it would enable me to discover whether the school had any hidden agenda. I could also see what was going on behind locked doors. (Hartleb, 2007)

Having opted to focus on a school for his longitudinal investigation, Hartleb quickly decided that the optimum time to start filming would be at the children's point of entry into the system. This would enable him to chronicle the experiences of a generation of children as they made their way through the whole nine years of their basic schooling. The study would thus, he hoped, be able to lay claim to some sociological significance. Following the children in this way would give greater sociological validity to his findings and also provide the audience with food for thought as to how a period of rapid social change affects the lives of the youngest and potentially the most vulnerable members of that society.

In his efforts to find a suitable school in which to conduct his study, Hartleb was relatively fortunate. As it happened, a friend who was working in one of the Jordbrö schools was able to secure a number of introductions for the aspiring documentarist. Having persuaded the head teacher of one school to give their consent for filming to take place in the school, Hartleb still had some difficulty in finding a teacher willing to allow him to spend extended periods filming the children in the classroom situation. As Hartleb concedes, this proved to be more difficult than he had imagined: 'I asked six teachers – all of them women – if they would allow me to film in their class. And only one [Inga-Britt Jonés] was willing. But I liked her immediately, so that's why I didn't look any further.'[16]

The other point to bear in mind about the genesis of the Jordbrö project is that, from the outset, Hartleb was convinced that he could only achieve his aims over a much longer period. The problem was that Swedish Television was not willing to commit at this stage to a whole series but was only prepared to provide the funding for one film that would cover the children's first year of schooling. Any further funding would depend on the success of this first film. Fortunately for Hartleb, the film *From a Child's World* (1973) received a positive audience response, so the way was now clear for him to proceed with his plan to produce a series of regular Jordbrö updates. During the period 1972–81 he produced no fewer than twelve hour-long films. The Jordbrö chronicle was well and truly underway.

In many ways the conditions under which Hartleb operated during this initial period were optimal from the point of view of a long doc filmmaker. Early on, he had established a good working relationship with a sympathetic class teacher and the children in her class. He had the blessing of the school authorities and had also got the institutional support of Swedish Television. Even the fact that the broadcasters were not willing to enter into an open-ended funding commitment was proving to be salutary, as it forced him to be constantly on his mettle. As he once commented to a journalist: 'It meant I was forced to deliver. Without that constraint, I might not have stayed so focused' (Weman, 2006: 5). It was, however, probably the absence of external pressures from any 'higher authority' (such as those that constantly bore down upon Winfried Junge and his team) that made it possible for Hartleb to develop the sets of practices and techniques that were to become the hallmark of his film-making style.

Right from the launch of the Jordbrö project, Hartleb began to display many of those qualities that are often considered to be essential for a filmmaker tracing developments over the longer term. Just as he had predicted, he quickly discovered that he was indeed far more at home doing this kind of film work than he had been in the fast-moving world of television journalism. Temperamentally Hartleb is – as all those who have met him will testify – a quietly spoken and somewhat retiring man. In company he has a particular talent for listening attentively to the views of others before offering his own. He has in this respect many affinities with the late Studs Terkel, the legendary chronicler of American life in the twentieth century, about whom one obituary-writer wrote: 'He was maestro of that most precious craft in the practice of both journalism and history: listening' (Vulliamy, 2008: 34).

Having started work on the project Hartleb spent a considerable amount of time familiarising himself with the school environment and talking with Jordbrö residents. One of his first tasks was getting the children accustomed to his presence and that of other members of the team (one camera-operator and one sound person). Hartleb and his crew sought to remain relatively unobtrusive and there was never any attempt to orchestrate events (in stark contrast to the first film in the *Children of Golzow* series).[17] The children quickly adjusted to Hartleb being there and they soon accepted him, rather as they would a benevolent uncle. According to Hartleb: 'We didn't belong to the official school hierarchy. We were the film lads: the nice uncle figures.' From the children's perspective, then, the film team became just another feature of the classroom landscape.

Hartleb also spent a lot of time during the early phase of the Jordbrö project visiting the children and their parents in their homes. Not only did he want the film to be a study of how children are formed by an education system, he also wanted it to chronicle the experiences of an emergent community and the challenges that families face when they move to a new area. As he recalls:

> The first year I was out there [in Jordbrö] almost every day and we filmed for perhaps two or three months ... We tried to get a maximum of presence, but we didn't calculate or anticipate what events would

occur ... Then I also visited all the parents at home and we talked about their background and what their plans were ... and that I did without camera, person to person. Then I saw the children on their own in their homes, and suddenly you see quite different personalities than at school. (Hartleb, 2007)

Operating in this way not only enabled Hartleb to establish a strong bond of trust with his subjects; it also made it possible for him to show the formative influence that the family environment can have on a growing child's attitudes and values.[18]

The twelve one-hour films that Hartleb produced in just short of a decade not only chronicle the progress of a generation of Swedish youngsters through the formal education system; they are also an attempt to explore what impact the recent move to Jordbrö had on the children's parents (mostly blue-collar workers). In this respect the films also represent as much a sociological exploration into the strains and stresses imposed on incoming families as an account of individual life-journeys.[19] It may be of some significance, however, that when Hartleb later decided to edit down these twelve films into two medium-length feature-films *The Children of Jordbrö* (1972–75) and *Living in Jordbrö* (1975–81), he decided to strip out much of the 'sociological content' in order to concentrate more on the tracking of individual life journeys (Hartleb, 2007).

These early Jordbrö films were generally well received by Swedish audiences and they also got favourable reviews. Like other long doc filmmakers, however, there were some responses to the films that could, potentially, have had damaging consequences for the further development of the series. Firstly there were the reactions of the children themselves. Just as with other serialised documentaries (most notably Paul Watson's *The Family*), once subjects had begun to acquire media celebrity status, their attitude towards their involvement in such a project changed. As Hartleb explains:

Once the children had been seen on television, they became mini-celebrities. And it was impossible to approach them in a serious way. It took me a full year to get back to a more natural state of affairs where they were not playing up to the camera. (Hartleb, 2007)

An additional and potentially more serious problem arose immediately after the broadcast of the first film. Though many in the Jordbrö community considered that the picture that emerged from Hartleb's account was a true reflection of how things were, there were some who felt that the film totally misrepresented Jordbrö and the views of those who lived there. This carried with it an implied threat that they would refuse to co-operate in any planned sequel. With the wisdom of hindsight Hartleb now accepts that he would have been better advised to arrange for a pre-broadcast screening of the film, which all those who had been involved in the project could have attended. This would have allowed any issues of possible misrepresentation to be aired and for Hartleb to carry out some judicious re-editing before a final version of the film was prepared for transmission.

All long doc filmmakers have to be extremely sensitive to how they represent those who agree to appear in their films, since if they get embroiled in a battle over alleged distortion or misrepresentation, this can easily jeopardise the long-term future of the whole enterprise.[20] They are after all absolutely dependent on the continuing co-operation of subjects and their families. Hartleb was much chastened by this experience and considers it to have been an important lesson in his apprenticeship as a long doc filmmaker. It immediately set him thinking about some of the implications of working in the longitudinal mode. One outcome of these thoughts was the realisation that there were distinct advantages in being able to paint on a larger canvas (or possibly on a series of canvasses). Above all it enabled the filmmaker to work incrementally and to produce a more nuanced picture than would have been possible through the 'snapshot' view provided by a one-off programme. As Hartleb once quietly observed in the course of our extended conversations (even in interviews he never gives the impression of being in a hurry):

> I needed to realise that I had time on my side. I had to tell myself that each film was not a definitive statement. Each film was part of a much larger, slowly emerging picture. (Hartleb, 2007)

Notes

1 Stella Bruzzi, for instance, makes the point that '*Seven Up* is a significant *document* – both within the annals of television and documentary history and as a record of social and political history' (2007: 116, original emphasis).

2 The classic example of a serial narrative form is, of course, soap opera. I shall have more to say about the latter's affinity with long docs in Chapter 5.

3   When considering the question of how funding can be secured for long-term ventures, it is, however, worth reminding ourselves that in today's filmmaking and broadcasting climate it is becoming increasingly difficult to obtain money for any project that requires extensive research or an inordinately long preparation time. For more on the funding of contemporary documentary work, see Kilborn, 2003: 24–36.

4   It is perfectly possible to conceive of a one-off documentary that explores the world of a group of seven-year-olds as they enter the school system. Nevertheless, such an exploration will almost inevitably include a series of conjectures about what consequences this system will have for the children concerned and how they will cope with the educational and life challenges that lie ahead. Having been introduced to a number of personable young individuals, viewers develop a natural interest in what will become of them. For more on narrative anticipation, see Branigan, 1992: 1–2; Kilborn & Izod, 1997: 115–21; Nichols, 1991: 19–20, 125–6.

5   Hewat had long wanted to produce such a film himself. Knowing, however, that he was soon to leave Granada, he handed over the responsibility for making it to others in the *World in Action* team.

6   It is possibly no coincidence that, in the case of both *Seven Up* and *The Children of Jordbrö,* the idea for conducting what some would regard as an ethnographic study of the indigenous population came from two individuals (Hewat and Hartleb) who were themselves incomers.

7   Apted is especially rueful about the relative absence of women and also that there are so very few middle-class representatives in the series.

8   As a *World in Action* 'Special', the *Seven Up* programme had a slightly longer running-time (40 minutes) than standard *World in Action* programmes. As such, it was able to take rather more of a documentary approach to its subject than some of the weekly half-hour *World in Action* programmes that one would classify more as current affairs reporting.

9   Viewers cannot fail to have been charmed by young Neil's enthusiastic: 'When I grow up, I want to be an astronaut'; by Lynn's bold assertion: 'When I leave school, I want to work at Woolworth's'; and by Bruce's poignant declaration: 'My heart's desire is to see my daddy'.

10   Part of DEFA's original mission had been that of assisting in the task of 'removing all traces of the fascist and militaristic ideology from the minds of every German … and re-educating the German people – especially the young – to a true understanding of genuine democracy and humanism' (cited in Allan & Sandford, 1999: 3). In formulating this mission statement, the underlying assumption was that the GDR could lay a more legitimate claim to represent the German people than West Germany because of its explicit commitment to a thoroughgoing anti-fascist programme.

11   The history of GDR filmmaking is, in no large measure, marked by the

struggle between apparatchiks working to ensure that film was being 'constructively' employed and filmmakers seeking to express their views on a range of contemporary issues. The tensions between state-appointed officials and creative artists in the GDR are most poignantly illustrated in Florian Henckel von Donnersmarck's acclaimed film *Das Leben der Anderen* (*The Lives of Others* – Germany, 2005).

12   Eleven films were affected by these measures, including *Jahrgang 45* (*Born in 1945*) the first fiction film of Jürgen Böttcher, who went on to become one of East Germany's leading documentarists. For more on these so-called 'cellar-films' see Allan & Sandford, 1999: 11–14).

13   Despite the many obstacles and challenges that confronted them, DEFA filmmakers in some respects enjoyed working conditions that were the envy of many filmmakers in the West. Not only were they able to make their films using 35-mm equipment; they also received the kind of logistical and technical support that stood them in very good stead for the longer type of project such as the Golzow series.

14   Gass happily concedes that the envisaged project was something he himself would have undertaken if he had been several years younger (see Junge, 2004: 12).

15   The growing institutional support for the project can also be gauged by the fact that the DEFA authorities agreed that *Eleven Years Old* should be allowed to have a much longer running time (30 minutes) than the first two Golzow films.

16   What strikes one is the relative ease with which Hartleb was able to gain access to a school where he could film. This is in stark contrast to the Golzow project, where the search for a suitable location was subject to far more constraints and directives. Hartleb himself admits that the gaining of consent from participants might be more difficult in the changed media environment of the early twenty-first century, where both individuals and organisations are more wary of all forms of media intrusion.

17   Hartleb's approach also differs markedly from that of Apted. He is much less intrusive and generally refrains from being in any way confrontational with his subjects.

18   This is in striking contrast to the other long docs under consideration in this book. Apted for instance, studiously avoids interviewing children's parents, even though this would have arguably provided some possible explanations for the kind of people the children turned into!

19   According to Hartleb, one of the questions posed in these films is what it felt like to grow up in a place like Jordbrö where, out of 6,500 inhabitants, there were only eleven pensioners.

20   The normal compromise that a filmmaker strikes is to show subjects a rough-cut version of the film to allow them to check for factual inaccuracies.

4

Gaining and maintaining momentum

This chapter seeks to explore how long docs develop after they have achieved initial lift-off. As I have already noted (Chapter 1, pp. 12–13), two of the best-known long docs in the history of film had quite modest beginnings. It is therefore of more than a little interest to discover more about the processes by which long docs gain and maintain the momentum necessary to sustain their further progress.[1] As well as discussing such key issues as how film and programme makers maintain good working relations with subjects, I will also be examining some of the textual properties of these works. What are the principal narrative devices used in structuring these works? To what extent are the contributions of individual subjects played off one against another, as they would be in a piece of dramatic fiction? How do filmmakers resolve the problem of working with an increasingly complex time-structure in terms of managing the relationship between the parts of the text that relate to the present day or the recent past and those which bring reminders of much earlier times?

Just as in the previous chapter, I will be devoting individual sections to each long doc in turn, paying particular attention to the challenges that film and programme makers face as they move into what one might term the more mature phases of the projects.[2] One of these challenges relates to the management of the ever-increasing amount of recorded material that filmmakers accumulate. Not only does this throw up certain archiving and storage problems, it also means having to keep the later films within reasonable proportions as far as length is concerned. The main difficulty lies in the fact that that there will quite often be differences of opinion between filmmakers and sponsoring agents as to just how long individual episodes should be. Filmmakers like Winfried and Barbara Junge were certainly of the opinion, for instance, that, as the Golzow chronicle developed, their films would need to get progressively longer. Broadcasters and other sponsoring agencies, on the other hand, will almost always take the view that excessive length can prove to be counter-productive and that certain narrative economies should be observed.[3]

One further general issue that we will need to take into account when we consider the longer-term development of long docs concerns their alleged chronicling function (see also Chapter 1, pp. 17–19). I use the word 'alleged' here, because, as long docs develop, it is clearly the case that their focus of interest changes and that they become progressively more concerned with the tracking of individual lives. It is a moot point whether such a shift of emphasis can be considered as a generic feature of long docs. It does seem, however, more than simply a coincidence that in all three of the works under scrutiny in this book, the same shift is observable. Different explanations can be given for the growing preoccupation with individual life-journeys. Firstly there is what one might term the socio-geographical consideration: the strong likelihood that a group of individuals who have been brought up in a particular locality and who have gone through school together will go their separate ways once they have completed their formal education. Secondly, there is the growing recognition that, as the volume of recorded material expands, it will become increasingly difficult to maintain a twin-track approach, one that traces the lives of individuals *and* chronicles socio-historical developments.

Institutional relations

Throughout this work I have placed particular emphasis on the role played by various institutions in the origination and nurturing of these projects. In the case of all the works currently under consideration, each of them has been exposed to the shaping influence of an institutional sponsor. Let me therefore briefly indicate the ways in which the impact of certain institutions and agencies is discernible as each of these long docs gradually gathered momentum.

One way in which the influence of an institution can be discerned is by considering how the works in question can be perceived to fit in with the programming or production policies of particular organ-isations. In the case of *Seven Up*, for instance, Granada Television was well aware that a follow-up to the original *World in Action* programme would be the kind of programme likely to speak to members of its core audience. In the course of the 1960s Granada had rapidly acquired a reputation for itself as a pioneering broad-caster with a particular aptitude for creating programming across a range of genres with which its audience could instantly connect. As one commentator has written: 'Granada quickly established itself as the most socially conscious of the commercial companies making distinctive programmes that included innovative drama and ground-breaking coverage of current affairs' (Finch, 2003: 1). Granada prided itself especially on programmes that set out to explore aspects of working-class life that had been relatively neglected in some of the BBC's programming output. Two years after the broadcast of *Seven Up*, for instance, Granada launched *This England*, a docu-mentary series that was to run for the next two and a half decades. The series explored the everyday lives of working-class people and gave viewers the opportunity of hearing ordinary people giving their views on life and the world around them without the intrusive commentary of a narrator (see also Goddard, Corner & Richardson, 2007: 43). Mindful, then, of all that was happening at Granada in the late 1960s and of the programming portfolio that this broad-caster was developing,[4] it is not all that surprising that someone in the organisation (the then Head of Programming, Denis Forman) should have approached Apted to ask whether he would be inter-ested in making a follow-up programme to the original *Seven Up*.[5]

With *The Children of Jordbrö* the relationship between filmmaker and sponsoring institution is of a slightly different order insofar as the original idea for the series came from Hartleb himself rather than the broadcaster. Even here, however, the institution (Swedish Television) exercised a controlling influence over the future course of the project in that it first needed to be persuaded that this was the kind of subject that lent itself to longitudinal treatment. It was some time before Swedish Television felt able to make a longer-term commitment to the project, but again it is worthwhile conjec-turing what additional grounds the broadcasters may have had for supporting Hartleb in the way they did. What may have proved instrumental in helping them to reach this decision was the fact that the early films in the Jordbrö cycle, besides focusing on the lives of individual children, are demonstrably concerned with wider social issues such as housing and employment policies, equal rights for women and attitudes towards immigration.[6] Engaging with these topics manifestly lies within the remit of a public service broadcaster such as Swedish Television. It is not difficult, therefore, to see why Hartleb – once he had shown proof of his capacity to deliver programmes in a timely fashion – should have received the kind of support from the national Swedish broadcaster that allowed him to pursue the project in the longer term.

With *The Children of Golzow* the progress of the work was even more subject to institutional pressures than was the case with the Swedish and the British long docs. Junge and his team were always aware that they were working under a set of tight constraints and that each time they were granted permission to make another film, it was coupled with particular expectations as to the kind of work that would emerge. When one reads Junge's own account of how the individual Golzow films came to be made, for instance, one is made constantly aware of the compromises that were entered into and the general level of uncertainty as to what would be possible under the prevailing political conditions (see Junge, 2004). One gains the strong impression, indeed, that throughout the whole DEFA period of the Golzow project Junge and his team were involved in a cat-and-mouse game with the state-appointed cultural officials whose responsibility it was to ensure that documentarists (and others) always remained 'on message'.

Seven Up

Asked what he thought were the main differences between *The Children of Golzow* and the long doc with which it is most frequently compared, Apted's *Seven Up*, Winfried Junge responded thus: 'For someone who is interested in the sociological and psychological aspects of the children's development, there are distinct advantages in Michael Apted's approach' (Junge, 2006). Junge went on to say that he thought Apted also had the advantage over him insofar as the latter's more 'economical' approach had allowed his British 'rival' to develop two parallel filmmaking careers.[7] As Junge somewhat ruefully observed: 'If I had adopted the same approach, I too would have had the chance to make more feature films than I have done' (ibid.). However, possibly the biggest difference between the two works is that, whereas Junge's long doc was conceived as a work intended for cinematic exhibition, Apteds' *Seven Up* series bears all the hallmarks of a series designed for television. In opting to take a largely interview-based approach Apted has also been able to capitalise on the intimacy of television's appeal. Likewise, the regular episodic mode of presentation employed in *Seven Up* is one of television's classic strategies for maintaining audience attention (see also Chapter 5, pp. 128–31).

Going longitudinal: *Seven Plus Seven*

Once it had been decided that Apted would take over responsibility for the follow-up to the original *Seven Up* programme, Granada seems to have given him considerable freedom as to the exact approach he would take. The resultant programme, *Seven Plus Seven*, though relatively unsuccessful as a programme in its own right, enabled Apted to put his own particular imprint on the emergent *Seven Up* series. Doubtless influenced by the experiences he had gathered while working in the field of dramatic fiction, Apted quickly recognised that the potential appeal of such a programme would lie in how it juxtaposed segments of an individual's life-journey in such a way as to make a powerful and dramatic statement. This already became apparent when he began to bring together footage he had shot for *Seven Up* with material he had gathered for *Seven Plus Seven* (or *14 Up*, as it came to be known). According to Apted, the act of juxtaposing sequences from these two films 'in a sense set the seed for the whole series. I suppose we knew then we were on our way' (Apted, 2007). By the time he came to make *14 Up*, then, Apted had already made certain key decisions that were to have a significant impact on the whole series. He had elected to employ a largely interview-based approach and had also decided not to muddy the waters by attempting to make it too much like a chronicle (by introducing too many references to contemporary events) in order to remain focused on more existential issues affecting the lives of his *Seven Up* subjects.

Though there may have been an element of serendipity in the way in which Apted became reacquainted with *Seven Up* some six years after making the first *World in Action* programme, no sooner had he made the first follow-up programme than he quickly began to realise what remarkable potential such a series might have. *14 Up* has a particular landmark status in the development of *Seven Up*. As

Apted remembers:

> Once we'd done *Seven Plus Seven* we had a sense we were on to something, that there was a bigger idea at work here. And so we kept on going, even though I moved to Los Angeles to live round about the time we did *28 Up*. (Apted, 2007)

The 'bigger idea' to which Apted refers, centres on those seven-yearly visits that have become the cornerstone of the whole *Seven Up* enterprise. To some, no doubt, allowing so much time to elapse between visits may have seemed quite a daring strategy, especially to those in the television industry who believed that viewers have to be supplied with material at far more regular intervals in order that they develop desirable viewing habits. For Apted and his team, however, the benefits of opting for the seven-year method only properly came to be appreciated in the longer term. Having such a space between visits not only allowed ample time for a significant amount of narrative material to accumulate, it was also long enough for those tell-tale physical signs of ageing to be discernible on subjects' faces. As a consequence, the contrast between the 'Then' and the 'Now' thus acquires much greater poignancy than if, say, only a single year has elapsed between visits.

Although *14 Up* established the basic parameters for the *Seven Up* series and also confirmed Apted in his newfound role of director, it was, nevertheless, a difficult film to make. As Apted now freely admits:

> *Seven Plus Seven* was a nightmare. It was kind of spotty, monosyllabic and all that but – very difficult to make and embarrassing to do – but then you see the beginnings of a powerful idea. From then on it was frankly down to whether Granada and I would hang in with it. And they did. And I did. (Freedland, 2005b)

As was to be the case with all subsequent *Seven Up* films, *14 Up* involved Apted in having to address two distinct constituencies of viewers: those who had encountered the original *Seven Up* programme when it was first transmitted in the *World in Action* series and those who were joining it for the very first time. The first part of *14 Up* is given over to (re)-acquainting viewers with the aims of the original *World in Action* programme. It also provides a series of visual and verbal reminders of the day that the *Seven Up* subjects had spent together in various London venues. Having informed viewers about the circumstances out of which the project grew, the film moves swiftly on to its own narrative agenda. How have the children changed in the time since we last encountered them? Are they developing in ways we might have anticipated? Answers to these questions are provided in the form of a number of short scenes in which images of the wide-eyed, enthusiastic seven-year-olds are juxtaposed to those of the generally more tongue-tied and some-times anguished fourteen-year-olds they have become. The sense of time passing (or having passed) is further reinforced by switching between the *World in Action* black-and-white footage and the *14 Up* colour footage. (As the credits proudly proclaim: '*Seven Plus Seven* is a Granada colour production'.)

Special interest in the first part of *14 Up* is centred on the extent to which the hopes and aspirations expressed by the children as seven-year-olds are being realised as they enter their teenage years. One of the central questions that the programme poses is whether their progress, as the original programme would have had us believe, has continued to be largely determined by their class or family back-grounds. How have their attitudes changed since we last encoun-tered them? Not surprisingly, in view of *Seven Up*'s scarcely veiled political agenda, the unequivocal answer to these questions is that the children from the more privileged backgrounds, who have had their education pre-planned and paid for, have mostly remained on course to achieve their stated goals, whilst those from less advan-taged homes confront a 'far less certain future' (*14 Up* commentary). The other theme that emerges with some force in *14 Up* is how – again as one might have anticipated – several of the children have had to revise some of their more extravagant ambitions. Peter, who – like his fellow-Liverpudlian Neil – had wanted, at the age of seven, to be an astronaut, now has more realistic aspirations. As he says: 'I've changed my mind completely of course. It was just the imagi-nation of a seven-year-old.' Likewise Bruce, who at seven wanted to be a missionary, has now changed his mind: 'I wouldn't be very good at it and I wouldn't enjoy it.'

In certain ways *14 Up* also anticipates some of the problems and challenges that Apted would face over the longer term. In inter-views he has always been very candid about the difficulty he had in securing the willing co-operation of his subjects.[8] For instance, when he asks Suzy about how she feels about participating in the programme, he gets the sullen reply: 'I think it's ridiculous. I don't see any point in it.' John and Andrew, two of the trio of posh boys in the *Up* films, when asked the same question, complain – with some justification – that the programme seems to be operating with very stereotypical categories.[9] In a not dissimilar way, Jackie and her two friends, all of them from working-class East End of London backgrounds, feel as fourteen-year-olds that Apted is putting them into class-determined boxes, especially when it comes to assessing their future prospects. There is one telling moment, for instance, when Apted directs the following provocative question at the three girls: 'There's a danger you'll get married in your early twenties and have children quickly and then be stuck at home. Any thoughts?' Judging by their body language, Jackie and her friends are extremely resentful at being pigeonholed in this way, as indeed they should be. It is only many years later, however, in a memorable sequence in *49 Up*, that Jackie (always the most feisty of the three) is able to articulate the huge irritation that such crass class-based assumptions aroused in her at the time and how the resentment has continued to rankle ever since.

Also striking about *14 Up* is the degree to which – even at this relatively early stage of the project – Apted actively encourages his subjects to indulge in extended acts of reflection. Apted's subjects have not been slow to recognise that the requirement to be reflective is part of the unwritten contract they have entered into when they became involved in the project. All of them know that, when Apted comes calling, they will be asked to give their considered views on a range of more or less predictable questions. This knowledge that Apted's subjects will be required to discourse at some length on a number of standard topics also belongs to what Robert Allen has called the 'horizon of expectations' with which readers confront a particular type of text (Allen, 1985: 149). To give just one example of this from *14 Up*, when Nicholas the still shy Yorkshire lad is asked whether he has a girlfriend, both he and many in the audience have been anticipating just such a question. As he observes: 'I thought that [question] would come up. What do you want me to say? I don't know what to say.' Likewise, Bruce at fourteen is also aware that, because in *Seven Up* he mentioned he wanted to become a missionary, he is likely to be asked in subsequent programmes whether he still has this ambition. Judging by his well-considered response to the 'missionary' question in *14 Up*, Bruce has clearly been able to formulate some thoughts on this matter before the interview took place.

From the long doc filmmaker's point of view, one can immedi-ately see the attractions of adhering to the same line of questioning. It makes it that much easier, when editing the films, to compare and contrast a subject's views on a range of issues at various stages of their life and to show how attitudes may have changed in the light of experience gained. A possible limitation of the method, however, is that some subjects will, in anticipation of particular questions being asked, have engaged in a certain amount of mental rehearsal, thereby depriving the responses of the spontaneity they might otherwise have had. When asked about this, Apted has always argued that it is one of the *Up* films' strengths that his subjects are able to give their *considered* reflections on what has been happening in their lives. He also regards it as inevitable – given the significance that subjects attach to this septennial conversational exchange – that they will have gathered some of their thoughts in preparation for the interview. As Apted once observed:

> Yes, they are ready for it. They know what's on the table. But they don't spend six and three quarter years rehearsing for it. They don't live their lives preparing for it. (Apted, 2006)

For Apted, then, the key question is not whether his subjects go through a mental rehearsal for the event but how articulate they become at expressing their thoughts on camera. Apted is of the opinion, indeed, that the facility that most of his participants have developed over the years for articulating their thoughts is one of the particular strengths of the series. In his own words:

> The fact that my subjects have turned out to be so articulate is in a way a tribute to what the programme is, which in a sense celebrates ordinary life. I've always thought that the one thing these films do is to *honour the drama of ordinary life ... When you talk to people in bars and on buses, they're remarkably articulate, but they hardly ever get the chance to say anything in public.* (Ibid., my emphasis)

From the *Seven Up* subjects' point of view, being given the oppor-tunity – in the case of the *Seven Up* series once every seven years – to reflect on what they have achieved and possibly on what forces have shaped their lives, becomes part and parcel of being a long doc participant. Some, like Jackie, in spite of the occasional abrasiveness that has crept in to her relationship with Apted, still regard their involvement in the project in largely positive terms. 'I don't think I'd ever have kept a record of my life in the way that we have with this programme' (*42 Up*). Others, like Suzy, view their continuing partic- ipation with much greater trepidation: 'There's a lot of baggage that gets stirred up every seven years for me … and I have to deal with it all over again' (*42 Up*).

21 Up

From *21 Up* onwards the original programme's overtly political stance (about Britain being socially divided according to class affili- ations) becomes progressively more muted and the series begins to be more concerned with the tracking of individual life-journeys (see also Bruzzi, 2007: 15; Moran, 2002: 390–1).[10] With the shift in emphasis from a more sociologically oriented to a distinctly person- centred approach came the recognition on Apted's part that the series would henceforth become increasingly interview-based.[11] As he later observed:

> I've always latched on to the fact that the interview is the centre of it, the core. I never tried to get it [*Seven Up*] on its feet and take it into the world. I also realised that the close-up was going to be my main currency. It's watching that face change that's the real story. Watching England change – through its streets, parks, buildings and politics – is *not* my business. My business is these people changing. Therefore the interview and the close-up become the core of it, so the manner of the interview has determined the tone of the film(s). (Apted, 2006)

In developing the methods that would be most appropriate for charting the progress of his subjects' lives, Apted was also aware that, as the series evolved, he would have to constantly refine his filming and editing techniques. By *21 Up* he may already have settled into his seven-year rhythm, but he also recognised the dangers of becoming overly formulaic in his approach and accepted that some of the strategies that had stood him in good stead in the past would need to be revised. Among other things, for instance, he realised that, now that most of his subjects had concluded their formal education and were beginning to lead more independent lives, he would have to develop new dramaturgical means to take account of the changing trajectories of their lives. It was also clear to him that he would have to adapt some of the narrative techniques he had employed hitherto in order that material drawn from the rich 'sediment' of the past could be productively incorporated into the latest *Seven Up* episode.

Though Apted never seeks to disguise the fact that his *Seven Up* subjects, from their late teens onwards, are striking out on ever more divergent paths, he often goes to some lengths – for the purposes of the film – to foster and maintain the illusion of family togetherness. As far as the audience is concerned, the individuals who feature in these films will, for all their manifest differences, always remain members of the *Seven Up* family that Granada, Apted and his team have brought into being.[12] It is partly to preserve this illusion of togetherness that, in the opening sequence of *21 Up*, Apted gathers his participants in a cinema auditorium and films their responses to watching excerpts from some of the earlier films. Besides offering a reminder of the occasion when the children were first brought together in London almost a decade and a half previously, the scene in the cinema provides Apted with a neat way of (re)introducing all his *dramatis personae*. As they confront their former seven- and fourteen-year-old selves, some respond with squirming 'theatrical' embarrassment whilst others remain quietly reflective. This is an important narrative consideration, given that some viewers will be joining the programme for the very first time. Besides serving an expositional function by setting the scene for all that is to follow, the sequence also provides an opportunity for the voice-over narrator to inform viewers about the purpose of the *Seven Up* project and for viewers to contemplate the degree to which subjects' physical appearance has changed in the decade and a half that the series has been running.

Encouraging self-reflectiveness

Having filmed the subjects watching themselves on screen, Apted then provides them all with the opportunity to consider how *they* feel that they have been represented in the series so far. Bearing in mind that they only have two programmes on which to base their remarks, what is striking about subjects' observations is how many insights they have gained already into how film produces a mediated version of reality. John and Charles, for instance, are both very critical of how the programme employs what they regard as crass stereotyping. They resent being portrayed as individuals who are simply sailing through life as a result of an 'indestructible birthright'. They prefer to think that they achieve what they do through sheer hard work rather than because they have been born with a silver spoon in their mouths. Nicholas has also become aware of the programme's capacity for distortion, complaining that: 'Viewers tend to read significance into it that doesn't really exist.'

In general, participants in *21 Up* have become increasingly conscious that *Seven Up* has its own agenda and that they, as protagonists in this unfolding drama, are subject to the constraints that this agenda imposes. They are also aware that they are, to some extent, manipulated in accordance with the programme's dramaturgical requirements and its changing thematic focus. As is so often the case in the *Up* films, it is left to Neil, the complicated, fragile personality who is already emerging as the central protagonist in the series, to provide the most perceptive comments on what he sees as a clear shift in the programme's original, more political concerns: the desire to demonstrate the perniciousness and rigidity of the class system. In Neil's words: 'The fact that we're all here today [in this cinema] has broken class barriers that might have existed. Therefore the film may have defeated its own purpose' (*21 Up*).

Memory work

One of Apted's constant preoccupations in the *Up* films is to encourage subjects to keep working on their memories. It is, however, important to consider how all this memory work actually gets absorbed into the texts themselves. From *21 Up* onwards, all the *Seven Up* films include a number of sequences where subjects are actively coaxed into acts of remembering. In *21 Up* Neil is prompted by Apted to start digging into memories of his childhood. In *35 Up* Tony, still mourning the recent death of his mother, recalls life in the family home when he was a boy, whilst Paul in *42 Up* reflects back on his 'dislocated childhood'. In addition to the occasions when subjects are guided by Apted into acts of recollection, there are the many instances where the moments preserved from a subject's past are strung together into sequences that Apted refers to as 'golden highlights'.[13] Sequences such as these may simulate the act of memory recall – and they may at times create the illusion for the viewer that the subject is bringing to mind significant moments in their past. On closer inspection, however, these sequences are significantly different from flashbacks in fiction films with which they have a certain superficial resemblance. Fiction-film flashbacks, which have become an accepted part of filmic language, involve a sudden, filmically motivated switch from present to past or from a conscious to a more dreamlike state. The intention is often to apprise the viewer of an event in or an aspect of the character's past that is of particular narrative significance. In long docs on the other hand, the 'golden highlights' sequences have a markedly different function. To start with, the interpolated images will almost always carry documentary status insofar as they are recognisably (at least to long-stay viewers) ones that have already been used in earlier episodes and are simply being remobilised here as a reminder of what is already known. The fact that the images are recycled in this way means that, for the viewer, the effect of re-encountering these representations of the documented past, is somewhat akin to the act of rapidly leafing through an album of family photographs. In terms of how the past is being remembered, however, these images are clearly accorded the status of documentary archive material rather than being interpreted as belonging to a subject's personal memory store.[14]

The primary purpose of these 'golden highlights' sequences is to stir the memories of viewers and to remind them of the routes that subjects have taken to reach their present destinations. The same sequences can sometimes be used by the filmmaker as a means of getting subjects to start delving in their memories or to indulge in other forms of retrospective conjecture. At the beginning of *21 Up*, as we have seen, Apted shows his subjects excerpts from earlier films in order to be able to film their reactions. This strategy for activating participants' memory flow has the additional benefit of directing their thoughts towards parts of their past with which viewers are likely to be familiar. Another strategy that long doc filmmakers will occasionally employ to prompt subjects' memory flow is to show them photographs of their youthful selves or to take them back to locations that have strong childhood associations for them. Apted does this with Paul and Symon in *21 Up* when he arranges for them to revisit the children's home where they had spent their early boyhood.[15] In *42 Up* he brings Nick (as he is now known) back from America, where is presently located, to the Yorkshire Dales, where he grew up.

Towards the individual portrait: the biographies of Bruce and Neil

The structural feature that we have discovered to be characteristic of most long docs, as they mature, is their tendency to privilege the individual biography (see also Chapter 2, pp. 25–6). As individual subjects begin to go their separate ways in life, so filmmakers find themselves having to develop new narrative strategies. In the first two *Seven Up* films, attention had been regularly switched between individual protagonists. By the time he came to make *21 Up*, however, Apted had developed a markedly different narrative approach: one that gave greater precedence to the individual life-journey. Beginning with *21 Up* and continuing with *28 Up* and *35 Up*, Apted divides the films up into a series of individual 'chapters', each devoted to a single character or group of characters. In *21 Up*, for instance, almost half the film is given over to extended accounts of just four of the *Seven Up* subjects (Tony, Bruce, Nick and Neil). What is quite striking about the way in which these mini-biographies are presented is that, with each successive update, viewers are able – thanks to the incremental mode of presentation – to revise the image they have formed of individual subjects.

Also noticeable in the *Seven Up* series from *21 Up* onwards is the frequency with which subjects themselves are encouraged by Apted to offer their opinion on how they feel they have been represented. There is, for instance, a point in the opening sequence of *21 Up* (the one where subjects are gathered in the cinema) where Nick remarks: 'People tend to read significance into the film that doesn't really exist.' This acts as a cue for Apted to move into a longish (almost five-minute) sequence in which we (re)-encounter Nick at 7, 14 and 21, which in turn prompts Apted, as narrator, to make the flattering assertion: 'I suppose of all the seven-year-olds, the original ones, you are the big success.' Nick quickly responds that he is 'not inclined to agree with that' and goes on to suggest that Apted's criteria for measuring success (educational achievement or the ability to move swiftly up the career ladder) may not necessarily be ones that are shared by the public at large.

Bruce's story

With Bruce, we also confront a similar disjuncture between the image that the subject feels is being projected of them and their own perceptions and understandings. From early boyhood Bruce has come across in the films as a thoughtful, sensitive person who – though he has enjoyed certain educational privileges – has always sought to involve himself in activities where he can be of service to others. Even though Bruce is not as critical as, say, Jackie about the manipulative tendencies of the programme, he still feels that he has been somewhat stereotypically depicted, in his case as an archetypal do-gooder. It is only in the later *Up* films that a more detailed and rounded picture of Bruce emerges, one in which some of the more complex aspects of his personality begin to be revealed. Bruce is one of the *Seven Up* subjects who manifestly does not conform to the programme's original thesis that class background determines the kind of people they become. Bruce has proved that it is possible to outgrow the narrow class confines into which one is born and to live one's life according to a value system that places a high premium on using one's talents in the service of others.[16] As Apted has commented:

> Bruce is also interesting because, in a way, he's the exception to the class rule. Most people in the film tend to have stayed in their own class and done very much – at least superficially – what's predicted for them. But Bruce didn't do that. He didn't throw in his lot with the system he grew up in. He went into state education to help the poor, the disenfranchised. He turned his back on the riches he could have made out of private education. (Apted, 1998)

As with several other *Seven Up* subjects, however, further developments in Bruce's life have illustrated that it may be unwise to deliver such sweeping judgments on a subject's life when events are still in progress and significant changes are still possible. Apted made those remarks shortly after completing work on *42 Up* and a couple of years after Bruce had got married to Penny, also a schoolteacher. By the time Apted came to make *49 Up*, Bruce and Penny had two children. Bruce had stopped teaching in an inner-city comprehensive in the East End of London and had moved to what was presumably a much less stressful job in a boys' independent school in St Albans. Bruce is well aware that this move back to a more protected environment exposes him to the charge that, in so doing, he is betraying the socialist beliefs he has professed on a number occasions in earlier films, including the time in *35 Up* when he observed: 'This is a class society; and I think that public schools may help its continuance.' In certain respects, then, the turn that Bruce's life has taken would appear to lead credence to the original *Seven Up* thesis that subjects' class affiliations, will – sooner or later – have a determining impact on their lives. Longer-stay viewers of the *Seven Up* series may well be more disposed, however, to interpret Bruce's move not as originating from a long repressed desire to return to a world in which he ultimately felt more comfortable but rather as stemming from the realistic assessment that he would not have the physical and mental stamina to carry on teaching in the tough inner-city environment till he reached pensionable age.

The case of Bruce throws some interesting light on how, as the *Seven Up* series develops, viewers are given more space to contemplate how subjects have become the people they are and what compromises they have been required to make in the course of their life-journeys. One such opportunity for reflection comes at the end of Bruce's 'chapter' in *49 Up* when Apted asks him 'Do you have a dream?' to which Bruce replies: 'I'd have probably liked to have played international cricket, but I just wasn't good enough. You know, one's dreams go in the day-to-day living of ordinary life – and family life takes over. I think we just learn to live without our dreams.'

Neil's story

Ever since he took responsibility for the *Seven Up* series, Apted has, like any good programme maker, always had to consider what are the best strategies for structuring and presenting the material at his disposal. From *21 Up* onwards, for instance, he has had to decide how much film-time to allot to each of his protagonists and in what sequence to present their individual stories. As someone with considerable experience of television drama production and making fiction films, Apted quickly came to recognise that some of these lives had considerably more dramatic potential than others. From a fairly early stage in the series, it became apparent that, of all the *Seven Up* protagonists, Neil's story was the one most likely to evince an empathic audience response, partly because his life was filled with so many dramatic ups and downs. As Apted later commented:

> Neil's roller-coaster of a life has been one of the most memorable parts of the film, from the bright seven-year-old who everyone wanted to take home and cuddle to the down-and-out of *28 Up* and *35 Up*. Neil has had the most huge of audience responses. (Apted 1998)

The story of Neil is one that has continued to attract considerable media interest, with constant concern being expressed about whether he would be able to prevent his life from spiralling out of control. There was also some discussion at the time that *28 Up* and

35 Up were screened as to whether Neil's case in any way reflected what appeared to be the increasingly uncaring attitudes of a materialist society.[17]

Measured by the criteria of a drama production, Neil has acquired 'lead character' status in the *Seven Up* series and has, accordingly, had the most screen-time allotted to his story.[18] For a number of years Neil appeared to be on the brink of psychological or emotional collapse, though throughout these troubled times he has always exhibited an acute self-awareness and an ability to talk honestly about his problems in a manner that viewers have found deeply affecting. Apted himself refers to Neil as 'in some ways the emotional core of the whole thing' (in Freedland, 2005b). It is for this reason that he chose in the last three *Seven Up* instalments (*35 Up, 42 Up* and *49 Up*) to give pride of place to Neil's story by introducing it as the final 'chapter' of the film.

It is not difficult to see why Neil should have acquired such narrative centrality. Gradually, in the course of several extended sequences in *21 Up, 28 Up* and *35 Up*, audiences are made aware of the precariousness of Neil's situation. Since dropping out of university, Neil has become increasingly isolated and disorientated and his future has begun to look increasingly bleak. During these years Apted tracks him down in various far-flung places. Often the bleakness of the locations in which he is filmed seems to reflect the apparent hopelessness of Neil's position.

Since Neil turned out to be such a troubled soul, part of the narrative quest is to throw some light on how he has come to be this way. More so perhaps than in any other *Seven Up* biography, Neil's story becomes one in which, to an increasing extent, understanding is sought for the psychological origins of his 'condition'. There is an illuminating moment towards the end of *21 Up* when Neil starts talking about the possibly detrimental effect that his upbringing may have had on his capacity to face up to some of life's challenges. In his own words:

> I don't think I was really taught any sort of policy of living by my parents. This is one of their biggest mistakes: that I was left to myself in a world which they seemed totally oblivious of. And I found, even when I tried to discuss problems which were facing me at school, my parents didn't seem to be aware of the nature of the problem.

It has been Apted's good fortune as a filmmaker that Neil has seemingly always been willing to open up to him in this way. On the other hand, Apted has also shown considerable skill in the way he has gone about constructing Neil's biography. Early on in the series, for instance, Apted came to understand that a key aspect of the story was the rapid decline in Neil's fortunes after what appeared to be such hopeful beginnings. On several occasions, therefore, in later *Seven Up* episodes, Apted is keen to elicit from Neil what he feels and thinks about that earlier, less troubled period of his life, in the knowledge that the subject's responses will provide the cue for the insertion of interpolated images depicting that happier past.[19] There is a good example of this towards the end of *21 Up* when Apted asks Neil what goes through his mind when he sees the images of himself as a seven-year-old when he was 'bright, perky and full of life'. This is Neil's measured response:

> I find it hard to believe I was ever like that – but there's the evidence. I want to know why I was like that. I wonder what it was inside me that made me like that … I don't know what sort of stumbling block should be put in a child's way to get him used to living in the outside word. I think maybe this was something that was wrong with my up-bringing: I didn't have enough obstacles to get over to toughen myself up against.

Of all Apted's *Seven Up* subjects, Neil has continued to be the one who has proved to be most willing to articulate his thoughts and feelings on a whole range of issues. He has shown a capacity to produce a series of thoughtful and at times almost philosophical reflections on the nature of existence and on individual responsibility. As such he has proved to be one of the most challenging of the *Seven Up* participants in the sense that the course that his life has taken raises uncomfortable questions about developments within the wider society and the apparent ease with which vulnerable individuals like him can find themselves all too easily thrust out on to society's margins. Because he has had such a 'rollercoaster' of a life and because there has always been a high degree of uncertainty about his future, Neil has long established himself as the narrative lynchpin of the *Seven Up* series. As John Corner has perceptively written: 'Neil's apparent lack of "progress" in matters of career and of family, endless changes of location and depressive tendencies have given the series its most anxious "hook" of narrative anxiety' (Corner, 2009).

The role of partners and spouses

By the time Apted came to make *28 Up*, most of his subjects (with the exception of Bruce and Neil) were living in a settled relationship with a partner or spouse. Forming as they do such an important part of subjects' lives, these relationships have assumed major importance in the conversational exchanges between Apted and his *Seven Up* participants. Apted has been able to exploit these liaisons in another sense in that, wherever possible, he has drawn partners and spouses (if they are willing) into the interviewing process. The potential gain for the series has been twofold. Firstly, partners or spouses constitute a valuable narrative resource in that they are able to give new insights into subjects we have previously got to know largely on the basis of accounts they themselves have given. Secondly, the contributions of a number of wives and girlfriends provides a measure of compensation for what Apted had come to recognise as a major weakness of the series: the relative absence of women among his original cast of subjects. Though not all the spouses and partners agreed to take part (interestingly, none of the partners of the three East End girls Jackie, Sue and Lynn would agree to be interviewed), the contributions of Jane (Andrew's wife) Susan (Paul's wife) and especially Debbie (Tony's wife) introduced an important new element to *Seven Up's* narrative structure. Apted has, however, been careful not to recruit too many new members to his existing cast of players. Unlike Winfried Junge, who clearly felt that his chronicle would gain from seeking the views of more than one generation, Apted has always been convinced that broadening the scope of his inquiry beyond the initial cast of *Seven Up* subjects would lead to unnecessary complications. Just as he has rigorously adhered to his seven-year filming cycle, so too he has always insisted on keeping a handle on the project by limiting the number of foregrounded subjects. In his own colourful phrase: 'I was terrified about it all getting out of control, so I limited it to those who are the nearest and dearest and kept away from interviewing [the] children' (Apted, 1998).

The inclusion of partners and spouses from *28 Up* onwards has one further narrative benefit for the *Seven Up* project in that the views that they express about their dearly beloved will, on occasions, coincide with those that members of the audience have also formed about that person. With Paul, for instance, one of the boys who spent part of his childhood in a children's home, there are several references to his vulnerability, beginning with the scene in the first *Seven Up* film in which Paul is introduced to us as the little lost boy from the children's home. Viewers' memories of this and other sequences in subsequent *Up* films where Paul's vulnerability is touched on, are likely to be re-awakened in the scene in *28 Up* when, in answer to Apted's question about what it was in Paul she fell in love with, his wife Susan responds: 'It was his helplessness, I suppose. It was the mothering instinct in me just to pick him up and cuddle him.'

Continuity and change

One of several consequences of the longevity of long docs is that viewers are, in many cases, able to follow subjects whom they first encounter as children through to the phase in their lives where they are bringing up children of their own. For this reason the 'middle' range of *Up* films (*28 Up, 35 Up* and *42 Up*) all have as one of their central themes issues relating to child-rearing and parental responsibility. The topic of conversation between Apted and his subjects frequently revolves around how they are coping with the challenges of family life, but it also touches on what the having of children means to them. Greater depth and meaning is given to some of this discussion by the opportunities, made possible by the long doc form, to draw viewers' attention to the way that successive generations have brought up their children. As one might have anticipated, whilst a number of continuities are discernible, there are some significant differences, many of them rooted in subjects' determination that mistakes of the past will not be repeated. Paul, for instance, who comes from a broken home and has had very few educational opportunities, is determined that his own children will be given a better start in life (*28 Up*). Suzy, on the other hand, who was brought up by a nanny and later attended a boarding school, is not at all comfortable with the thought of her own children sharing the same fate, though she is still in favour of them being privately educated when they are older. Asked by Apted to explain her reasons, she responds: 'I suppose it's what we had; it's what we know' (*28 Up*).

A further consequence of long docs' concern with inter-generational issues is that the theme of human mortality will inevitably come more into prominence as the long doc narrative unfolds. Most long docs have death – or perhaps better, the transience of life – as one of their major themes. From *28 Up* onwards, we witness several

Seven Up subjects coming to terms with having lost one or both of their parents. For viewers, witnessing how subjects cope with bereavement carries with it a special poignancy, since they are able to see the event in the wider frame of a whole life-history. It may even prompt thoughts of a more philosophical nature, especially where the death of a parent occurs at the same time as the birth of a subject's child, as is the case with Suzy (*28 Up*).

Future developments?

Since the *Seven Up* films have brought such regular reminders of life's transitoriness, viewers are naturally intrigued to know when and under what circumstances the project itself will move to a conclusion. Apted himself is, as we know, determined to continue with the series for as long as he is able and has suggested that the best conclusion that he can envisage for the project will be one that is enforced by his own demise and not by the loss of too many of his *Seven Up* subjects. As he put it, when asked about the possibility of one or more of his subjects dying: 'As we all get older, I have to deal with that possibility ... I always hope I'll be the first to go and that none of them will pre-decease me' (Apted, 1998).[20] All long doc film-makers sustain the loss of one or more participants in the lifetime of a project. In Apted's case, the loss of a few of his original subjects had a tangible impact on certain aspects of the *Seven Up* project. So far, however (up to and including *49 Up*), Apted has always been able to compensate for the departure of these participants by adjusting the narrative structure of the films to accommodate for such losses. Though he admits to having a little anxiety about the longer-term 'loyalty' of one or two of his remaining subjects, one gains the impression that the project has now gathered sufficient impetus that only some *force majeure* could halt its further progress.

The Children of Golzow

According to Karl Gass, it took some time and effort to persuade the still youthful Winfried Junge to continue work on the Golzow project once the first Golzow film had been completed. Gass conjectures that his young *protégé* either had misgivings about whether he possessed the necessary experience to complete such a potentially onerous task or else was anxious about the impact that such a long-haul involvement might have on his filmmaking career (Junge,

2004: 12). However, by the time Junge had completed the third film in the cycle (*At the Age of Eleven*) in 1966, the project had evidently gained sufficient momentum to convince him that this was a project to which he would be prepared to devote a considerable portion of his working life.

In committing himself to the project in this way, Junge demonstrates that he has come to share Gass' belief that a longitudinal study of children growing up in the GDR would be an appropriate means of showing the impact on a generation of the so-called 'socialist experiment'. Junge has never made any secret of the fact that he was broadly sympathetic to many of the ideas that lay behind this experiment. In Junge's own words:'We wanted to chronicle how socialism was developing, how it impacted on individuals and how all these changes effected a whole generation growing up under socialism' (Cited in Jordan & Schenk, 1996: 116). Like many in the GDR, however, in the course of time Junge was to become increasingly critical of policies being undertaken by the Socialist Unity Party (SED)'s regime, though he never went as far as the singer Wolf Biermann in actively expressing his opposition to or disapproval of what was happening in the GDR (see Molloy, 2009: 23–7).[21]

In the decade following the production of *When I First Go to School* (1961), Junge and his team produced four more Golzow films. All of them are relatively short (the longest is 36 minutes) and each of them chronicles what is seen to be a key stage in the children's development. All these films rely on largely observational techniques. As Junge later remarked: 'The only real way of tackling this material was by the use of observational means. Whether I was conscious of this or not, I felt that this would result in a genuinely documentary study' (Junge, 1962: 432, my translation). The films are mainly focused on chronicling various classroom activities, though sometimes we accompany the children on class excursions to sites of historical interest or to industrial plants. All this is in keeping with the films' chronicling imperative, as are the attempts to provide a flavour of life in the wider Golzow community and to show how the children are being actively prepared to be good GDR citizens. This is best exemplified by *At the Age of Fourteen* (1969), the film which focuses on the event known as the *Jugendweihe*, the formal ceremony at which young GDR citizens were required to declare their unswerving allegiance to the state and all that it stood for.

Institutional relations and expectations

Many of the challenges that Junge faced during the first decade of the Golzow project were similar to those confronting other long doc filmmakers. Like them, Junge was concerned with building good working relationships with the children and their families and with developing the filming and editing strategies that best suited the task in hand. The larger challenge remained that of producing the kind of work that, within the limits of what was possible at the time, could still lay claim to have genuine documentary validity. This was certainly no easy task. Junge, like all his fellow GDR filmmakers, was acutely aware of the constraints under which he was required to operate, but was nevertheless concerned to do all in his power to prevent his work from becoming ideologically complicit.[22] As the Golzow project slowly gathered momentum, however, Junge and his team became increasingly aware of the expectations that were being placed upon them concerning the picture of 'everyday life under socialism' that the series was projecting.[23] Where the filmmakers knew they would have to practise extreme vigilance, if they were to avoid accusations of ideological complicity, was in all matters relating to any attached commentary.[24] In the first three Golzow films it had been possible to maintain a discreet compromise between providing a limited amount of signposting commentary and allowing the image sequences to speak for themselves. Once the children had spent four or five years in the school, however, the filmmakers evidently came under greater pressure to make more explicit links between the school's educational programme and the wider aims of the 'socialist experiment' being practised in the GDR. By the same token, Junge knew that we would have to pay careful heed to what visual material he chose to include that depicted everyday life in the school or in the small township of Golzow. There was, for instance, an understanding that the filmmakers would practise some self-censoring discretion and that nothing should be revealed about the external fabric of the town and its institutions that did not reflect well on the Party's desire to be seen as an engine of social change.

During the first decade of its production *The Children of Golzow* series became relatively well known in GDR documentary circles, which resulted in the relevant authorities paying more attention to the films than they had done at the outset. Within the ranks of DEFA officialdom, indeed, there began to be mutterings of discontent that the films were not living up to expectations and that the filmmakers might have to pay greater heed to the more positive aspects of GDR life. In one unpublished internal memo written at the time, for instance, a DEFA chief editor writes:'What the children have to say in these films isn't really what one could legitimately expect of young GDR citizens at this stage. The Golzow educational authorities should set about improving the situation' (cited in Moreno, 2000: 12). Such remarks are highly revealing in the light they throw on documentary filmmaking in the GDR, especially with respect to the tension between the desire to project a positive image of what was being achieved in the name of socialism and the rather more mundane reality that the filmmakers were documenting. As Junge has commented:

> DEFA would have probably preferred to bury the project after the first three episodes, but the films were already becoming known in documentary circles at home and abroad. If the authorities had put a stop to them now because they were not pointing in the right direction, then they would also have had to admit that something was fundamentally awry with socialism. (Cited in Moreno, 2000: 12)

It was decided therefore to allow work on the series to continue, though Junge was left in no doubt that, from now on, his work would be exposed to particularly close scrutiny.

The impact on Junge and his team of all this was that they always had to second-guess the impact that their film would have on various constituencies of viewers (including of course members of the Party hierarchy). Junge was, however, sometimes able to turn to his own advantage the requirement that his film be seen to be chronicling contemporary GDR realities. When planning a future film in the Golzow cycle, for example, he would often time the making of the film to coincide with a particular GDR anniversary or with an event considered to have special significance in the lives of citizens (such as that of the *Jugendweihe*). *At the Age of Fourteen* was scheduled to coincide with the twentieth anniversary of the GDR, whilst *Spare No Charm* (1979), the film intended as a summary of the previous six Golzow films, was conceived partly to celebrate the GDR's thirtieth anniversary.

Working relationships with subjects

Like all long doc filmmakers, Junge and his team not only had to remain sensitively attuned to what was expected of them as DEFA documentarists, they also had to maintain good working relations with the children and their parents.[25] It did not take long for the children to become accustomed to the presence of the filmmakers. Bonds of trust began to be established between Junge and his subjects and there was a sense in which the filming, in part, became a collaborative venture. By the time he came to make the third Golzow film, for instance, Junge had begun to encourage the children themselves to have more of a say in what was filmed and how certain topics should be approached. As Junge observed at the time:

> As the children grew older, we had to devise new ways of approaching them. From film to film we gained valuable lessons about what worked well, but by the same token I also became aware of some of the dangers of working with authentic heroes [sic]. (Cited in Hesse, 1974: 18)

During his work on his fourth Golzow film _At the Age of Fourteen_, Junge also discovered, just like other long doc filmmakers, that there are particular difficulties of filming and interviewing children as they are going through the trials and tribulations of puberty.[26] He has even suggested that one of the reasons that this film acquired a rather intrusive commentary was the need to compensate for the children's taciturnity.

Once the children had left school, one of Junge's biggest challenges was that of continuing to persuade his chosen subjects to participate. As already noted, GDR society was not characterised by a high level of trust, and there was a widespread anxiety about how openly one could express one's opinions.[27] This was doubtless one of the reasons why one or two of the original Golzow children began to have doubts about the wisdom of remaining involved in the project. At the age of twenty, Petra, who according to Junge was one of the most intelligent pupils in the class, was the first to turn her back on the project. Like several other long doc subjects, she could not reconcile herself to the prospect of having her life under more or less constant surveillance for such an extended period (see Junge, 2004: 48–9). She was also, apparently, critical of the way that the film had manoeuvred her into the role of 'model pupil', once again echoing the criticism of other long doc subjects about stereotypical representation. With Ilona it is a rather different story. She did not finally sever her ties with the project till the mid-1980s, though her misgivings had probably surfaced much earlier. Two reasons are usually cited for her decision to withdraw. First and foremost, Ilona is a naturally shy and retiring person and, in normal circumstances, would be eager to keep herself to herself. This has meant that she found the filming and interviewing process more intrusive and disturbing than many others. In addition, however, Ilona had already in her teens become a Party member and this in itself may have led to certain apprehensions on her part concerning how she would be expected to respond in a conversational exchange that she knew was destined for public consumption (see also Chapter 6, pp. 167–8).

The examples of Petra and Ilona tell us a good deal about the challenges faced by long doc filmmakers in managing their relationships with subjects over the longer term.[28] It is difficult, for instance, to avoid concluding that, in whatever socio-political context the long doc is being produced, there will always be some participants who experience the regular intrusion of a film crew into their lives as an unsustainable burden, whilst there will be others who regard their involvement in much more positive terms, either for the kudos that this brings or simply out of recognition that they are making a contribution to a worthwhile project that also has historical value. In seeking further reasons why some participants are able to stay the course whereas others feel compelled to withdraw, one can also surmise that much depends on whether subjects feel any temperamental affinity with the filmmaker. Several of the Golzow subjects, for instance, especially some of the women, did not take to Junge s manner, finding him too schoolmasterly in his approach. Others, most notably Jürgen and Willy, established good relations with the filmmaker from the outset and remained on friendly terms with him for more than four decades. Just like Tony and Bruce in the *Seven Up* series, Jürgen and Willy have been subjects on whom the filmmaker has always been able to rely, even though there have been certain areas of their lives that they have found it difficult to talk about (with Jürgen his alcoholism and with Willy his relations with women).

Individual portraits: the biographies of Marieluise and Elke

When all is said and done, maintaining good relations with one's long doc subjects is always going to demand a considerable measure of trust on both sides. As Junge has observed on several occasions: 'Trust belongs to the aesthetics of documentary film' (Junge, 2004: 54). The following section discusses developments in the working relationship of Junge with two of his subjects, Marieluise and Elke, who are arguably the two leading female participants in *The Children of Golzow*. Just as in other long doc series, there is a sense in which the unfolding cycle of films not only chronicles the experiences of a particular generation but can also be regarded as documenting a developing relationship between a filmmaking observer and those on whom the filmmaker's attention is so unremittingly focused.

Marieluise

All the evidence suggests that, in Marieluise, Junge had found an ideal long doc subject with whom he enjoyed a fruitful working relationship for more than four decades. Right from the outset, like several participants in other long docs (most notably Tony in *Seven Up* and Slovodan in *The Children of Jordbrö*), Marieluise appears to have been a very co-operative subject. She has hardly ever given the impression that she has found the filming process overly intrusive or threatening and, unlike some of her contemporaries, has always been willing to talk in quite open terms about her relationships and her plans for the future. It was, therefore, no surprise that Marieluise emerged as the central protagonist in the film *I Spoke With a Girl*, which took as its starting point a class reunion of the Golzow children in 1975.[29] Marieluise was to continue to be a leading light in later Golzow films. Some two decades later the Junges produced a long (141 minutes) film biography *I'll Show You My Life: Marieluise, Child of Golzow* that traces Marieluise's life from her early years spent as a citizen of the GDR to her post-*Wende* life in (West) Germany as the wife of a *Bundeswehr* officer. Given the tensions that can often enter into relationships between filmmaker and participant, Marieluise belongs to the category of subjects who have been willing to declare that they are 'largely content' with the way in which their life has been represented on screen.[30]

Broadly speaking, there has been a very positive audience response to the 'character' of Marieluise in the Golzow films. This is, in part, doubtless attributable to the remarkable frankness that she displays when talking about herself and her life. It may also be connected with the fact, however, that certain facets of Marieluise's life can be seen to provide some most revealing insights into some of the more problematical aspects of GDR society. In one of the early films *Eleven Years Old*, for instance, Marieluise is shown in the company of her father and one of her sisters as they return home after attending a service at the local Protestant church. Churchgoing in the GDR, though tolerated, was certainly not encouraged.[31] If anything, it was regarded as a somewhat deviant pursuit. Junge was, thus, aware that he would have to tread most warily when dealing with this topic. What made the situation still trickier for Junge was that Marieluise's father was a man who not only held firm religious convictions but was also prepared to voice his principled opposition to many of the policies being followed by the SED regime. As long as the GDR remained in existence, Junge always had something of a struggle with his conscience about how to deal with Herr Hübner. The filmmaker knew that the state authorities would never tolerate the expression of such heretical thoughts in a DEFA documentary. At the same time Junge recognised that he had a responsibility as a documentarist to signal to the audience that there were some in the GDR who held contrary views to those that were being propagated by the Party leaders[32] (see also Chapter 6, pp. 163–4).

The other area of Marieluise's life about which the earlier (pre-*Wende*) Golzow films are relatively silent is the occupation of her husband, Hans-Steffen. Only after the *Wende* does it come to light that Hans-Steffen had for several years been attached to the so-called 'government squadron', a special division of the GDR air force. Since everything relating to the military in the GDR was considered a matter of state security, nothing could ever be revealed in the Golzow films about what Hans-Steffen did. This created a number of headaches for Junge during the later 1970s and the 1980s since Hans-Steffen effectively became a structuring absence in the films of this period.[33] Just as was the case with Marieluise's father, however, the full truth about Hans-Steffen can only emerge at a much later date – thereby once again revealing the advantages of being able to take the long view. In *Screenplay: The Times* Junge is finally able to put the record straight about the role that Marieluise's husband played in the East German military. Junge is also able to show the remarkable process by which Hans-Steffen gets converted into a fully-fledged member of the (West) German *Bundeswehr*, the self same force against which, as a GDR officer, he had been so implacably opposed.

Elke

Marieluise's openness and her readiness to allow herself to be filmed over such a long period are in stark contrast to what appears to be the much less obliging attitude displayed by Elke, one of the other female protagonists in the Golzow films. Elke is one of those participants who has found certain aspects of her role as a long doc subject difficult to cope with and has clearly felt intimidated by being so frequently 'called to account'. In spite of all this, Elke remained with the Golzow project for almost its entire duration and, like several other participants, also had an individual film devoted to her – *My Life Is My Own Affair: Elke, Child of Golzow* (1996). Like many other long doc subjects who have reservations about being regularly put on public display, Elke has devised her own coping strategies. Instead of opting to withdraw completely from the project, she has (rather like John in the *Seven Up* series) made it clear that she would be the one who would dictate the terms of her further participation. In a practical sense this has meant that, over the decades, she has chosen to make what one might call a number of strategic with-drawals, either declining the invitation to be filmed or simply staying out of communication with Junge and his team. Elke's reluctance to be interviewed at times when Junge would have welcomed contribu-tions from her manifestly has less to do with any natural diffidence on her part (as was the case with Ilona) and is more connected with the principled stand she is prepared to take on the more intrusive aspects of long doc participation. Her disinclination comes especially to the fore during those periods of her life when she is forging new relationships or settling down in new marital partnerships (of which there were several). Just like Jackie in *Seven Up*, Elke is of the firm belief that certain areas of an individual's life should be off-limits.[34] Quite often she only informed Junge about important events in her life long after they had taken place and even then only in the most general terms. One of the consequences of this is that viewers get the impression that Junge is constantly involved in a game of 'catch-up' with the elusive Elke. It has also meant that, more so than with any other Golzow participant, Junge has been driven to interview one or more of Elke's partners in the attempt to throw at least a little light on her enigmatic persona.

Elke's apprehensiveness about being filmed became stronger as the years rolled by and she proved progressively more reluctant to expose herself to the probing eye of the camera. In the immediate post-*Wende* period, a time of great uncertainty for all East Germans, Elke completely disappears from view for a while and she only allows herself to be filmed again in 1991. According to Junge, the events leading up to the fall of the Berlin Wall and the aftermath of these events had rendered her 'speechless' and she wanted some time to consider whether she wished to have any further involvement in the Golzow project.

Elke's role in the Golzow cycle of films in many ways provides an object lesson in the strengths and possible limitations of adopting the long doc approach. As we follow her progress from a childhood spent in a relatively nondescript East German town till the point when, in her mid-forties, she marries a West German property developer, we begin to get some idea of what life must have been like for somebody whose formative years were spent in the GDR but who has now had to adapt to living in radically changed circumstances in a re-united Germany. As with most other long doc subjects, Elke provides plentiful scope for considering how an individual's life course is subject to the forces of heredity and environment. Born into a Catholic family, Elke – even at a comparatively youthful age – shows all the signs of being single-minded and forceful in her attitudes. As depicted in the early (pre-*Wende*) Golzow films, Elke's life will also have carried particular resonance for East German audiences in that it exemplified the type of the challenge that many in the East faced as they sought to reconcile personal hopes and aspirations with what was expected of them as GDR citizens. Junge's attempt to chronicle the various stages in Elke's life as she seeks to assert herself in both a professional and a personal sense also provides some most illuminating insights into everyday life in the GDR. When viewing these films, for instance, one finds oneself constantly speculating on whether the many false starts in Elke's life are more the consequence of her strong-mindedness or have more to do with the socio-political and cultural environment in which she was nurtured.

Viewed with the benefits of hindsight, the story of Elke also draws attention to some of the more problematical aspects of long doc filmmaking. In spite of having remained a participant for many years and of feeling at least some sense of obligation towards Junge and his team, Elke evidently believes that the only way she can maintain an element of control over her personal privacy and prevent herself from becoming a victim of unwarranted media intrusiveness is by effecting those aforementioned strategic withdrawals.[35] This in turn points up what some would see as a more general problem of longitudinal filmmaking: however diligently and persistently a filmmaker and their team attempt to track the life-journey of an individual through its many phases, certain aspects of that journey will never become visible. It is almost as if the very longevity of the exercise serves merely to point up the impossibility of the task.[36]

Changes of trajectory

Not surprisingly, given the different sets of conditions under which they were produced, the long docs in this study reveal different developmental trajectories. One of the most striking features of *The Children of Golzow*, for instance, is that it was only after Junge had been working on the project for a decade and a half that he began to employ some of the narrativising ploys that Apted and Hartleb had started using at a much earlier stage. It was only from the mid-1970s, for instance – more precisely with the making of *I Spoke With a Girl* – that Junge began to move away from the more observational style of the early films towards one that is significantly more interview-based. Describing the particular turn in the development of the Golzow cycle, Uwe Kant, the man responsible for scripting the commentary of many of the Golzow films, has commented: 'Locations started to multiply and there was greater emphasis on solo performances' (cited in Junge, 2004: 207).

In spite of the greater emphasis on the tracing of individual life-journeys, Junge is at some pains to perpetuate the myth that the Golzower 'children' are still members of that very special club that he and his team had called into being when they initiated the Golzow project. Once the children had left school, opportunities for filming them in interaction with each other were limited to those occasions when the subjects got together for class reunions (as in October 1978) or when the filmmakers themselves contrived to bring the Golzow subjects together for various media-initiated events.[37] The first such event was in 1975, some four or five years after the children had completed their formal education. A far more important reunion came, however, in 1991 when the filmmakers succeeded in persuading their subjects to participate in a specially arranged excursion to Hamburg, timed to coincide with the first anniversary of German (re)unification. The significance of this event, in filmic terms, was that it provided a platform for both filmmakers and subjects to discuss at some length how the events of the previous two years had touched and transformed their lives.

By the late 1970s, it had become clear to Junge and his team that – in spite of these occasional attempts to reunite the members of the 1961 primary class and film their interactions – the Golzow films would, from now on, have to focus more on tracing the progress of individual participants. The two works that most clearly exemplify this change of narrative trajectory in the Golzow films are *Spare No Charm* (1979) and *Biographies* (1980/81). The two films are, structurally and thematically, closely related. Not only are they substantially longer than any of the previous Golzow films; they also provide evidence of how Junge and his team have sought to develop a more flexible type of narrative structure that does justice to the ever-expanding body of material. The essential aim of both films was to continue the task of chronicling a set of historical developments, but at the same time to give more detailed accounts of the life-journeys of individual Golzower. As Junge soon realised, this was no easy task. As he began work on the film that was eventually to become *Spare No Charm*, his initial concept had been to start by giving a summarising overview of the six previous Golzow films and then go on to provide a series of updates on most of his protagonists (Junge, 1981: 63–6). Having discovered, however that such a film would run to more than four and a half hours, Junge decided that a better approach would be to produce two separate films that would stand in complementary relationship to each other.

Of the two films, the later one *Biographies* has had by far the greatest resonance. It is also the work that brought the Golzow cycle of films to the attention of a wider international public and is the one that most clearly demonstrated what could be achieved by longitudinal means. *Spare No Charm*, by comparison, as well as revealing certain structural deficiencies, provides a good deal of evidence about the difficulties encountered by filmmakers working in a state-controlled media environment. Junge has written at some length about the circumstances under which this film was produced (Junge, 2004: 60–9). What emerges very plainly from this account is that, during the making of this film, Junge and his team were forced into a series of concessions and compromises. Since *Spare No Charm* was to be linked in with anniversary celebrations, for instance, there were expectations not only that it would draw attention to the contributions being made by the young folk of Golzow towards the building of a socialist society but also that it would contain at least some references to the growing importance of the GDR as a freedom-loving state that was playing its part in securing the peace of the world.

Not surprisingly, in view of these high expectations, *Spare No Charm* had quite a fraught production history and a mixed critical reaction when it was first screened (Junge, 2004: 212–14). The consensus was that it was a not wholly successful attempt to combine historical chronicling (three decades of GDR history) with brief biographical updates on more than a dozen of the Golzower. Particular criticism was levelled at the tendentious commentary that was always seeking to draw generalising conclusions from the experience of individual Golzow subjects (Roth, 1981: 31). The film did, however, apparently give rise to some lively debate amongst members of the cinema and television audience, possibly because it was the first of the Golzow series to attempt to make connections between the lives of individual subjects and the broader sweep of historical events.[38] There are, moreover, reasons for believing that *Spare No Charm* created a sufficient ground-swell effect to make it that much easier for Junge and his team to argue for a continuation of the project when sceptical voices were raised.

Biographies is generally regarded as a more successful film than *Spare No Charm*, not least because it can be seen to exploit some of the perceived strengths of the long doc form. In *Biographies* the major part of the film is taken up with nine individual biographies, presented in a way not dissimilar to the separate 'chapters' of films in the *Seven Up* series. As with the Junges' previous film, however, there were once again certain problems concerning how the filmmakers approached their subject[39] (see also Richter, 1982: 59). This time most of the controversy centred on whether the lives of those who were highlighted in this film were exemplary enough in the eyes of the state authorities. By the same token, when the film was finally screened, questions were raised by some members of the audience about the criteria according to which just nine of the original twenty children were selected. Could there have been political calculations in the choice of some and the rejection of others? What reasons lay behind the effective deselection of half the original Golzow cast?

In presenting the life-journeys of his nine chosen protagonists in *Biographies*, Junge still adheres to a chronological mode of presentation – one that has no recourse to the backwards-and-forwards time-shuttling seen in other long docs. Short scenes from a subject's life are condensed into a brief filmic biography that is supplemented with some narrative interlinking or some explanatory commentary, some of which contains reflections on the filmmaking process itself. *Biographies* has also acquired landmark status in the development of the Golzow project in that it is arguably the first film in which Junge begins to exploit some of the particular expressive possibilities of the long doc form. In each of the biographical segments there are significant ellipses as a series of life-events are reprised.[40] The events are presented in such a way, however, that the viewer has a strong sense of encountering them as if they belonged to the living present rather than the rediscovered past. The narrative viewpoint is, in other words, not one that is primarily retrospective but one that seeks to evoke the vibrant actuality of lived experience. Though each of these biographical sketches is marked by significant temporal leaps, viewers of films such as *Biographies* get a strong sense of immediacy as, for a few brief moments, they lock into consecutive developmental phases of a person's life. Whilst the viewing experience is somewhat reminiscent of leafing through a photo album, the particular properties of film mean that these highly compressed bios are able to secure a much greater degree of viewer involvement. As Rolf Richter has perceptively commented:

> In this film (Biographies) we experience a series of life-situations, actions and events. Nevertheless we perceive each separate phase as if it were a present-day event. What we experience is rooted in this sense of immediacy. The film doesn't so much attempt to reproduce past events by means of retrospective reconstruction or re-enactment. It provides an account in which events unfurl sequentially as they would have done in real life. (Richter, 1982: 57, my translation)

Another major theme in *Biographies* is a concern with time and its inexorable progression. The passage of time and the transitoriness of all things are recurrent features of many long docs and they acquire considerable thematic significance in *Biographies*. Already in the prologue to the film we are introduced to the countryside outside Golzow as winter turns to spring, whilst in the epilogue we are once again made aware of the cyclical nature of life, as summer gives way to autumn. In order to prompt further reflections on the wider import of such changes, viewers are also reminded, via the commentary, of the wise words of the Greek philosopher to whose teachings the children had been exposed at the tender age of eleven: 'Everything is in flux, the only constant factor [in life] is change.'

The art of the possible

In the course of working on *Spare No Charm* and *Biographies*, the Junges had once again been made aware of the many compromises they were having to make in order to ensure that the films met with the approval of the state authorities. Just as Bismarck had once remarked of politics, filmmaking in the former GDR was also very much the art of the possible. Certain types of material might provide some telling insights into everyday life in East Germany, but these might be the very scenes whose inclusion would lead to objections on the part of cultural officials. Thus, the Junges always had to be alert to giving too many hostages to fortune in these matters and would often err on the side of caution. They were, however, able to derive at least some consolation from the knowledge that – given the characteristically incremental nature of long docs – they would possibly have the opportunity of including in a later film scenes that they had decided it would be impolitic to include in the film they were currently working on. There were, even in GDR times, marked fluctuations in the attitude of the authorities to what could and could not be shown. For instance, Junge recalls a scene he had wanted to include in *At the Age of Fourteen* (1969), where the children are shown rehearsing for the *Jugendweihe* (pledging their allegiance to the state). At the time it was not considered politic to include this sequence, but ten years later in *Spare No Charm* the authorities clearly took a more relaxed view and the whole scene was allowed to be shown. As Junge later remarked, with tongue very much in cheek: 'you see, certain things that once seemed impossible later proved to be possible. Sometimes, even in the GDR, people got a little wiser' (Junge, 2004: 47).

Biographies was produced exactly two decades into the Golzow project and has become one of the most highly regarded of the Golzow films. By presenting within a single film biographical accounts of nine of the Golzow subjects, the Junges were also effectively inviting viewers to draw comparisons between the individuals whose lives were thus foregrounded. Among other things, this was likely to lead to conjecture as to why, given that they all share the same point of departure and have been subject to very similar socialising stimuli, they should have developed in such remarkably different ways. As Barbara Junge observed in a later interview:

> I always find it intriguing when you compare our subjects and consider that they all come from the same background and have all had the

same chances in life at the outset. What's so striking is to see just how differently their individual lives have developed. So you begin to ask yourself how much of this is attributable to 'nurture' and how much is down to 'nature'. (Richter, 1996: 5)

By highlighting the lives of individual Golzower in this way, the Junges knew that they were sailing very close to the wind as far as the authorities were concerned. The Golzow project had never received the wholehearted endorsement of senior officials in the film ministry, largely, one imagines, because it also drew attention to some of the shoddier aspects of life in East Germany. Junge himself has ruefully concluded that, even though *Biographies* provides a 'realistic balance' of the thirty-year socialist experiment in the GDR, it was still regarded with suspicion by the powers-that-be in East Germany. In Junge's opinion this was 'because the many insights that it gave into social developments and into everyday life in many ways contradicted those more acceptable, but nonetheless one-sided views that artists and filmmakers were expected to project' (Junge, 2008).

For audiences in the GDR the primary appeal of *Biographies* (and for that matter probably of all the other films in the Golzow cycle) may well have been that so much of what the film depicted had the ring of truth about it. They could thus identify with this film far more than with the more openly propagandistic work of which there was certainly no shortage in the GDR at the time. Audiences far beyond Germany's shores have also found much with which they can connect in these accounts of individuals attempting to manoeuvre their way through life with no great certainty as to where they are heading and with no evident enthusiasm for the tasks and duties they are required to perform. In a celebrity-obsessed age it is argu-ably these depictions of quietly pursued, less than heroic lives that evoke such a powerful response from audiences.[41] As Elke Schieber has written about *Biographies*:

> In spite of many compromises *Biographies* gives an honest, true-to-life account. It depicts situations and events in the everyday lives of many different sorts of people. Illnesses, weddings and divorces, not liking one's job, poor living conditions, fear of saying the wrong thing or feelings of distrust when confronted with fine phrases and prom-ises: you can find all these in *Biographies*. All this reveals how different people's attitudes were, but it also shows that people's lives were not totally overshadowed by always having to toe the Party line. (Schieber in Jordan & Schenk, 1996: 184, my translation)

As well as acquiring the status of a key film in the Golzow cycle, *Biographies* is also regarded by many as a landmark film in the history of East German documentary. For as long as the GDR remained a communist state, East German filmmakers were simply not able to comment at all openly on many of the issues affecting the lives of GDR citizens. It is much to the Junges' credit, therefore, that in *Biographies* they succeeded in producing a film which – like much of the work of their East German contemporaries Volker Koepp and Jürgen Böttcher – offered revealing insights into everyday life in the GDR.[42] Focusing as it does on a group of unheroic, ordinary individuals attempting to muddle through as best they can in less than optimum conditions, *Biographies* gives what many saw as a more accurate picture of living under socialist conditions than many other types of account (Lölhöffel, 1982). It would certainly be going too far to claim that the picture projected evidence of a society in the first stages of disintegration. The mood seems more one of resigned acceptance that this is simply the way things are, with no real prospect of change. What *Biographies* does us alert us to, however, is that at the beginning of the last decade of the GDR's existence there was an ever-widening gulf between the inflated rhetoric of Party officials and the actual lived experience of most East Germans.

The Children of Jordbrö

Having had his first film *From a Child's World* screened in 1973, Rainer Hartleb proceeded to produce a series of regular Jordbrö updates in the course of the next eight years, all of which were broadcast on Swedish Television. The starting point for the series, it will be remembered, was Hartleb's wish to examine the impact of a new policy introduced by the government in the late 1960s which was designed to provide suitable housing for all Swedish citizens. Hartleb's view was that the best way of tackling this subject was via a longitudinal study that chronicled the experiences of a group of incomers shortly after they had moved into one such housing development in Jordbrö on the outskirts of Stockholm. Just like its German and British counterparts, then, the initial intention of *The Children of Jordbrö* was in part a sociological investigation. As well as drawing attention to a possible gulf between political rhetoric and the reality on the ground, the series also set itself the more specific goal of exploring the ways in which the move to a completely new living environment had affected some of the younger members of the incoming families. To these ends the original series set out to accompany a group of Jordbrö youngsters through their nine years of elementary education from the time they first entered the school until their leaving at the age of fifteen or sixteen. The conscious-ness-raising aim was to discover what it was like to be growing up in a pioneering community such as Jordbrö and to show how a new generation of children were being prepared for life in a rapidly changing world.

The regular flow of one-hour Jordbrö updates produced and transmitted over this period (1972–81) had the predictable conse-quence of generating a considerable level of audience interest in how the children were developing. Thus, even though there were some in Jordbrö who were concerned about what they saw as an unduly negative portrayal of their community (see Chapter 3, pp. 66–7), Jordbrö was now well and truly on the map as far as the larger, nationwide television audience was concerned. Having become acquainted with this group of mostly quite endearing personalities, viewers were understandably eager to be kept in the picture as to how the children would develop in the longer term.[43]

The Jordbrö Children and *Living in Jordbrö*

The relatively high profile that the Jordbrö cycle of films had gained as a television series also made it possible for Hartleb, at a later date, to get the funding for two feature-length films based on material he had gathered for the television series. The two films *The Jordbrö Chil-dren* (covering the period 1972–75) and *Living in Jordbrö* (1975–81) combine some of the elements we would expect to find in a tradi-tional documentary account (engaging with issues in the socio-historical world) with others that are more typical of a longitudinal work (the focus on subjects' development over a significant period of time).[44]

The Jordbrö Children and *Living in Jordbrö* put a clear marker down for all the Jordbrö films that follow in that they introduce us to the characteristic features of Hartleb's filmmaking style. In stark contrast to the hectic narrative tempo and in-your-face commentary of the first *Seven Up* programme, for instance, these first two Jordbrö films are altogether more restrained in their tone and their whole approach. Above all, viewers get no sense that the films are seeking to win them over to a particular point of view. Hartleb has never perceived his role as a filmmaker as one that requires him to loudly persuade or exhort, but rather has sought to present his audience with a body of evidence on the strength of which they can draw their own conclusions.

Already in these first two Jordbrö films there is plenty of evidence to suggest that Hartleb has all the qualities required of a long doc filmmaker. Patient observation, quiet attentiveness and tenacity are very much his watchwords. When registering events, he always remains an unobtrusive presence. Never once in the whole history of the Jordbrö cycle does he emerge from behind the camera. Likewise in his role as interviewer, Hartleb gives every indication that he has the ability – or has cultivated the technique – of making subjects feel comfortable in his presence Above all, Hartleb always remains empathically aware of what it must feel like, as a subject, to have one's life exposed to such regular scrutiny. The Jordbrö participants' willingness to share many of the more intimate details of their lives with him is, thus, testimony not only of Hartleb's ability to be a good listener but also of the trusting relationship that they have developed with him over a considerable period of time.[45]

As befits a filmmaker who is seeking to encourage the audience to reach their own interpretation of what they hear and see, *The Jordbrö Children* and *Living in Jordbrö* have very little commentary or expository narration. Scenes filmed in the classroom and in and around Jordbrö are mostly allowed to speak for themselves, and there are, at this stage, relatively few interviews with subjects. The main intention is, in Hartleb's words, 'to convey, in words and pictures, the hopes and dreams of these "wild" little 7-year-olds and how their ideas about life and their own place in it are constantly changing as they grow older' (Hartleb, 2007). The films employ largely observational techniques, though the material is edited in such a way as to enable the viewer to gain some insights into the methods by which the children were taught and into an educational practice that put considerable emphasis on child-centred learning.[46] Also particularly striking are the efforts made by the school to develop the children's awareness of their responsibilities as citizens, which include encouraging them to take an interest in political affairs. On one occasion, for instance, we see the children involved in a lively role-playing exercise based on the possible outcome of the upcoming Swedish General Election. A little later in the same film, we see other children debating the pros and cons of nuclear power with their teacher.

Though part of Hartleb's remit in the early Jordbrö films was evidently to chronicle the educational milieu to which the children were exposed, his other main concern is to show how the children – under the influence of various shaping forces – begin to develop as individuals with their own distinct personalities and attitudes. Having been able to observe them in a variety of situations, viewers begin to feel that they are getting to know more about individual children: their character traits and their idiosyncrasies.[47] Some, like Camilla, already have problems in relating to their peer group. Others, like Ulric, are already beginning to show signs of the behavioural problems that will make life difficult for them in future years. In seeking to throw some light on how the children develop in the way they do, Hartleb also extends his inquiry to their lives outside the classroom, in the wider Jordbrö community.

In both these films, viewers are also provided with plentiful opportunities to reflect on the ways in which family circumstances and parental outlooks may have affected or determined the development of their offspring. (This is in striking contrast to Apted's and Junge's work, where only limited information is given about the children's home environment.) Conducting extended interviews with the children and their parents in the family home also enables Hartleb to elicit a number of responses to questions regarding what they see as the gains and losses of their move to Jordbrö. As one might have anticipated, whilst the children appear to be adapting quite well to this new environment, their parents are more divided in their views. Some are grateful that it has enabled them to move out of cramped living conditions into relatively spacious new apartments. Others are far more critical about what they see as the soullessness of the place. In one extended interview, for instance, a young mother pointedly remarks that the advantages of having additional living space are more than outweighed by the sense of growing isolation she is experiencing. As she observes: 'Everything is plotted out for you, it shouldn't be like that. The thrill of the week for me is when the illustrated magazine is delivered.' (*Children of Jordbrö*)

The immigrant experience

Many of those now living in Jordbrö are immigrants who have moved to Sweden from countries such as Finland, Greece, Turkey and the former Yugoslavia. Hartleb is evidently keen to explore what life was like for those who had come to Sweden looking for a better future. Four of the children, who, in the fullness of time, will become protagonists in the Jordbrö films, are the sons or daughters of immigrants. In the very first film, for instance, there is an extended sequence focusing on Slobodan, the son of a guest-worker couple from Yugoslavia. As a bright-eyed seven-year-old, just starting school, he is made to feel most welcome in this alien environment by the teacher Inga-Britt. This is the same Slobodan who, not so very many years later, we will witness going through the trauma of seeing his homeland ravaged by internecine warfare. Slobodan's story graphically illustrates some of the split loyalties that members of immigrant families experience: how to reconcile a growing attachment to the country in which they have settled with their feelings for the country from which their parents originate.[48]

The stories centred on the children of immigrants are made more meaningful because we first encounter them at a tender age and then follow them through their formative years as they seek, among other things, to clarify the sometimes-ambivalent feelings they have for their homeland. Encountering the children at regular intervals, viewers are given the opportunity to reflect on the immigrant experience from the incomer's point of view. What is especially striking, for instance, is that, whereas the children appear to have fewer problems of integrating themselves in the host culture, the parents often experience much greater difficulty. For Slobodan, for instance, becoming assimilated into Swedish society appears to be a more or less natural process. He remains acutely aware, however, that for his parents the decision to build a new life in an alien environment must have involved them in considerable sacrifice. There is, for instance, a memorable sequence in a later Jordbrö film (*Back to Jordbrö*) where we hear Slobodan – now a smart personable young teacher, in charge of a group of Swedish primary schoolchildren – quietly reflecting on how, mindful of his parents' sacrifice, he is now firmly resolved to 'do something with his life'.

Just as with the *The Children of Golzow* project, one of Hartleb's major concerns in the first phase of the Jordbrö cycle is to track the children's progress through their nine years of compulsory schooling. As the children enter their teens, the teachers are confronted with ever more challenging behaviour, all of which Hartleb chronicles with a fine eye for revealing detail. Not once does he allow any note of false optimism to creep into this chronicling of his subjects' early teenage years. Already, several of the youngsters are beginning to express considerable disenchantment with everything the school represents. Rebelliousness is in the air and viewers are left in considerable doubt as to how some of the children will fare when they complete their studies and move into the much less predictable world of work and adult responsibilities. As their class teacher observes, only half-reassuringly, while the children collect their school-leaving certificates at the end of the film: 'Most of them will be alright. I hope so, anyway.'

Back to Jordbrö

Once the children had left school and begun to embark on their separate life-journeys, this could well have signalled the end of the Jordbrö film project. Hartleb could easily have seen it as the end of his Jordbrö mission and as an opportunity to move on to fresh woods and pastures new. Just as we have seen with other long docs, however, such projects tend to acquire their own kind of momentum that makes stopping them more difficult than might have been anticipated. And so it proved to be with *The Children of Jordbrö*. Some five years after the youngsters graduated from school they met for a class reunion to which Hartleb was also invited. When he turned up to this event without his camera, there were apparently voluble protests. This set him thinking about the possibility of reconnecting with the Jordbrö project.

As Hartleb began to make plans for the film that would become *Back to Jordbrö*, he soon realised that he would need to make some adjustments to the filming and editing techniques he had employed hitherto. In practical terms this meant the same kind of shift we have witnessed in other long docs: moving from an earlier more sociologically oriented approach to one that privileged individual biographies. As soon as the youngsters leave the contained environment in which they have spent their early years, the filmmaker really has no other option than to follow them to their new living or working locations and to start thinking in terms of individual rather than group portraits. *Back to Jordbrö* thus represents a turning point for Hartleb in that it is the first film in the cycle to be made up of a succession of individual 'chapters', each providing a foreshortened account of an individual's life-journey to date, with attention being drawn to both continuities and discontinuities.[49] The subjects, now in their early twenties, have moved away from the protective or controlling environment of the family home into situations where they have taken on new responsibilities and challenges.

The passing of time and the subjects' move into adulthood also brings changes in the relationship between the filmmaker and his participants. Generally speaking, participants will often have been less than co-operative subjects during puberty and adolescence. By the time they have reached their early twenties, however, subjects who have maintained links with the project will usually be prepared to enter into more mature conversations with the filmmakers as they reflect back on the road thus far travelled. For the filmmaker too the passing of time opens up new possibilities in terms of how material is structured and presented. In the case of *Back to Jordbrö*, for instance, this is the first film to make extensive use of what I have referred to elsewhere as the 'time-shuttle device' (see Chapter 1, pp. 26–7). By means of this device, viewers are either reacquainted with earlier phases of a subject's life, before being brought up to date with more recent events or, alternatively, are first updated with the subject's contemporary situation before being shuttled backwards in time on a journey of rediscovery.[50]

What is striking about *Back to Jordbrö* is the extent to which Hartleb exploits the narrative potential of being able to juxtapose material gathered in the course of more than a decade and a half of filming. Just as in Apted's *21 Up*, audiences are encouraged or cajoled into making connections between the various pieces of 'back-story' information about early and more recent phases of subjects' lives. It is as if we are being asked to consider whether we can pick up on anything in a subject's earlier attitudes or behaviour that provides clues as to why they turned out to be the people they have become. In order to give readers a better idea of how the time shuttling works in practice, let me therefore examine in some detail how one such life-journey (that of Uffe) is presented in *Back to Jordbrö*.

Uffe's story

Most of the biographies in *Back to Jordbrö* are structured according to the 'retrieving-the-past' principle. We are first introduced to a subject in the time and space frame of the present before being then escorted back into the subject's past. Occasionally, however, this pattern will be reversed and the past provides the starting point and the present the destination. This is how Hartleb chooses to present Uffe's story in *Back to Jordbrö*.

Uffe is a long doc subject, rather like Neil in *Seven Up*, to whom one is tempted to attach the label 'troubled soul'. He finds it difficult to forge relationships and, especially during his teenage years, always seems to be in some danger of going off the rails. In the segment of the film devoted to Uffe's story in *Back to Jordbrö*, Hartleb first reminds viewers of their first encounter with him in the first year of primary school. For the experienced Jordbrö viewer this is a fondly remembered and touching scene where seven-year-old Uffe is seen being reassured by the kindly teacher Inga Britt after he has had a violent temper tantrum. Subsequent sightings of Uffe in the programmes broadcast during the following nine years tend to reinforce the idea of his vulnerability and also hint at possible deep-seated emotional problems. It therefore comes as no surprise, when – at the end of his school career – Uffe once again appears to be having difficulties in conforming to what is expected of him. The scene in question comes towards the end of the film, when all the other Jordbrö children are shown receiving their certificates at a special leaving event. In the midst of the general rejoicing, Hartleb then rapidly cuts to a shot of a track-suited Uffe running by himself along the side of a lonely highway. Initially, it is not clear whether we are meant to interpret this as a show of recalcitrant defiance on Uffe's part (playing truant on prize-giving day) or whether we should see it more as a bold bid to free himself from the constraints of socially imposed norms. It does, however, carry strong echoes of that much earlier show of rebelliousness. Here Hartleb is clearly seeking to trace lines of continuity between past and present behaviour but recognises that the image of the lonely roadrunner could prove all too enigmatic for his audience. He therefore does something he only very rarely does in the Jordbrö films; he includes the following voice-over statement: 'Two weeks before term ended, Ulf vanished. He didn't come to the prize giving either. With his particular talent for achieving goals, he was travelling the length and breadth of Sweden with his new friend the truck-driver.'

For those viewers who have followed the Jordbrö films from the outset, these are the sort of memories of Uffe that they will be able to tap into when meet him again halfway through *Back to Jordbrö*. Having first reminded viewers of what Uffe was like as a recalcitrant seven-year-old by replaying part of the scene where he refuses to rejoin his fellow pupils, Hartleb swiftly moves to the present and (re)introduces us to Uffe as a twenty-something-year-old quietly and thoughtfully reflecting back on all that has happened in his life since we last encountered him.[51] One of the most significant events is that he has become a father, although he and his partner Anne have now separated. In *Back to Jordbrö* Hartleb includes some footage of Uffe in the company of his daughter, which anticipates a further sequence in which he mulls over the responsibilities of fatherhood. This in turn triggers a series of memories of the difficult relationship he has had with his own father. As he confides to Hartleb: 'I didn't want to see what happened between me and my father repeated ... I had a father, but it was years before I found out what he was like; but now I don't want to see him again.'

In *Back to Jordbrö* Uffe's story is related with considerable narrative economy (some three minutes of film-time) and there is no attempt to offer any psychologising explanations as to why Uffe's life should have taken the course it has. Hartleb simply allows us to draw our own conclusions from the subject's remarks. Like many other long doc subjects, Uffe seems to have developed a remarkable capacity to talk about himself and his problems in a highly articulate way.[52] And just as with the others, so in Uffe's case, the newfound articulateness seems to have been partly inspired by the trust he has in Hartleb as empathic confidant, but it is also linked to what he clearly understands to be his role as a performer in a long-running film and television series.[53]

Problems that subjects have had in their relationships with their parents become one of the central themes of *Back to Jordbrö*. Throughout the film, indeed, there is a strong sense of how the past casts a long shadow over present-day lives. Uffe, as we have seen, is still struggling with his repressed anger relating to how he was treated by his father. Likewise, Camilla and Mona are bearing the psychological burden of knowing that their fathers abandoned the family when they were both young girls, whilst Maria is having to come to terms with the discovery that she and her sister have different fathers. For viewers, the confessional scenes, in which subjects give expression to the emotional pain these memories cause them, take on greater resonance and significance by being juxtaposed to scenes from yesteryear where the subject may have appeared less vulnerable or less burdened by sorrow.[54] In other words, because viewers first become acquainted with these subjects at an age when they were first being exposed to some of these psychological pressures or traumas, it is more likely that they will be affected by hearing the twenty-something-year-old talking about a life-experience that has had a profound impact on them.

Nowhere is the affectedness more keenly felt than in those sequences where a subject is witnessed reflecting on the loss of a parent or a loved one.[55] As participants look back on what the deceased meant to them, viewers will not only gain privileged access to subjects' emotional worlds but will often discover more about a person's past than the information they held until this point. There is, for instance, one instance at the beginning of *Back to Jordbrö* when Petra talks at some length about the recent death of her father. Viewers are cued for this event by shots of Petra standing pensively by her father's grave. We then cut to shots of her in her own home, as she begins to talk to Hartleb (as ever out of frame) about what her father meant to her and about the qualities she feels she may have inherited from him. No sooner has she begun to speak, however, than she breaks down under the weight of the released emotions. With the words 'I can't do this. It's hard to talk', she temporarily leaves the room where Hartleb is filming in order to collect herself. On her return, she proceeds to give a highly articulate and moving account of several deep and meaningful conversations with her father shortly before his death.

Sequences such as these illustrate one of the particular strengths of the long doc form. Revelations such as Petra's are not designed to appeal to a confession-hungry audience but emerge rather out of subjects' desire to articulate deeply held feelings to someone they know they can trust. As Hartleb once observed when he was asked why his subjects always seemed ready to lay bare their souls in response to his promptings:

> Normally there's no one who will ask such questions. But I'm someone who they recognise is taking a serious interest in their lives. It was clear to them from the time they were still quite young children that I was interested in serious matters. (Cited in Borchert, 1995, my translation)

Connecting past and present

With *Back to Jordbrö* and the earlier films behind him, Hartleb had firmly established his credentials as a long doc filmmaker. Having worked for almost two decades on the project, one of the biggest challenges he faced was how to cope with an ever-expanding volume of life-story material and how to structure any new Jordbrö film in such a way that it did not collapse under its own weight. In practical terms this meant retaining a keen awareness of what material had already been collected and of assessing its usefulness for upcoming films.[56] The problem that Hartleb faced – in common with most other long-haul operators – was having to decide what kind of narrative vehicle was best suited for the next update. As more and more material accumulated, one of the possible options for a long doc filmmaker was to opt for the individual as opposed the group portrait, thus allowing far more detailed coverage of the subject's back-story. This was the route that Hartleb elected to take in his next film *Once Upon a Time There Was a Little Girl* (1992).

Once Upon a Time There Was a Little Girl

In *Back to Jordbrö* Hartleb had opted for what one might call the multi-bio approach, in which attention was regularly switched between sixteen Jordbrö subjects. For the filmmaker, the advantages of adopting such an approach are the opportunities for shuffling and juxtaposing characters according to particular dramaturgical criteria (just as in soap opera). Strong and forceful subjects can be set against others who have much less to say for themselves. Eventful roller-coaster lives can thus be contrasted with ones in which there is a marked absence of any drama. The potential draw-back of this approach, of course, is that it provides little opportunity for exploring an individual's life in any depth. This explains why, as in the case of *Once Upon a Time There Was a Little Girl*, long doc filmmakers occasionally decide to produce a film centred on the life of just one subject. *Once Upon a Time* is an hour-long film providing a biographical account of the life of Mona Jönsson. Like most of the other later Jordbrö films, the film is characterised by its quietly reflective tone and its multi-plane narrative. Using the fairy-tale 'Once-upon-a-time' conceit, the film follows a broadly chronological sequence. Having made Mona's acquaintance as a seven-year-old, we accompany her through the storm and stress of her rebellious teenage years until we finally re-encounter her in her late twenties in the latter stages of her first pregnancy. Much of the last part of the film is taken up with juxtaposing scenes from the present day, where Mona is organising the home in preparation for the birth, with scenes from her childhood, in which Mona and her mother talk about the having of children and the difficulties of being a good parent. This is a classic long doc tactic to encourage conjecture on the part of the viewer about the nature of the links between past and present attitudes and behaviour. In addition, however, the juxtaposing of different time-planes – almost a defining feature of long docs – has the further effect of drawing attention the cyclical character of life itself. Thus the shots with which Hartleb chooses to end this film, those of a happy and contented Mona breast-feeding her new-born child, bring reminders that the continuity of life itself is assured.

Giving viewers space

Hartleb is a serious-minded filmmaker and would like to think that he has given his Jordbrö participants, through their involvement with his long doc project, the opportunity to reflect on their lives in ways that viewers of these films will find thought-provoking. In the course of his conversational exchanges with participants, Hartleb is also always at pains to treat his subjects in such a way that they do not feel that they are being called to account or are otherwise being required to justify their actions. As a viewer, one has the distinct impression that Hartleb enters these conversations with absolutely no preconceived notions about what he expects his subjects to divulge or how he would like them to shape their narrative performances. As he explained to me when I asked him to describe his interviewing technique:

> I simply encourage them to talk about their lives, because it could be of interest to other people. I don't empower them [the subjects]. When I come into their lives, I have no other goal than hearing from them what their life is like and what they think and feel about it. (Hartleb, 2007)

Hartleb adopts a similar attitude with respect to what he appears to expect of the audiences at whom these films are directed. Viewers are also given time and opportunity to reflect on, or make connections between, these separate lives and to draw their own conclusions as to why individuals should have developed in the ways they have. Narrational intrusion is limited to the minimum that is required for the viewer to understand the situational context in which the subject made the remarks they did. Never, at any point, however, is there any attempt to impose any authorial interpretation upon what is being shown or spoken about. Viewers are made aware of the filmmaker's presence as interlocutor, but they are equally conscious that they are being called on to consider some of the more imponderable aspects of human existence. How do we become the people we are and in what ways does the environment in which we were originally nurtured continue to have a shaping influence on our present-day perceptions and attitudes?

What also begins to come through quite strongly in films such as *Back to Jordbrö* and *Once Upon a Time There Was a Little Girl* is the increasing preoccupation with the theme of life's transitoriness. This in no way means that the films are full of gloom and despondency, since Hartleb is, as ever, concerned to introduce material that strikes a more optimistic note. It does have the consequence, however, that the later Jordbrö films have a characteristic undercurrent of melancholy running through them. As Hartleb once confided to a Swedish journalist when he was asked to explain why the Jordbrö films engendered such melancholy responses: 'It could be something to do with knowledge that each moment of our lives is gone for ever once it has occurred' (cited in Borchert, 2006: 4, my translation). It is not just that the subjects themselves will frequently be heard lamenting or reflecting on the irretrievability of all that has been. It also has to do with the fact that the narratives of the films are organised in such a way as to prompt a general mood of reflectiveness on the part of the viewer. Viewers are always allowed the time and the space to consider the import of a subject's remarks, especially when it is clear, from the person's body language or facial expression, that the mere act of giving voice to these thoughts and feelings has been a painful or draining experience.

Several times in the course of the later films, Hartleb includes scenes in which subjects lapse into silence, either in the process of gathering further thoughts or as they reflect on the implications of what they have said. Rather than breaking in upon these silences with another question or a response, Hartleb deliberately maintains the camera's gaze upon his subjects' faces as they continue their reflections. It is a clear invitation for the viewer to do likewise.

Notes

1 Tracing the history of each long doc production provides some telling insights into wider developments in broadcasting or film production. It is certainly questionable, in this respect, whether, in today's more com-

petitive media world, long docs such as those of Apted, Hartleb and Junge would have gained the support necessary to sustain them.

2 In the course of long docs' development, they appear to grow in cultural significance. It would seem to be the case that nationally or regionally defined groups of viewers begin to develop especially empathic relationships with subjects whose concerns are not so very different from their own.

3 In the case of Winfried Junge, battles over the length of individual films became ever more intense as the series advanced. *Screenplay: The Times* (1991), for instance had a running time of almost five hours, which the Junges sought to justify on the grounds that only a film of this length could properly engage with the issues they were seeking to address.

4 Of particular importance for Apted's work on the *Up* films is the experience that he gained in directing several episodes of *Coronation Street*. It provided him with some valuable lessons in the art of story telling and in how to create maximum dramatic impact by the artful editing of material.

5 As Apted remembers it, Forman simply came up to him as he was sitting in the Granada canteen and said 'Why don't we go back and see what's happened to them [the *Seven Up* children]?' (Cited in Freedland, 2005b)

6 Hartleb once made the comment that 'It began as a sociological study, but then the emphasis slowly changed and there was greater concern with individual lives' (cited in Borchert, 1995, my translation).

7 Though their work is often mentioned in the same breath, Apted and Junge have, interestingly enough, never met. A meeting was once planned in 1986 when the Junges were touring the United Kingdom with their Golzow films, but the meeting never came about because of Apted's filming commitments.

8 Apted has remarked on several occasions that, as the series has worn on, the age gap (approximately 16 years) between him and his subjects has become of much less importance than it was at the outset and that his relationship with them has become far more equal (Apted, 1998).

9 It is presumably on these grounds that John and Andrew decide at a later stage to sever – or, in John's case, temporarily suspend – their involvement with the programme.

10 As the series continues, subjects generally show an acute awareness of the extent to which their lives have been shaped by their respective family or educational backgrounds. By the same token, however, the *Up* films bear witness to the fact that class-consciousness is a much less significant phenomenon in today's consumer society than it was in Britain of the 1960s.

11 The fact that so much of the *Seven Up* narrative consists of one-to-one interviews, mostly filmed in close-up or medium close-up, sometimes

leads to the distinct impression that subjects are involved in some form of confessional performance (see Kilborn, 2003: 61–2).

12 Insofar as all the *Seven Up* subjects were all initially brought together for the purposes of a television programme, the whole series could, in some respects, be looked upon as a (very) extended media event.

13 The term 'golden highlights' is possibly not the most accurate descriptor to apply to these sequences. In some cases, the interpolated sequence of images will contain scenes from a subject's life associated with times of discord and distress.

14 English has no precise word or expression to convey the idea of a memory that has a strong visual or image-like quality. German on the other hand has the term *Erinnerungsbild* (memory-image), suggesting that a memory has lodged in the mind's eye and has acquired the status of an image.

15 One of the most poignant moments in the whole of documentary film where a subject re-encounters a place redolent with memories comes early in Claude Lanzmann's film *Shoah* where a Holocaust survivor returns to the site of the Nazi death-camp where he had once been imprisoned.

16 For some more reflections on the role played by Bruce in the *Seven Up* series see Bruzzi, 2007: 100–8.

17 The 1980s, it will be remembered, were a time when the then British Prime Minister, Margaret Thatcher, famously disputed that there was any such thing as society.

18 It is significant in this connection that images of Neil, one in black-and-white and the other in colour, are given pride of place on the cover of the DVD recording of *49 Up*. Over the years Neil's image has achieved the kind of iconic status to enable it to stand as representative of all the *Seven Up* protagonists.

19 Apted claims that he feels a special parent-like responsibility towards Neil, knowing him to be probably the most vulnerable of all his *Seven Up* subjects (Apted, 1998).

20 The issue of project endings (actual and envisaged) will be dealt with in more detail in the final chapter, where – among other things – I will be considering the subject of character attrition.

21 On the 'Day of German Unity' (3rd October 1990) Junge had an open letter read out on a German radio station (Antenne Brandenburg) in which he makes an eloquent statement concerning the extent to which he identified with much that the GDR sought to achieve, though wishing to disassociate himself from what he calls 'dictated socialism'. The letter is reproduced in full in Junge, 2004: 243.

22 The media system in East Germany, which during the Cold War period was often painted by Western observers as a monolithic propaganda machine, was actually somewhat more differentiated than some would

have had us believe. For more on this point see Silbermann, 1994: 23.

23 German has the expression 'real existierender Sozialismus' to describe
    the 'socialism that actually exists'. For a revealing account of how
    individuals in the GDR perceived the socialist experiment, see Molloy,
    2009.

24 The filmmakers knew, for instance, that – sooner or later with a work of
    this type – they would be expected to provide an explicit message about
    the aims and purposes of the education the children were receiving (see
    Moreno, 2000: 12).

25 In such a suspicion-laden society as the GDR there were some who
    believed that the families of children who were featured in the Golzow
    films were able to secure material and other benefits for the assistance
    they were providing to DEFA filmmakers.

26 Some of Apted's subjects were positively hostile and most were gener-
    ally unforthcoming when he interviewed them for *14 Up.*

27 There was a well-known saying in the GDR: 'Vertrauen ist gut, Vorsicht
    ist besser' (It's good to be trusting, but it's wiser to err on the side of
    caution.) Mindful of the huge network of informers operating in the
    GDR, many East Germans were fearful of speaking their minds at all
    openly. The resultant atmosphere of mutual suspicion is powerfully
    captured in Florian Henckel von Donnersmarck's rightly acclaimed film
    The Lives of Others (Germany, 2005).

28 Junge has had much more to say about the ups and downs in his rela-
    tions with his participants than any other long doc filmmaker. One of
    the most detailed accounts is provided in a very long interview repro-
    duced in Junge, 2004: 17–181.

29 When, almost thirty years after the event, Junge looked back on the
    making of this film, he admits that Marieluise may at this stage have
    found him a rather intimidating interlocutor. Conceding that he as-
    sumed too dominant a role when he was interviewing Marieluise, he
    suggests – just as Apted does with respect to his *Seven Up* participants
    – that the twenty-year age gap between him and his subject is more
    apparent at this point of a long doc's development than later when sub-
    jects were more disposed to treat the filmmaker as an equal (see Junge,
    2004: 51).

30 She voiced this sentiment at the film premiere of *I'll Show You My Life* in
    1997.

31 One of the consequences of her father's religious convictions is that
    Marieluise does not participate in the *Jugendweihe* ceremony which
    most of the other children attended.

32 Junge devotes considerable time in his first post-*Wende* film *Screenplay:
    The Times* (1992) to discussing the various compromises he was forced
    into as he sought to accommodate a man with such 'uncomfortable'
    views. *Screenplay* is also the film in which Junge includes previously

unscreened material taken from interviews from the 1980s, in which Herr Hübner voices his vehement opposition to many of the regime's ideas and policies.

33   The films of the period only make the most general reference to his position as a 'Captain in the People's Army'.

34   Elke's reticence to talk about certain aspects of her life becomes a central motif of the Golzow films. It also comes over in Junge's voice-over commentary in which he frequently makes references to his frustrated attempts to make contact with her.

35   In spite of their 'professional' differences, Junge and Elke have remained on amicable terms with each other. The only problems that have arisen have been when the personal and the professional have entered into conflict. Or, as Elke once remarked to Junge: 'I'd be happier if you sometimes came to see me and didn't bring your camera' (Junge, 2004: 262).

36   One German critic makes a similar point about the longitudinal form when she writes in a film review of *My Life Is My Own Affair*: 'The film is an attempt – one that is, however, always doomed to fail – to achieve some convergence between an act of observing and the object of observation' (Nguyen, 1997: 80).

37   Other long doc filmmakers have used the same ploy for regrouping their subjects. One recalls how Michael Apted gathered his subjects together as 21-year-olds and filmed their reactions to seeing excerpts from earlier films.

38   It is important to remember that GDR audiences, at whom these films were primarily addressed, were well versed in the art of 'reading between the lines' when it came to interpreting DEFA films (both fiction and non-fiction). There was recognition of what dues may have been paid in order to ensure that the film got produced and also alertness to any sub-text that the film may have contained.

39   As with almost all the Golzow films, the production of *Biographies* was prefaced by a period of intense discussion involving the filmmakers, senior members of the DEFA hierarchy and high-ranking State officials, including on this occasion the Deputy Minister of Culture, Horst Pehnert (Junge, 2004: 60).

40   Junge himself has used the term *im Zeit-raffer* ('speeded-up effect') to describe the effect created by such ellipses.

41   Michael Apted, it will be recalled, was quite surprised at the positive response of American audiences to the *Seven Up* series when the films were first shown in the United States. It was this response that made him aware of the universal relevance of issues raised by the *Up* films (in Singer, 1999: xi).

42   Junge belongs to a small group of East German documentary filmmakers, including Volker Koepp and Jürgen Böttcher, whose work provides some telling insights into the lives of ordinary GDR citizens. In spite of

regular attempts by the state apparatus to mobilise them for more propagandist types of film work, all three filmmakers succeeded in maintaining their artistic integrity, primarily as a result of their overriding
concern to focus on the lived experience of unexceptional individuals
(see Kilborn, 1999: 267–82; Jordan & Schenk, 1996: 108–27; 152–79).

43 For more on the importance of the 'revisitation' in long docs and in other
forms of contemporary programme making, see Chapter 1, p. 12.

44 These two films form part of a four-disc DVD set comprising all the
Jordbrö films.

45 Of all the long doc filmmakers surveyed in this book, Hartleb is the one
with whom subjects appear to be most at ease. Particularly in the later
Jordbrö films there is a degree of intimacy in his exchanges with participants that one sometimes misses in those between Apted and Junge
and their subjects (see also Borchert, 1995). Above all, Hartleb shows
great sensitivity to the difficulty that subjects often experience when
talking about certain aspects of their lives.

46 There is a very stark contrast between the progressive teaching methods
that we witness in this Swedish primary school and the much stricter
regime of the East German classroom.

47 Hartleb is much more reticent in his interviewing style than Apted.
When he involves the children in conversation, Hartleb allows the children plenty of scope to respond on their own terms, whereas Apted's
subjects are required to answer a series of very specific questions.

48 Slobodan, as we are to discover from later films, decides to make his
home in Sweden. Krisoula, on the other hand, one of Slobodan's class-
mates, decides to go back to Greece and make her life there.

49 Apted's *Seven Up* films are similarly structured. In *21 Up*, *28 Up* and
35 Up he even uses the word 'chapters' to describe the individual biographical accounts.

50 Sometimes in *Back to Jordbrö* it will be a subject's apparently chance
remark about some past event that triggers the memory sequence. On
other occasions, Hartleb will simply juxtapose past and present time-
planes in the attempt to reinforce the idea of 'distance travelled' or to
pick up on certain continuities in a subject's development.

51 This is one of the sections where Hartleb underlines the reflective mood
by some judicious musical accompaniment. Throughout the Jordbrö
cycle he makes extensive use of Chopin s piano music, especially the
nocturnes. This not only helps to establish a quietly reflective mood
but is also employed to convey that sense of moving fluidly backwards
and forwards through time, which some would regard as a generically
specific trait.

52 John Corner makes a similar point about some of the *Seven Up* participants' capacity for 'sustained self-reflectiveness' (Corner, 2009).

53 Analogies might be drawn between some of the more confessional

exchanges between subject and filmmaker and psychotherapy sessions where clients are likewise given permission to unburden themselves with no fear of being interrupted or contradicted.

54 These acts of disclosure in the Jordbrö films are of an entirely different order from the confessional moments in television talk shows and reality programmes. In the latter the major focus is on the drama of the confessional or self-revelatory moment. With long docs the interest is more in discovering more about the possible underlying causes of the emotional or psychological affliction and its impact on subjects over a long period. For more on this issue see Dovey, 2000: 103–32.

55 Bereavement is an experience that almost every subject confronts in the course of their long-term attachment to a long-term project. In the *Seven Up* series, for instance, Tony, Suzy and Lynn speak at some length about the death of a parent.

56 The systematic archiving of material is a vital part of any successful long doc operation, Michael Apted has now arranged for all the extant recorded material (from *21 Up* onwards) to be digitised. The Junges, whilst they were working on the Golzow saga, accumulated a veritable arsenal of film material, which they are now in the process of transferring to the Federal Film Archive.

5

Never-ending stories?

There comes a point in the life of most long docs when, just as with long-running soaps, one gains the impression they might have achieved a state of perpetual motion. As sure as night follows day, we are returned to familiar locations and reacquainted with characters whom we might not have seen for quite some time but instantly recognise when they reappear. Any thought that long docs have discovered the secret of eternal life is, however, tempered by the knowledge that all of them are, in reality, destined to be of finite duration. The only uncertainty concerns when the ending will come and what manner the ending will take.

Several critics have noted, in this respect, long docs' kinship with soap opera, though on those occasions when it is mentioned, it is usually in the form of a general reference to their status as 'never-ending stories' rather than to any deeper structural affinity.[1] It is difficult to see why critics should have been so reluctant, generally, to press the analogy between long docs and soaps. One reason may lie in the fact that soap opera has, for the most part, been held in relatively low critical esteem (Geraghty, 1991: 1–2). Claiming a strong family resemblance between the two forms might therefore be seen as tantamount to tarnishing the reputation of a form of documentary filmmaking that is quite highly regarded. A more likely reason for not emphasising the kinship, however, is that there are, at first sight, such marked dissimilarities between these two (sub)genres. Soaps are fictional works with an inbuilt tendency to melodramatic excess; long docs, by contrast, are works of non-fiction that can be clearly assigned to the more sober documentary domain. Likewise, there are significant differences in the way in which each form seeks to engage the attention of the viewer. Whereas a soap opera will rely on the constant drip effect, with relatively short intervals of time between the screening of individual episodes, in a long doc there will be a significantly larger gap between successive episodes or instalments. For the viewer, therefore, being reacquainted with a character in a long doc after a long absence can bring timely reminders of the physical toll the passing years exact on all of us. With soap opera the very frequency with which we encounter characters means that the impact of the ageing process is far less discernible.

Despite the marked differences between long docs and soaps, there remain a number of striking resemblances. First and foremost, both require a relatively large cast of characters. In the case of soaps, this is in part to ensure that scriptwriters have a sufficient number of persons at their disposal to generate the multiple storylines on which all soaps depend. Having a large central core of characters (typically 15–25) is also useful for reinforcing the illusion of a real-life community. Long docs likewise operate with a sizeable number of protagonists. This guarantees, just as in soaps, that there will be a diversity of narrative interest and that it will be possible to play off subjects, one against the other, in order to make for a more varied viewing experience.

In terms of their formal structure, soaps and long docs resemble each other insofar as both are divided into a series of individual narrative segments, with each of these segments being focused on one or more *dramatis personae*. And whilst a television soap scriptwriter will be more concerned to produce a dramatic effect by the constant interweaving of multiple storylines, long doc filmmakers will likewise have given most careful thought to the artful sequencing of the sections or chapters devoted to individual life-stories. Particular attention is paid to the manner in which the various entrances and exits of subjects are managed. In soaps the switch to a new location is as often as not signalled by an internal narrative cue provided in the dialogue. In a long doc, on the other hand, the move to a new subject will more often be indicated by some external marker such as an intertitle or the name of the new character superimposed over their on-screen image and possibly reinforced by a reference in the voice-over commentary. Nevertheless, just as soap opera audiences have come to expect that each episode will spread the narrative interest across a number of different characters, so most long doc viewers anticipate there will be a veritable parade of subjects, with each of them being allocated a due amount of screen time before being superseded by another player.

Viewer empathy and identification

Both long docs and soaps rely on viewers being able to form relatively strong empathic bonds with a number of central characters. Much has been written about the nature of this relationship with regard to characters in soaps (Allen, 1985: 61–91; Geraghty, 1991: 9–10; 14–18; Kilborn, 1992: 68–84). In seeking to explain the strong imaginative hold that soaps are able to exert over their audiences, critics have also drawn attention to the duality that seems to be operating in viewer response. The claim is that soap opera viewers desire to relate to characters as if they were real people but will always retain an awareness of the soap's status as a fictional construct. As the American critic Robert Allen has commented:

> The soap opera consciously walks the line between texts that can be read as fiction and those which, for various reasons, constantly spill over in to the experiential world of the viewer, as few, if any, other fictions do. (Allen, 1985: 105)

With long docs, viewers relate to subjects not *as if* they were real people but in the sure knowledge that they are. The nature of the relationship is, however, bound to be affected to some degree by the recognition that the way in which these life-journeys are represented owes much to the mediating influence of the film or programme maker. In spite of this, it is still quite remarkable how strong the response of audiences to long doc subjects can be, especially when fate has dealt them especially heavy blows. Marcel, one of protagonists in the Golzow films, for instance, is one such figure. His mother Brigitte, one of the original Golzow children, died at the very young age of twenty-nine, when Marcel was only twelve. After Brigitte's death, the Junges continued to track developments in Marcel's life, which has also, sad to say, been marked by a number of setbacks and difficulties. Just as television viewers are known to be emotionally affected by sad events in the lives of soap opera characters, so the screening of the 1998 Golzow film *Brigitte and Marcel* elicited a considerable number of letters from viewers who had been deeply touched by witnessing a life racked by adversity (Junge, 2004: 284).[2]

Likewise in the case of the *Seven Up* series, after the screenings of *21 Up, 28 Up* and *35 Up*, thousands of viewers were moved to write to Apted or to Granada Television to express their concern at what was happening to Neil, the once perky little boy whose life now appeared to be spiralling out of control (Apted, 1998).

What increases the likelihood that audiences will be moved to express their concern in this way is that longer-stay viewers will have developed a strong sense of sharing in subjects' lives. The idea that we have an imaginative involvement in the life of an otherwise unknown individual is further encouraged by our ability to speculate on what may be happening to them during the often long periods of 'unrecorded time' when filming is not taking place. (This again mirrors the way in which viewers can imagine how characters are faring in the parallel world evoked by soap opera narratives where we are encouraged to believe that what is being enacted is unfolding in real time.) Over time, then, the faces of long doc subjects become almost as well known as those of characters in several of the better known soaps. This has, in turn, inevitably fuelled journalistic interest in discovering more about some of the prominent long doc protago-nists such as Neil in *Seven Up*. It has also led to much speculation as to what effects this particular form of media exposure may have had, in the longer term, on subjects' lives. Would their lives have developed along different lines if it had not been for the historical accident of having become a long doc subject?[3]

Episodic and serial mode of presentation

One of the more obvious similarities between soaps and long docs is that both employ an episodic form of presentation that in itself draws attention to viewers' real-life experience of time passing.[4] As Christine Geraghty has written:

> The time which elapses between the episodes of a soap is not dependent on the organisation of the story (what happens next?) but on the sense of time passing in the programme which parallels the time which has passed for the viewer between episodes. (Geraghty, 1991: 11)

By the same token, long docs – even though they appear with nothing like the same regularity as soaps – also mark the passing of time episodically. Just like producers of television soaps, therefore, long doc filmmakers quickly become sensitively attuned to the potential that lies in long docs' serial mode of presentation.

Long docs' particular mode of address also has implications for the way that they are read. Though not appearing with the same regularity as the episodes of a soap, the individual instalments of a long doc are all embedded in the same time frame as the one occupied by the audiences at whom they are directed. Long doc viewers, especially those belonging to the long-stay category, are therefore able – if they feel so inclined – to make comparisons with how their own lives have panned out over the same time span.[5]

Just as producers of soap opera know that, over a long period of time, viewers will have constructed a detailed mental map of diverse life-stories and relationships, so too long doc filmmakers know that they can rely on substantial numbers of viewers having built up an extensive knowledge of subjects' lives from their previous viewing experience. One of the consequences of this is that both long docs and soaps are able to gain some specific narrative benefits by encouraging conjecture as to how past events and relationships have impacted on subjects' present lives. Once again, however, long docs do this in slightly different ways from television soaps. In soaps the narrative priority will always be to keep viewers *au fait* with developing relationships or to feed them information concerning the storylines currently in play.

Time and space are seldom found in soaps for active reminiscing about the past. References to earlier times are more surreptitiously and allusively worked into inter-character dialogue, in order to evoke in longer-stay members of the audience the memories of much earlier events in the life of that soap community. In long docs on the other hand the main narrative trajectory of each episode will focus on the retrospective exploration of subjects' life-journeys thus far taken, with special emphasis on the ground covered between the previous and the present encounter. Memories of the past are thus evoked more directly, either through flashback sequences or through a person's own recollections. It follows that, with long docs, there will usually be a more conscious attempt to draw connecting lines between past and present. In long docs, past episodes or events are *literally* re-invoked, whilst in soaps there is simply a more general sense of the past casting its shadow over present lives.[6] One of the consequences of this is that, whilst soaps' actual historical starting point will tend to be lost in the mists of memory, each successive long doc episode will bring explicit reminders of 'When It All Began'.

In the case of long docs, then, what is sometimes referred to as 'narrative backfilling' assumes a far more important structural role than it does in soaps. Viewers, even as they are brought up to date with more recent events in a subject's life, will know that they will soon be reacquainted with (in the sense of being shown) a series of defining moments from the earlier stages of that subject's life. There is, in other words, a strong, generically determined expectation that the individual biographical accounts will include what Michael Apted has called those 'golden highlights' (Apted, 1998) – namely, a sequence of images that rapidly traces over a series of allegedly defining moments in a subject's life that have already been captured on film.[7]

Knowing that each film or programme they produce is part of a larger unfolding narrative, long doc filmmakers are always aware they will need to gather, assemble and present material in such a way that it allows some kind of dialogic relationship to be established between material relating to the more distant and the more recent events in a subject's life. Long doc filmmakers have devised different strategies for achieving this goal. In conversations with his subjects, Rainer Hartleb, for instance, has always refrained from asking them very specific questions about their earlier lives (or for that matter their future aspirations) but has preferred to let memories of the past be triggered more associatively in the course of his conversations with them (Hartleb, 2007). Apted, on the other hand, has always adopted a more strategic approach. When he interviews his subjects, for example, he ensures that he includes a number of specific questions relating either to their past and their future plans or to their memories of how they have been represented in earlier films. This means that for each *Up* film he will always have the requisite amount of recorded material that he can employ when juxtaposing past and present scenes. A good example is seen at the end of the sequence given over to Jackie's story in *42 Up*. After Jackie has talked at some length and in very moving terms about having to come to terms with her discovery that she has rheumatoid arthritis, Apted asks her whether she remembers those earlier moments (captured on film in *21 Up*) when life appeared to be so full of promise. In response to Apted's question: 'There was so much hope back then, wasn't there?' Jackie provides the typically feisty riposte: 'Oh, there still is. Don't make that mistake, Mike. I'm down and I am depressed about my illness, but I'm certainly not down and depressed about my life.' Not only has Apted set up an opportunity for a revealing flashback (the scene from *21 Up*); he has also elicited from Jackie the kind of response that he can use as a means of bringing to a close the latest chapter in this particular life-journey.

'Closed' and 'open' narrative forms

Both long docs and soaps are classic examples of an open form of narrative that addresses its audience in a markedly different manner from 'closed' narrative forms. Unlike the various forms of fictional entertainment that move purposively to a point of resolution where all the narrative threads are drawn together in a final act of closure, in long docs and in soaps the emphasis is on perpetual postpone-ment of an ending.[8] Soap storylines, just like individual instal-ments of long docs will, of course, be brought to a close, but there is always a sense in which this act of closing is accompanied by, or is heralding, some new beginning. By contrast, closed narratives tend to be very goal-oriented and self-contained. This leads to an expectation on the part of viewers (or readers) that they are going to be moved, with relative swiftness, through the various parts of the story towards some final resolution.[9] Since closed narratives have to exercise a particular form of narrative economy, they will typically have to operate with far fewer characters. In open narrative forms, interest can be fairly evenly distributed across a comparatively large number of characters, thereby enabling there to be multiple points of narrative interest.

One of the other defining features of these more open-ended forms of narrative is that they allow for, or actively encourage, different forms of viewer engagement with the text than 'closed' narrative modes. Producers of such texts recognise, for instance, that they will need to make allowance for the different levels of textual knowledge that particular constituencies of viewers will have accu-mulated. Some members of the long doc or soap audience will have been following the programme or series from the very beginning. These early adopters will, in some cases, have become so intimately acquainted with the work in question that they may feel they have come to know the featured characters or participants almost as well as if they were members of their own extended families (Geraghty, 1991: 14; Allen, 1985: 39). There will, on the other hand, always be a substantial number of viewers who have started viewing the programme or series at a much later point. The upshot of this is that producers of long docs and soaps pay careful attention to presenting their material in such a way as to ensure that the needs of both early adopters and relative newcomers are met.[10] With soaps, there will be fairly frequent references to earlier events that have occurred within that particular soap community.[11] The difference between soaps and long docs in this respect is that, whereas in the former the 'time-when-it-all-began' will tend, even for the longest-serving viewers, to be lost in the mists of memory, each successive long doc episode will bring explicit reminders of 'journey beginnings' in the form of those golden highlights sequences.

Real-world connectedness

One feature of open narratives that is often remarked upon is that most of them seek to create a strong sense of here-and-now reality. In works belonging to the British soap opera tradition, for instance, considerable care is taken to ensure that a number of textual markers are included that reinforce the illusion that on-screen events are taking place in a domain that viewers can accept has real-world status.[12] The desired outcome is to enhance the reality effect of these works and to create the illusion of a 'parallel world' in which persons not wholly unlike ourselves are playing out their lives (Kilborn, 1992: 85–103). Whilst some effort is needed to maintain this sense of pseudo-reality in soaps, no such elaborate efforts are required in long docs to persuade viewers that what they are witnessing is a recording of real-life actuality. Everything about a long doc – from the style of filming the interviews to the constant references to actual external events – contains the assurance that this is essentially a documentary rather than a fictional mode of address.

Long docs are clearly not driven by the same dramatic imperatives as soaps. Nevertheless, the claim could still be made that there is something about the manner of long docs' address that encourages viewers to relate to them in ways not so dissimilar from the ways in which they respond to soap opera. This may have something to do with the fact that both soaps and long docs are concerned with the lives and activities of ordinary people rather than those who have already – by whatever means – acquired celebrity status. A large part of the continuing appeal of soaps to audiences is that most of the action is centred on the drama of everyday life as reflected in the lives of the cast of characters brought together in a particular soap community. Likewise, the principal concern of most long docs is with tracing the life-journeys of individuals. The emphasis is not so much upon the contributions they make to the public good (though this can sometimes be touched upon) but rather on what they are like as individuals and how they relate to their fellow human beings.[13]

The major thematic focus of both soaps and long docs is best illustrated by considering the locations in which most of the action occurs. In soaps it is almost axiomatic that the preferred locations are family homes and various meeting places within the 'contained' soap community which can provide the backcloth for characters to indulge in all the gossipy exchanges and other bits of dramatic business to which audiences have become accustomed.[14] The existence of a world outside the narrow confines of this community is acknowledged, but it is only rarely that this world is seen to directly impinge on the everyday lives of the community-dwellers.

With long docs the situation would appear, at first sight, to be somewhat different. Here there would appear to be a greater concern with showing how external events occurring within the wider socio-historical world inevitably have a determining impact on individuals and communities. On closer inspection, however, long docs are not always as interested as it is sometimes claimed they are in investigating the ways in which individual lives are shaped by external forces. They may, as shown in *The Children of Golzow*, contain a certain amount of speculation about the impact of significant political change. They may, as illustrated by *The Children of Jordbrö*, be concerned – initially at least – to show the impact of a new government housing policy. They may indeed, as is the case with the *Seven Up* series of films, attempt to reveal how particular structures and practices within a social system give certain members of that society a head and shoulders advantage over less fortunate individuals. In the course of their development over the longer term, however, long docs seem much more at home when exploring and tracing the lives of individuals: their relationship with a significant other, their ability to overcome adversity and their degree of success at achieving a balance between work and life.

Thus, notwithstanding that certain long docs will devote (considerable) time to showing the public face of individuals, most of these works generally display a natural gravitational pull towards the personal rather than the public domain. A very high-profile, political event such as the fall of the Berlin Wall may seem to offer an exception to the general rule in that a legitimate claim could be made that the post-*Wende* Golzow films are providing a record of how a society comes to terms with such an epoch-making occurrence. Once again, however, there is relatively little discussion of the lead-up to and the aftermath of these events. The focus is on revealing how individuals are adjusting to living under a new political system, how some of them are coming to terms with their sense of quite considerable disorientation and how all of them, in both a professional and personal sense, are having to build their lives anew.

The major similarity between long docs and soaps remains, however, their future orientation. Seriality is, if you will, a part of the generic DNA of long docs, as it is of soap opera. Just as one of the pleasures of soap viewing is that of perpetually delayed gratification, so too long docs trade to some extent on audience expectations as to what revelations the next update will bring. Everything is, as in life itself, tantalisingly unresolved and in a state of transition towards an uncertain future. Joe Moran, in his perceptive study of the *Seven Up* films, speaks of the 'necessarily provisional nature of the project' and goes on to suggest that: 'The films ultimately avoid any sense of coherence and finality because, as the 'Up' suffix in their titles indicates, they are an indefinitely timetabled project about ongoing lives' (Moran, 2002: 402).

Notes

1   Junge himself refers to the fact that, by the 1980s, the Golzow project was already being referred to as 'Dallas in the East' ('*Ost-Dallas*') (Junge, 2004: 102).
2   The strength of the empathic bond that can develop between soap opera audiences and fictional characters is demonstrated by the extent to which some viewers feel genuinely bereaved when one of their favourite soap characters departs from the scene. Some go so far as to send bouquets of flowers or wreaths to television stations as a way of extending their condolences (see Kilborn, 1992: 85–98).
3   There has, for instance, been speculation about whether the dramatic change that comes about in Neil's life following his move to London

after *35 Up* was in any way attributable to his long-term involvement in the *Seven Up* series. Would the change of fortune have occurred, for instance, without the timely intervention of fellow subject Bruce that allowed Neil to get his life back on track again?

4   A key feature of soaps' appeal is the manner in which they emulate the basic human experience of the quotidian. Soaps tend to focus on those routine activities and events that can allegedly give our lives a reassuring structure.

5   Michael Apted once commented: 'I think the *Up* films have ultimately been so successful, because audiences can always find somebody, some event, some relationship, some idea in the body of the film that they can identify with. I think it's an enormously audience-friendly project' (Apted, 1998).

6   Soaps will occasionally introduce sequences with the express intention of taking viewers for a trip down memory lane when characters will nostalgically recall life as it was once lived in their respective soap communities. One of the best examples of nostalgic reminiscence came in a late 1980s episode of *EastEnders* which took the form of a two-hander featuring two of the older women characters Dot and Ethel remembering their early days in the East End and recalling what it had been like to live in a genuinely close-knit community.

7   Certain affinities can be drawn between these sequences and various contemporary forms of morphing. The intention in both cases is to create a special 'time-eradicating' effect by means of an editing or computer-generated device. The difference between the long doc time-shuttling and morphing, of course, is that in the latter the transitions are made to appear seamless (thus drawing attention to the technological skill of the effects-generator), whilst with the former the ellipses remain evident, thus artfully drawing attention to the effects of time having passed.

8   Possibly because he gained valuable experience working on *Coronation Street*, Michael Apted proves himself to be highly adept at contriving acts of partial narrative closure at the end of individual chapters in the *Up* films.

9   Scriptwriters working in closed narrative forms will often start by contriving an ending of the story, which in turn acts as the 'destination point' for the story trajectory.

10   It is well known, for instance, that scriptwriters who join the production team of an established soap are usually provided with a so-called 'bible' that chronicles major developments in the soap's history and provides a wealth of information on the lives and relationships of some of the key characters (see Allen, 1985: 70).

11   A distinction needs to be drawn between , on one hand, more general or more allusive references to events that are often to be located in the

soap's more distant past and, on the other hand, references to something that has happened in the more recent history of the soap. In the latter case scriptwriters will often need to reference an event that has already taken place because they realise that not all viewers will have kept up with all the episodes and will therefore not be *au fait* with certain key developments. It goes without saying that narrative redundancy is a characteristic feature of soap opera narratives.

12   The textual markers can take various forms but will typically include references to the passing seasons, to national holidays and to other events in the life of the nation, such as parliamentary elections, royal weddings and divorces.

13   Soaps and long docs place particular emphasis on major rites of passage in an individual's life. One's first encounter with the formal education system; the trials and tribulations of puberty; leaving home and starting one's first job; starting a family; coping with the death of a parent or a partner – all feature quite prominently in both soap opera and long doc texts.

14   When producers are devising a new soap opera, they pay special attention to the creation of a defined environment for their fictional community. This environment will have specific regional markers in order to heighten the illusion of authenticity (see Smith & Holland, 1987).

6

Towards an ending

Introduction

Among the questions I will be addressing in this chapter are the following: In what ways, given long docs' generically inbuilt resistance to closure, do filmmakers begin to contemplate the prospect of terminating these works? What role does the sponsoring agency or broadcasting institution play in deciding how and when a long doc should be terminated? In what ways are viewers actively prepared for being separated, once and for all, from subjects with whom they may have developed especially close relationships over the years?

As in previous chapters, I will once again be considering some of the special challenges that filmmakers face when working in the long doc mode. The possibility of losing the services of one or more of one's subjects remains an ever-present threat (see below, pp. 150–4). Therefore one of the skills that long doc filmmakers have to develop is that of disguising or compensating for the absence of such absconders in future instalments of the work. One of the ways in which this can be achieved is by explicitly drawing attention to the exit of a well-known subject and even – as in the case of Jochen from *The Children of Golzow* – to capture on film the highly dramatic moment when a subject announces that they intend to sever all future involvement with the project.

Critical retrospection

As well as examining how filmmakers prepare the way for the conclusion of such marathon works, I will also be considering in this chapter how, over the years, filmmakers have had to adapt their techniques as their projects have developed. Just like other documentarists, long doc producers have generally been willing to subject their filmmaking practice to critical review – especially when they have been working on their projects for several decades. Such critical activity can take diverse forms: participation in media inter-views, the writing of reflective articles or the production of supple-mentary materials (for instance audio commentary) to accompany the sets of commercially available recordings of their works. Whilst the underlying intention of such ventures is almost always that of maintaining and promoting a high level of viewer interest in the works in question, these contributions can also represent a serious attempt to explore the perceived significance of the series and, further, to reflect on the often not inconsiderable difficulties that filmmakers have confronted in the course of producing them.[1]

What is noticeable about many of these retrospective reflections is the extent to which the filmmakers concerned are ready to concede the number of mistakes they have made along the way. Michael Apted in particular, in the audio commentary he provides before each new 'chapter' of *42 Up*, is very open about some of the prob-lems he has had with several of his subjects. In the case of Winfried and Barbara Junge, as we have already discovered, the conditions under which the Golzow series of films were produced from 1961 till 1989 meant that the filmmakers had to be very circumspect in airing views on problems encountered during the filming and editing process. However, as they entered what was to be the final phase of the Golzow series, the Junges took every opportunity to review the development of the project. Just as with other filmmakers, the Junges concede that their work on the Golzow long doc has been a constant learning process. What it has taught them, above all, is that each new film contributes a few more brushstrokes to a much larger, slowly emerging picture. By the same token, however, the produc-tion of the new instalment in one sense merely seems to confirm that working in the long doc mode poses an almost impossible chal-lenge. As Barbara Junge modestly observed:

> For decades these [Golzow] films have been able to able to capture the attention of new generations of viewers. At the end of the day, how-ever, what these works represent is just an attempt to show what this particular type of documentary film can achieve. (Junge, 2008: 12)

As well as recognising that, like any artist, they have been subject to particular sets of constraints, seasoned long doc operators are also able to derive considerable satisfaction from having had the stamina to undertake and possibly complete such a journey. In a long, wide-ranging interview published in 2004, just before the conclusion of the Golzow project, Winfried Junge provides a wonderfully detailed account of how each film in the series came to be produced and against what odds. Towards the end of this account, he chooses to reflect on the role that the Golzow chronicle has played in this own filmmaking career. At one point during these reflections Junge suddenly remembers a scene from a book he read as a child. The book in question is Daniel Defoe's novel *The Further Adventures of Robinson Crusoe* and the scene is the one in which Crusoe, having arrived back in London, contemplates what awaits him now that his journeying days are over.[2] As Crusoe reflects: 'Here, resolving to harass myself no more, I am preparing for a longer journey than all these, having lived seventy-two years a life of infinite variety, and learned sufficiently to know the value of retirement, and the blessing of ending our days in peace' (Junge, 2004: 181).

As long doc filmmakers look back on their many years of involvement in these projects, most of them have also wanted to underline the extent to which their works have been impacted by very particular sets of circumstances, not only in the more localized media environment but also within the wider social sphere in which they have been operating. In many ways it is the very longevity of this form of documentary activity that has sharpened filmmakers' awareness of what their works have actually achieved. The original remit of *Seven Up*, it will be remembered, was to 'give a glimpse of Britain's future [in the year 2000]'. Now, when he looks back on how the project has evolved over the years, Apted is careful to use more circumscribed terms in describing what he sees as the actual achievement of the series. In an interview he gave in 2006 he suggests, for instance, that any attempt to extract a wider meaning from the work will have to take into account that what it documents are the experiences of a very particular generation. In Apted's words:

> It's a portrait of a generation, rather than [one of] England. Had it started five years later, it would have been different and if it had started now, it would be a lot different. (Apted, 2006)

In their more recent interviews, Winfried and Barbara Junge have also sought to sound a more cautionary note when evaluating what they consider to be the achievement of their Golzow project. Though aware that the production of more than twenty Golzow films over more than five decades represents, by any criteria, a considerable accomplishment, they are nonetheless conscious that the films have only really succeeded in scratching the surface of the lives they have sought to chronicle.[3] The recognition that they have had to exclude so much from their account has therefore led them to the following sobering assessment:

> Because the films can only last hours and never days, a lot remains unshown and unsaid. Of the original twenty-six children we were only able to trace the life-journeys of eighteen of them. There were, however, so many elements in the rich tapestry of these lives that the films failed to cover. Given the difficult conditions under which we had to work – lack of money, not enough time and limitations of the available technology – we were frequently not in a position to capture the rapidly changing realities that we confronted. (Junge, 2008: 6, my translation)

Resistance to closure

In attempting to close down a long doc, filmmakers confront similar difficulties to television drama producers when the decision has been made to bring the curtain down on an established long-running drama serial. In the case of both long docs and soap opera there is an inbuilt resistance to closure. As Robert Allen has written:

> The soap opera trades an investment in an ultimate narrative telos – the most characteristic feature of traditional narratives – for a series of overlapping 'mini-closures,' which resolve a particular narrative question but are in no way read as moving the overall story towards its eventual end. (Allen, 1985: 75)

It is not until the decision is taken to conclude a soap or a long doc that the problems of terminating the potentially interminable begin to emerge.[4] Speaking of the termination in 1981 of the American drama serial *Love of Life*, for instance, a soap that had been running for three decades, Allen suggests that it 'did not so much end as it expired defiantly in medias res' (ibid.). As we shall see when we consider the respective endings of *The Children of Golzow* and *The Children of Jordbrö*, the filmmakers concerned have resorted to similar 'expirational' strategies when seeking to conclude their own long doc works. Both have sought to emphasise the idea of leave-taking rather than the reaching of any narrative conclusion. In the circumstances, this seems an entirely appropriate way of arriving at an ending for these projects. It conveys unambiguously to viewers that the journey is now ended, but at the same time it enables the audience to indulge in some further imaginative speculation about the possible future course of subjects' lives.

Comparing the manner in which long docs and soaps are brought to a close also throws some light on the conditions under which the works have been made and the network of relation-ships between those responsible for their production. In the case of continuing drama serials there will be a relatively large production team, with each member of the team having a designated task. Indi-vidual members of the team, including producers and directors, will remain relatively anonymous, and over the lifetime of an average soap there will a fairly regular turnover of personnel (Allen, 1985: 45–60; Kilborn, 1992: 49–60). Directors of long docs, on the other hand, are guaranteed no such anonymity, principally of course, because they are perceived by the audience to be an active presence in, and contributor to, the ongoing long doc narrative. It is for this reason virtually impossible for long doc directors to think of passing responsibility over to any other person.[5] There is, in other words, something almost proprietorial about the relationship between filmmakers and their project. In their heart of hearts they cannot conceive of anyone else being able to take on the role they have so long performed.

Seven Up

With *Seven Up*, it may appear to be somewhat wanton to talk about 'endings', since Apted has very clearly signalled his intentions to continue working on the series for as long as he is able. Currently Apted, now in his late-sixties, shows no real sign of wanting to pull the curtain down on a project that has taken up a significant portion of his working life. He is, however, well aware that the question of 'how-it-will-all-end' is one that is beginning to exercise many of those who have followed the *Seven Up* story thus far. When asked after a special screening of *49 Up* at the National Film Theatre in 2005 about how he viewed the future of the project, he replied that he was going to soldier on for as long as the core members of his 'cast' were willing to remain with the project. In his own words:

> I think *Seven Up* is the most important work I'll ever do, more impor-
> tant than the movies I'll ever make. I think the series has such a reso-
> nance and a longevity that I'll carry it on as long as I can keep standing
> and as long as there are enough of them to make it worthwhile. (Cited
> in Freedland, 2005b)

Apted is convinced that extending the life of the project by just a
few more years will also enhance the significance that the *Up* films
have as a social chronicle. Since the series began in 1964, Britain had
gone through some very significant social changes. In Apted's view,
giving his subjects the chance to consider the impact that these
changes have had on their lives, from the vantage point of middle
age, will add to the documentary value of the series.

One of the other reasons that Apted advances for wanting to
continue with the project is that he now feels that there is a closer
bond between him and his subjects. As he observed at the time of
making *42 Up*:

> My relationship with them has changed over the generations. When it
> started, I was twenty-two and they were seven. I was a remote autho-
> rity figure who they would forget as soon as I left the room. But then,
> in *14 Up*, I became a sort of benevolent uncle to them and then, in *21
> Up* and *28 Up*, I was a big brother. Finally in the more recent films (*35
> Up* and *42 Up*) the age difference has narrowed down and we're very
> much equals or colleagues in this whole enterprise. And I think we're
> much closer. The interviews are much better than they ever used to be.
> Not just because the subjects are more thoughtful and more articulate.
> I think it's because their relationship with me is much stronger. We
> speak to each other as adults. (Apted, 1998)

Like the other long doc filmmakers featured in this work, the making
of the *Up* films for Apted has been a constant learning process. And,
as noted in the introduction to this chapter, the longer these projects
have continued, the more disposed filmmakers have been to engage
in some critical retrospection (see pp. 137–40). The production of *42
Up*, however, seems to have marked some kind of threshold in the
making of the series, as far as Apted was concerned. In this film not
only does Apted invite his subjects, for the first time, to reflect on
the personal impact of their continuing participation in the series, he
also uses the occasion to do some personal stocktaking concerning

his own involvement.[6] Apted's reflections, which cover a wide range of issues relating to both the production and reception of the *Seven Up* series, are contained in the audio commentary that prefaces each of the subject biographies in the DVD version of *42 Up*. These reflections, which are incorporated into extended prefaces that introduce each subject's story, contain both specific comments on the role that each participant played in the series and more general thoughts on how the whole series developed over the years. Among the issues he discusses, Apted provides some thoughts on why the series should have been so powerful in its appeal to successive generations of viewers. Interestingly enough, he concludes that, in his opinion, the series' core attraction is its capacity to produce in its audience a particular kind of self-reflectiveness. In Apted's words:

> I think [watching Paul's story] makes you ask yourself: Well, when did I grow up. When did I become mature? When did I develop some view of the world? I think these are dramas that everyone can relate to. We can see ourselves in these characters. They're not something special. They are ordinary people; that's why I think the film is successful. It's the drama of getting through the day; it's the drama of ordinary life. (Apted, 1998, my emphasis)

Apted's working methods

As he reflects back on the three and a half decades of involvement in the *Seven Up* project, Apted is among other things keen to talk about the methods he has devised for filming, editing and presenting the material. As ever, when he discusses these matters, Apted is anxious to remind his audience of the longer-term consequences of that early decision to select subjects from opposite ends of the social spectrum. Though he now admits that he would have handled things differently, if 'we had known at the beginning that we were in it for the long haul' (Apted, 1998), he is equally convinced that other strategic decisions taken at the planning stage have had a far more positive influence on the further development of the project. For Apted, the key decision in this respect was the one that led to him pledging himself to the seven-year method. What has enabled him to keep the project within manageable proportions over all the years has been, in his opinion, largely attributable to the discipline imposed by having to adhere to the seven-year intervals between individual updates.[7]

It is Apted's contention that only through exercising this restraint has he been able to prevent *Seven Up* from acquiring the inchoate quality that he claims to detect (perhaps rather uncharitably, it has to be said) in the work of some of his long doc competitors. When talking about the working methods he had devised for *Seven Up*, for instance, Apted took the following sideswipe at the work of those with whom he clearly felt himself to be in some competitive relationship. Referring to *The Children of Golzow* rather disparagingly as 'an East German version of *Seven Up*', he goes on to deliver what some would regard as over-harsh criticism: 'It [the Junges' film] just didn't keep the discipline I've kept. They didn't do it according to a strict time routine. They just did it when something important happened' (Apted, 1998).

Maintaining discipline for Apted also means always adhering to the same procedures when he (or another member of the team) conducts the interviews that provide the raw material for these films. Keeping to a routine also carries with it a measure of reassurance for subjects insofar as they know what to expect when Apted once again calls them to account. Ever conscious of the need to be economical with the time he allocates to this part of the process, Apted – or in certain cases his producer Claire Lewis – will normally spend two full days with each participant. The first day will be spent conducting an extended interview with the subject, normally within the familiar surroundings of the person's home. This will be shot in close-up or medium close-up, in order that viewers gain a stronger sense that they are entering the subject's world. Apted has always considered these interviews to be the emotional core of the *Up* films, since they enable the viewer to gauge the extent to which a subject has changed, physically or emotionally, since last we met them.

Apted also admits that he has, over the years, introduced a few modifications to his basic interviewing technique. He has done this partly in acknowledgement of the way in which documentary itself has evolved. As he says:

> Most of the interviews are portrait style, but more and more as I've got into the project and documentary styles have changed, so I've done interviews on the hoof, interviews with people in different situations. I've done this to ring the changes a bit. It makes it a bit more complicated to edit the subsequent generations [of film material], but it adds some vitality to the film. (Apted, 1998)

Adding vitality to a film, as Apted is well aware, also makes for a more watchable documentary in that it brings some relief from the potential tedium created by a succession of talking heads. For this reason Apted will generally devote the second of his designated filming days to gathering some 'out-and-about' footage in order to introduce a little movement and variety into the overall mix.[8] By carefully choosing the locations in which the footage is shot, Apted can also, of course, provide some important contextual information about changes that have occurred in subjects' economic or living situations since we last encountered them. In Tony's case, it can point up the huge gulf between the milieu from which a subject originated (poor working-class background in the East End of London) and the comfortable middle-class environment in which he and his family now live.[9] In the case of Neil the bleakness of some of the locations in which Apted chooses to film him for *21 Up*, *28 Up* and *35 Up* almost become symbolic representations of the bleakness of his inner state.

In some cases Apted has accompanied his subjects (most notably Bruce and Paul) to relatively distant or even exotic locations in order to bring us information about some development in their lives. There is always a certain risk with such 'excursions', however, since one can never be certain whether there will be sufficient 'pay-off' in purely narrative terms to warrant the quite considerable investment in time and resources in obtaining this footage. On the other hand, as a highly successful commercial filmmaker, Apted is well aware that sequences shot in Australia (Paul) or Bangladesh (Bruce) can add what he calls 'colour and dimension' to the work (Apted, 1998), thereby potentially enhancing the films' appeal to an international audience.[10]

As well as sometimes filming his subjects in a variety of unfamiliar locations, Apted has also on a number of occasions arranged for his subjects to return home to the United Kingdom for their interview appointments. Of the filmmakers considered in this study, Apted is the only one to do this at all extensively, which raises some interesting questions concerning the legitimacy of the practice. In one respect it could be regarded as the kind of intervention that is not entirely consonant with sound documentary practice. Paul, for instance, the *Seven Up* subject who moved out to Australia in his mid-teens, has twice been brought back to the United Kingdom, once when he was twenty-one and again when he was thirty-five.

Reflecting on the implications of this interventionist act, Apted observes:

> I suppose Paul's done things he might never have done if he had not been in the film. I don't think Paul and his family could have afforded to come back to England unless I had bankrolled it. I admit that it's something artificial, but on the other hand it's something they wanted to do. (Apted, 1998)

The same kind of intervention occurs in *42 Up* when Apted brings back Nick from the United States, where he has been pursuing an academic career, to interview him in his former home in the York-shire Dales. Again the filmmaker is aware that this, for some, would be regarded as unacceptable practice, but seeks to justify it on what some would see as the slightly dubious grounds that he is enabling the subject to do something they really want to do. As Apted puts it:

> It's always artificial if I bring them back, since it might compromise any authenticity or reality the film might have, but I think that if the [subject's] reasons to come back are strong enough, it's probably worth doing. (Ibid.)

Staging the real

As the above examples show, long docs – like all other forms of documentary – will involve the filmmaker in different forms of constructive manipulation, as they find themselves working with an ever-increasing amount of material. In some senses, of course, a series such as *Seven Up* takes on its own kind of reality with the passing years. It is one that can resonate powerfully with viewers, but it remains, nevertheless, at heart a quasi-fictional reality. In real-life, for instance, individual *Seven Up* subjects – even those who lived near to each other or who attended the same school – would have probably gone their separate ways and would have been unlikely to seek out each other's company. For the purposes of the *Seven Up* series, however, the pretence has to be upheld that subjects are linked with each other by a special bond. It is therefore worth exploring some of the means by which Apted preserves the illusion of togetherness. The best example of this is provided by what Apted calls his 'famous sofa shots'. From *14 Up* onwards, Apted has been able to persuade his three female East Enders (Jackie, Lynn and Sue) who were brought up in the East End and, in the early *Seven*

Up films, his three posh boys (John, Andrew and Charles) to take up their time-honoured positions on a sofa similar to the one on which we encountered them as seven- or fourteen-year-olds. Apted himself is convinced that 'sitting them down in the same position generation after generation' works well in filmic terms, since it enables him to concertina time most effectively. As he observes, with reference to Jackie, Lynn and Sue, for instance: 'I think the intercuts between this three-shot at 7/14/21 etc are revealing, witty, and tell you so much about them just in one image' (ibid.). For the women themselves, however, this attempt to present them as if they were still all bosom friends is just another example of filmic manipulation. For this reason, it should come as no surprise to learn that Apted has encountered increasing resistance on the part of the subjects themselves to play along in this way.

The resistance of Jackie, Lynn and Sue to continue being filmed as a threesome is another pointer to the inevitable tension that arises when subjects' lives are exposed to this degree of scrutiny over such a long period. Subjects in more traditional forms of documentary will sometimes take exception to aspects of the way they are represented, but long doc participants may have more grounds for concern. With each successive update, an account of a subject's life is encapsulated in a sequence of images that are constantly re-invoked. The shorthand way of operating produces a version of subjects' lives that reinforces, with each iteration, the particular view that the filmmaker has taken of the life in question. Whilst most subjects will have learned to live with some of the distortions to which this inevitably gives rise, there are some cases where subjects have raised major objections to the way they have been represented. This is the topic I will be discussing in the following section.

Putting reality together

Some might argue that long doc filmmakers face a greater challenge than many other documentarists when it comes to editing their material. Not only do they have to cope with the ever-growing volume of material; they also have some especially tough decisions to make in connection with how to organise the filmic narrative.[11] Likewise, long doc subjects, after long years of involvement in these projects, become increasingly aware of the degree of control the filmmaker is able to exert, through the editing process, over how they are represented. As Jackie exclaims to Apted at a key moment in *49 Up*:

> You will edit this programme as you see fit. I've got no control over that ... this is your idea of what you want to do and how you see us. This one [*49 Up*] is maybe the first one that's about us rather than your perception of us.

Editing can, of course, be used to create a variety of effects, many of them involving the manipulation of time. For instance, long doc filmmakers employ elliptical editing not only to shuttle swiftly backwards and forwards in time; they also use it to provide various types of commentary on the way that subjects' lives have developed. A good example of this is when Apted picks up on something a subject says concerning what they think the future may bring and then rapidly cuts to a point in time, usually seven years later, when the reality turns out to be either much in line with or completely contrary to what they had hoped or prophesied. Thus in *28 Up*, Suzy who at twenty-one had boldly asserted, 'I don't like babies', is seen, in the very next shot, cradling a baby, whilst a two-year-old toddler plays in the background. Likewise, there is a sequence in *49 Up* in which Apted employs a similar kind of ellipsis to switch from a shot included in *42 Up* in which the recently married Bruce coyly declares, 'We may have children' to a present-day scene where he and his wife are revealed to be the proud parents of two boisterous boys.

Revisiting the past

All long docs involve constantly revisiting the past. Sometimes the revisitation effect is achieved by purely filmic means such as the employment of elliptical editing in which the past and present situations of a subject are contrasted with no form of commentary being provided. An alternative strategy for confronting a subject with their past is to get them, in the course of the recorded conversation, to reflect on a significant earlier experience or event and then, at the editing stage, to work in appropriate evidentiary images or utterances. In *42 Up*, for instance, Apted gets Symon to reflect back on his relationship with his first wife, Yvonne. Likewise in *42 Up*, when Lynn begins to talk about her experience of bringing up two teenage children, he uses it as a natural 'bridge' to get her to recall aspects of her own adolescent years, including how she related to her own mother. Yet one more strategy for reconnecting subjects with their earlier lives is to film them revisiting locations that have particular memories or associations. In *42 Up*, for instance, Tony is reacquainted with one of his happy hunting grounds, the Hackney Wick greyhound racetrack where he spent a lot of time as a boy.[12] On other occasions the revisitation sequence can be used to remind viewers of the extent to which lives are subject to the influence of both continuity and change. *49 Up*, for instance, has Tony showing us round the same suburban garden as in *42 Up*. Though much has remained the same, the trees are now much larger and Tony's hair is significantly greyer.

Undoubtedly, one of the greatest challenges that any long doc filmmaker confronts when updating their work is the creation of a narrative structure that can adequately reflect the interplay of past and present in a subject's life. The task becomes, if anything, harder with the passing years, since the amount of material increases exponentially whilst the length of the individual updates remains relatively static.[13] Apted is the first to admit that having to condense so much 'story-time' into relatively brief biographies has been no easy task. As he observes: 'One of the hard jobs of doing these films is to portray these people's lives in such a short time. It's very difficult to create an honest snapshot of their lives' (Apted, 1998).

What Apted always draws attention to when discussing the construction of the *Seven Up* series is how, when editing these films, his experience of working in narrative fiction has stood him in good stead. It is noticeable, for instance, that in each new *Seven Up* update, Apted is careful to build an appropriate level of narrative expectation in the audience before revealing the subject as he or she is today. Apted is nevertheless keen to point out where documentary and fiction part company. As he observes:

> There are some interesting differences between working in documentary and fiction. Because in some senses working in documentary is the reverse. With a story you have a script and my job as a director is to bring it to life. With a documentary you're really creating a script out of what you've already shot. I always find you don't really know what you have with a documentary until you've shot it and you begin to look at it and get a sense of it. In some ways it talks to you. And you start to fashion a script out of the raw material and discover it as you go along. (Apted, 1998)

Recognising that he will have to observe a strict narrative economy as the *Seven Up* project progresses, Apted has always paid especially careful attention to the time structure of these films. In both *42 Up* and *49 Up*, for instance, each subject is allocated 13–15 minutes for their story to be told. Since the focal point, in narrative terms, is always on the life-events of the immediate past (the past seven years), earlier episodes and events have to be squeezed in to a time frame that never extends beyond three and a half minutes of film time. As a consequence, with each successive update there is a progressive foreshortening of a subject's past. In *42 Up*, for instance, some two and a half minutes cover the twenty-eight years of the subjects' lives between the ages of seven and thirty-five. In *49 Up*, the same amount of time covers the thirty-five years between Tony at seven and at forty-two. In general terms, it might be said that Apted edits these films in such a way as to invite reflections from the audience on the multiple forces that have shaped subjects' lives and on how far they have travelled from their initial point of departure. The distance travelled by the participants is nicely illustrated in the final 'now-versus-then' sequence in *42 Up* in which shots of the subjects as seven-year-olds filmed during their day out in London are intercut with 'here-and-now' images of the people they have become.

Character attrition

One of the questions that long doc filmmakers get asked most frequently is what being involved in such a project has meant both for themselves and for their subjects. In responding to such questions filmmakers like Apted will generally seek to emphasise the degree of commitment, on both sides, that such a project calls for (see pp. 13–15). In common with his long doc colleagues, however, Apted is aware that in a number of cases – despite all the efforts that have gone into building and sustaining relationships – some subjects will decide to withdraw. By the time he completed work on the first five of the *Up* films, Apted had suffered a number of such casualties. This section will briefly examine the circumstances surrounding the departure of these subjects as well as discussing the significance that character attrition has for this particular form of documentary filmmaking.

The decision by any screen personality – whether that individual be an actor in a long-established soap or a subject in a long-running long doc – to withdraw from the show will always have a series of repercussions. In the case of an actor's departure, any potential damage can be mitigated by the writing-in of a new character or by the introduction of a replacement actor to fill the vacated role. With long docs no such solutions are available and filmmakers will need to resort to other means in order to compensate for the loss. In some cases it may be possible to signal a subject's impending withdrawal by getting him or her to make some form of valedictory statement prior to their departure.[14] The more normal course of events is that, following a long doc subject's intimation that they wish to pull out, there will be strenuous attempts by the filmmaker to get them to reconsider their decision. Once it becomes clear, however, that a subject is firm in their resolve, there is little else that a filmmaker can do other than to take what steps they can to cover the loss, usually by arranging for slightly expanded contributions from subjects who remain.

In the case of the *Seven Up* series, Apted has been reasonably fortunate in that, of the fourteen original participants, eleven have remained as more or less active members of his cast. One needs to apply the qualifying 'more or less', since there have been times when Apted has had to use all his powers of persuasion to keep some of his subjects on board. With Suzy, for instance, he freely admits that it has been a constant struggle to get her to maintain her involvement ('She's been very reluctant and awkward about taking part' (Apted, 1998)). Sometimes it has also happened that a subject has temporarily disappeared from view, only to re-appear in a later programme. This was the case with Symon, one of two *Seven Up* subjects who spent their early years in a children's home. At the time when Apted was working on *35 Up*, Symon was going through a difficult period in his life following the break-up of his first marriage and he chose not to appear in the film.[15] He does, however, return for *42 Up*, in the course of which he reflects very honestly on the breakdown of his relationship with his first wife and the anguish he went through. As Apted himself has acknowledged, the case of Symon is a pointer to the particular volatility of the long doc form. It also goes to show, however, that – given the characteristic open-ness of the long doc form – a subject's re-appearance and the reasons they give for their temporary absence – can also, on their return, be used as a means of providing additional narrative impetus.

Character attrition is an ever-present hazard in long doc production. In some instances the loss can occur with no apparent fore-warning. This is what happened in the case of Peter, a *Seven Up* regular who had participated in the series up to and including *28 Up*. In the first two *Seven Up* films Peter frequently appears together with Neil. Both attended the same primary school and both of them share a similar middle-class background. Peter's life has, however, been in many respects far more conventional than that of Neil. After school he went on to university, then did a teacher training course, and by the age of twenty-eight was working as a secondary school teacher. Asked by Apted in *28 Up* about his views on private, as opposed to state, education, Peter is outspokenly critical of private schooling and the privileges it supposedly buys, He then voices no less strong feelings about the policies being pursued by the government of Margaret Thatcher, referring to it as 'the most incompetent uncaring shower we've ever had'. Following the broadcast of *28 Up*, there was a very hostile press reaction to what some journalists saw as inappropriate utterances by a member of the teaching profession. Peter, clearly taken aback by the degree of hostility shown, decided that the only course open to him was to withdraw from the programme. He has never returned, though Apted maintains contact with him in the hope that one day he might decide once more to participate.[16]

While Peter and Apted have remained on amicable terms, the same cannot be said of others who have decided to part company with the programme. Peter's leaving may have resulted from a lack of appreciation of the consequences of making certain unguarded remarks, but with other subjects their withdrawal seems to have been more of a pre-emptive move. In the case of both Charles and John, for instance, two of the original trio of posh little boys, the decision to withdraw (in John's case temporarily) seems to have been principally motivated by the conviction that they could never really escape from the programme's stereotyping tendencies. In other words, they felt – in varying degrees – resentful that they had been used to provide 'evidence for the prosecution' that Britain was still a deeply divided, class-ridden society.

Charles, who had appeared in *Seven Up*, *14 Up* and *21 Up*, has never provided any detailed explanation about why he wished to part company with the programme, but from hints that he has given one can surmise that it had a lot to do with having so little control over how he was being represented, as well as a more general anxiety about this kind of insistent media intrusion (see Brooks, 1998: 2). As Apted has pointed out, however, there is a particular irony in Charles' decision to pull out, since the career that he has been pursuing in the last few years is that of documentary filmmaking (among other things he ran Channel 4's *Cutting Edge* documentary strand and he has also worked for the BBC). Apted's suspicion is that Charles, having become increasingly aware of how much manipulative power lies in the hands of the filmmaker, was no longer prepared to run the risk of being misrepresented. Apted has little truck with this point of view. His irritation comes across most pithily in the National Film Theatre interview, when he observed: 'Charles is incomprehensible to me. Because he's a documentary filmmaker – and although he lives by the sword, he won't die by the sword' (cited in Freedland, 2005b). Apted gives further vent to his irritation in the sequence in *28 Up* where he explains Charles' absence from the programme. Having replayed short clips from *14 Up* and *21 Up* in which Charles reflects on money-making and getting a suitable job, the narrator (Apted) makes the following laconic statement: 'Charles has found a job suitable for his talent. At the BBC he makes documentary films. He decided not to take part in this film' (*28 Up*).

John, one of the other posh boys, has managed his withdrawal more strategically. Like Charles, he decided to step down after *21 Up*, though since then he has appeared in two more of the films, once briefly in *35 Up* and again in *49 Up*. John's comings and goings illustrate some of the challenges that confront a filmmaker working in the long doc mode and are worth examining in a little more detail. Following John's initial withdrawal (after *21 Up*), Apted felt duty bound in the next film to provide some explanation for his absence and therefore includes a short sequence in *28 Up* where he offers a short *résumé* of John's life that concludes with the following statement: 'John declined to be interviewed at 28. He felt satisfied with what he'd had to say in the previous films and had nothing more to add.' To enable viewers to have something to remember John by, Apted then shows a photograph of John that the latter has kindly submitted in lieu of being interviewed. Nevertheless, John's absence was to be relatively short-lived since he agreed to participate once more in *35 Up*. This time, however, it is evident that he has made his participation dependent on a number of conditions. Aware of the large audience that is following the *Seven Up* series,

John seizes the opportunity that the programme affords to draw attention to the work of a Bulgarian charity in which he has been personally involved.[17]

John's fluctuating presence in the *Seven Up* series is a good illustration of what compromises a long doc filmmaker may be willing to enter into in order to secure the further participation of a subject. As far as Apted was concerned, it was worth paying a certain price in order to secure John's return to the *Seven Up* fold after a longish absence. Others might be of the opinion, however, that the very fact that a long doc participant can extract such *quid pro quo* concessions from a filmmaker illustrates the extent to which, in today's broadcasting ecology, individuals regard their participation in such programmes as little more than an opportunity to gain a promotional platform for themselves or for the organisations they represent.

Trials of the long haul

As is clearly shown by the number of casualties a long doc may sustain, the longer the subjects are associated with the project, the more aware they become of what this particular form of public exposure implies. As Suzy remarks in *35 Up*: 'It churns up happy and sad memories – and it all comes flooding back. Parts of it I'd rather forget; and it's all there for people to see.' John, who – as we have seen – has been highly critical of the programme's whole approach – is even more graphic in his account of what it is like for one's life to be publicly paraded on such a regular basis: 'I bitterly regret that the headmaster pushed me forward for the series, because every seven years a little pill of poison is injected.' By *49 Up* John has reached the jaundiced conclusion that the *Seven Up* series has only retained its popularity because it exhibits the same voyeuristic qualities as a tawdry reality show.[18] As he explains to Apted:

> I suspect that why the programme is so compelling and interesting for viewers is because it's like *Big Brother* and I'm a *Celebrity, Get Me Out of Here*. It's actually real-life TV, with the added bonus that you can see people grow old, lose their hair, and get fat. Fascinating, I'm sure, but does it have any value, that's a different question.

What several subjects have taken particular exception to is the degree to which they feel they are being defined by the terms and frames of reference the film itself employs. Of the original *Seven Up* subjects who have taken the most critical stance to the film, it is the 'posh boy' trio – who Apted refers to as his 'three wise men' – who have most frequently challenged the premise on which the programme is constructed and what they see as its stereotyping tendencies. John, as we have seen, is openly hostile to *Seven Up*'s aims, whilst Charles already withdrew after *21 Up* and there is little likelihood of his returning. Andrew, though appearing in all the programmes to date, has also become increasingly wary with respect to how much he is prepared to reveal about himself. As he says in *49 Up*: 'At 7, 14 and 21 we were fairly prepared to say what we thought. We've become more guarded over the years.'

In any long doc, a subject's long-term involvement in such a project can naturally have consequences for the spouses, children and other relatives of those whose lives are so regularly put on public display. I have already commented on how Apted has turned to the wives and girlfriends of some subjects to make up for the shortfall of women in the series (see Chapter 4, pp. 88–9). With Paul's and Symon's wives, the strategy appears to have worked well since in each case the confidence of the women acts as a counterbalance to the partner's relative taciturnity. In other instances, however, the introduction of a spouse has a far less favourable outcome, especially where the person concerned feels they are being less than fairly represented. The best illustration of this is provided by Nick's wife Jackie who severed her connections with the series after one brief appearance in *28 Up*. In Jackie's case, Apted admits that – just as he had done with Tony earlier in the series – he was guilty of second-guessing how a situation might develop and framing the narrative with this anticipated development in mind. The fact that, in *28 Up*, Apted represented her in what he concedes was 'not a very favourable or nice light' not only led to Jackie declining to take part in any more of the *Up* films but also to her withdrawing consent for her young son (Nick's child) to appear. As Apted dryly comments: 'I think I shot myself in the foot' (Apted, 1998). In other instances problems and discord can arise when a subject admits, on camera and in the partner's presence, to some lapse or indiscretion that can have implications for the partner and for other members of the family. This was the case when Tony revealed in *42 Up*, in the presence of his wife Debbie, that he had been guilty of what he calls 'regretful behaviour' (marital infidelity). Such a public admission proved to be a source of considerable distress both for his wife and for their children. According to Debbie in *49 Up*, his daughter Perrie was so upset by the revelation that she refused to go to school for three weeks.

In introducing these examples, I do not wish to give the impression that there has been a groundswell of disapproval among *Seven Up* subjects concerning the negative consequences of their participation. Some, like Tony, have positively revelled in the celebrity that the series has bestowed. Likewise Nick, the farmer's son who has built a successful career as an academic, has also spoken of his admiration for what the series has been able to achieve, even though he can 'hardly begin to describe how emotionally draining it is just to make the films and do the interviews' (*49 Up*).[19]

Faced consistently with the requirement to reflect back on their lives from the vantage point of their middle-years, Apted's participants have become increasingly aware of the processes of mediation to which they have become subject. In *42 Up* Apted saw fit to include a short epilogue section in which each participant provides a brief assessment of the personal impact of appearing in the *Up* films. As the series has continued, subjects have also displayed a greater readiness to comment on how they have been represented. Of all those who have seized this opportunity, by far the most sustained, insightful and persuasive critique is provided by Jackie (one of the East-End trio of working-class girls). Already in *42 Up* Jackie had acknowledged that, in spite of not always seeing eye to eye with Apted, she still enjoyed being involved in the programme, if for no other reason than it enabled her to 'keep a record of her life'. It was, however, precisely this recognition – Jackie's awareness that a record (albeit an imperfect one) was being kept – that made her much more determined to put the record straight when she was interviewed by Apted for *49 Up*. The nub of Jackie's critique is that she feels she has been consistently misrepresented by the programme: As she puts it to Apted in the course of their interview: 'I think in fact that I'm more intelligent than you thought I would be. I have reached a level in my life that I'm happy with – and I enjoy being me. But I don't think you ever really expected me to turn out the way I have (done).' She feels especially offended that Apted had, in her opinion, developed a class-determined view of her that resulted in a wholly inappropriate line of questioning. In Jackie's words:

> At twenty-one you asked me if I had had enough experience of men
> [before marrying]. And I thought that was actually an insulting ques-

tion. And I got very angry and we actually stopped filming because of it. And if you look at the tapes of me at twenty-one, I'm sitting there and to all intents and purposes I might not have been there.

Apted's defence when confronted with this type of criticism is the standard response of the documentary filmmaker: that any film that sets out to record people's lives in a reasonably honest way will occasionally run the risk of overstepping the mark. With respect to the particular criticism that Jackie raises, Apted does, however, concede that many of her points are well founded, especially concerning the power of editing (Apted 2005). What he does not explicitly acknowledge, however, is that a dramatic 'showdown scene' such as the one between him and Jackie – one in which filmmaker and subject square up to each other and the former gets his come-uppance – also works well in purely dramaturgical terms. Jackie has been given the opportunity to sound off about her long-held grievances.[20] Apted has been provided with the kind of material that can be worked into an attention-grabbing final sequence that can neatly and dramatically round off Jackie's story in the *49 Up* film.

The changing focus of *Seven Up*

Apted has constantly reiterated that the *Up* films have been an important part of his filmmaking life. On being asked whether he feels that the original *World in Action* thesis – that people's class origins have a determining impact on the rest of their lives – has been borne out by the *Seven Up* series, Apted is not persuaded that it has been. Whilst he feels that the thesis may hold good for members of the immediate post-war generation, such as those who feature in the films, he is less convinced that it has more general validity. As he says: 'This is a film about people who were born in 1956. I think if I had started the film seven, fourteen years later, it would have been quite different' (cited in Freedland, 2005b). Many observers are also of the opinion that the series has outgrown the programme's original aims and intentions that were themselves historically circumscribed. The consensus is that the series has become much less preoccupied with questions of class and far more concerned with 'Everyman' issues of life. As Stephen Lambert, the executive producer of *42 Up*, has observed:

The series is not as rigidly focused on class any more, but that's because the class system itself is not as rigid. So the programme has changed to become one about middle age and the problems of middle age which are marriage, divorce, children and death. (Cited in Brooks, 1998: 3–4)

Asked whether, after making the programmes for more than four decades, he had had any more thoughts on the validity of the Jesuit maxim: 'give me the child until he is seven and I will give you the man', Apted is slightly less cautious in his response:

For me the only real abiding generality is that there's something about that core personality at seven that never really changes. Whatever cards they get dealt, there's something about that personality that doesn't change. (Freedland 2005b)

Such a response, of course, raises a host of further questions relating to definitions of 'core personality' and to exactly how those cards get distributed. It also leaves conveniently out of account the questions of the means by which the 'core personality' is shielded from the environmental or economic influences which may threaten its existence (see Corner, 2009). But at least Apted can seek refuge in the defence that *Seven Up* is an ongoing project and that a little more light will be thrown on some of these questions when the next *Up* film comes along in a few years' time.

The Children of Golzow

Dividing any filmmaker's work into separate phases can some-times be a slightly arbitrary exercise. With long docs the difficulties are compounded by the fact that their development is characterised by slow exponential growth rather than being marked by distinct evolutionary stages. In the case of *Children of Golzow*, however, there is a clearly marked caesura in the work's development, one that coincides with the collapse of the GDR and the eventual re-unification of the two Germanys. The *Wende* was, among other things, a time of great economic uncertainty for many GDR citizens as they found themselves having to adapt to a new socio-political order. An increasing number of people in the East lost their jobs, and those who remained in employment had to adjust to radically different working practices and conditions.

These were indeed turbulent times, and the socio-economic and political reverberations of such momentous historical change are still being felt twenty years after the event. The demise of the GDR could also quite easily have signalled the end of the Golzow project. Not only was the country to which the Junges had always felt a considerable measure of allegiance in the process of being absorbed into an enlarged (West) German state; but DEFA, the film production company that had guaranteed them continuity of employment over all the years, was also being wound up.[21] In common with thousands of other East Germans, the Junges faced the prospect of losing their jobs, a fate that duly befell them in March 1991.[22]

Despite the many professional and personal uncertainties they had to confront in this period, the Junges were quick to realise that the very turbulence of the times provided them with a unique opportunity to report on how their Golzow subjects, individuals whose lives they been tracking for well nigh three decades, would manage during this period of major political and social transformation.[23] That the Junges were able, in the face of diverse logistical and financial problems, to continue working on their Golzow project *after* the demise of the GDR, has – in the eyes of some observers – considerably reinforced the historical significance of the project. As the East German critic Erika Richter, writing in 1994, has observed:

> The Golzow project is, in my opinion, actually gathering in importance as far as its cultural and socio-historical significance is concerned. It offers the unique possibility to trace the individual biographies of a group of unexceptional contemporaries at a time when the whole fabric of their society was being totally transformed (Richter, 1994: 20)

The final phase of *The Children of Golzow*

The impact of the *Wende* and the transformations it brought about have had a marked impact on all the post-1990 Golzow films. As Erika Richter rightly points out, the films provide us with the opportunity to witness a group of subjects with whom we are already well acquainted, going through the often painful process of adapting to radically changed circumstances. Disorientation, bewilderment, anger and sadness are all emotions that the Golzower experience during this time of transition, as they look back on the earlier part of their lives as citizens of the GDR and look forward, often with some trepidation, to what the future may hold.

For all those involved in the Golzow project – both subjects and filmmakers – this is a period during which all were forced into some form of reappraisal activity, especially with respect to what they both valued and despised about socialist experiment of which they had been a part. For the subjects, their further participation in the project enabled them (with a little prompting from the filmmakers) to reflect on the kind of society the GDR had been and consider why it failed to deliver all that it had set out to achieve. For the film-makers, the radical changes that had taken place in the conditions of film production, especially the lifting of censoring constraints, made it possible for them to undertake an extensive reassessment of both the Golzow series and, more generally, of documentary filmmaking in the GDR.[24]

Screenplay: The Times

For students of longitudinal documentary, doubtless the most signi-ficant of the post-*Wende* films and possibly of the whole Golzow cycle is *Screenplay: The Times* (1992). The film, which has the explan-atory sub-title: 'Three decades with the children of Golzow and with DEFA – a film about a film' reacquaints us with the Golzow protagonists as they embark on a specially arranged trip to Hamburg on the first anniversary of German re-unification. The Hamburg excursion acts as a point of narrative departure for an extended survey (278 minutes of running time) of what the Golzow chronicle has achieved in the first three decades of its existence and what awaits the Golzower in the new world they are entering.

If retrospective reflectiveness is a recurrent feature in most long doc films, then here it takes on a very special significance. *Screenplay* not only captures the reactions of the Golzower as a new era dawns; it also includes for very first time some extensive reflections by the filmmakers about the conditions under which the earlier films in the cycle were made and about the challenges they had faced while working for a state-controlled film company. The film thus has a dual focus. On the one hand it is an account of how re-unification has affected the lives of individual Golzower. On the other, it is a film with distinct essayistic overtones in which the business of docu-mentary filmmaking is subject to critical scrutiny. As such, *Screenplay* could legitimately be categorised as a reflexive documentary, a film in which the processes by which the filmmaker captures and incor-porates material into a particular representational form are themselves foregrounded (Nichols, 1991: 56–75; Kilborn & Izod, 1997: 75–80).

One of the most characteristic features of reflexive documentary is the readiness of the filmmaker to enter into a kind of dialogue with the audience about the conditions under which the film in question was constructed and the role that the filmmaker had in setting the agenda. To these ends, filmmakers will often elect to become a visible presence rather than a structuring absence in these films. This Winfried Junge does, for the very first time, in *Screenplay*. By entering the frame in this way, it would seem the filmmaker has two objects in mind. The first is, as suggested, to get the audience to reflect on the underlying aims of the whole long doc enterprise and on the difficulties of working under the kind of less than optimum conditions that prevailed in the GDR.[25] Secondly, being filmed together with one's subjects is a tacit acknowledgement that filmmakers and Golzow participants now confront the same existential uncertainties. All of them are, for better or for worse, having to bid farewell to a society which had powerfully shaped their lives up to that point. All are facing the sobering, even chilling, prospect of having to find their way in a society whose value system was fundamentally different from the one with which they had, perforce, become so familiar.[26]

Whilst every long doc update to some extent involves a critical evaluation[27] of all that has gone before, in *Screenplay* the evaluative component assumes major structural significance. *Screenplay* is, as stated in the opening credits, above all a 'film about a film'. Woven into the textual fabric of the film is an account of how the Golzow chronicle came to be made and the various circumstances that led it to acquiring the shape and form it eventually did. For these reasons, it is probably the most personal of all the Junges' Golzow films, in that it is clearly intended to give viewers access to what Junge refers to as his 'filmmaker's workshop'. The film, thus, not only performs the standard long doc task of providing updates on the lives of subjects but also initiates viewers into the problems and difficulties faced by East German documentarists.

At times in *Screenplay*, the film's concern to set the record straight, together with Junge's various musings on the role and responsibilities of the filmmaking chronicler, suggest that *Screenplay* could well have been the last film in the Golzow series. The filmmakers are careful, however, to leave the way open for the Golzow story to continue. Indeed, approximately two-thirds of the way into the film, Junge opts to deliver a carefully worded statement in which he expressly indicates that – in light of all the recent tumultuous events – he and his team feel under some obligation to carry on with their chronicling task. In order to make this announcement a little more memorable, he chooses to deliver it on the very day (3 October 1990) on which East and West Germany were formally re-united. Standing in front of the Golzow place-name sign on the outskirts of the village and holding up a copy of that day's local paper, Junge makes the following straight-to-camera address:

> On this day the paper I'm holding greets the citizens of Golzow and myself with the headlines 'Welcome to new Germany'. This is sup-posed to be a day of joy, but for me it's an occasion when I'm just curious to know how things are going to develop. It's also a day of mixed emotions. We have produced this chronicle with high hopes. We would have liked to have been able to show that the idea of a socialist society was capable of being realised. In the event, however, things have taken a different course and the chronicler has an obli-gation to show what is now going to happen. We are therefore going to continue. This is the first day of filming in the Federal Republic of Germany. I'm holding out hope for the good folk of Golzow and I wish all of them good fortune in these new times. (My translation)

This pronouncement by the filmmaker not only indicates an ongoing commitment to the Golzow project; it also reveals a greater readiness than at any time hitherto to ally himself with the citizens of Golzow. The emphasis has shifted, if you will, from the position in which the filmmakers presented themselves as detached chroniclers to one where they now identify themselves as involved participants. In consequence, from now onwards, subjects and filmmakers are able to interact with each other with much greater openness than in GDR times when people felt, with some justification, that they had to be much more guarded.

Putting the record straight

One of the most striking features of *Screenplay* is how it seeks to illuminate the difficult conditions under which the pre-*Wende* films had been made. Once again – though this time assisted by the remarkable turn of events in the socio-historical world – filmmakers have been able to take advantage of the opportunities provided by the long doc form. On this occasion they have set out to subject the

Golzow work produced thus far to a thorough-going review. This review is part of a more general attempt on the filmmakers' part to share with their audience some of the frustrations they experienced as GDR documentarists and to show what compromises they were often forced into in order not to incur the displeasure of state officials. Among other things, the Junges draw attention to the number of occasions when those in higher authority brought pressure to bear on them to include references to particular state anniversaries or some other significant event in the official GDR calendar. They also remember the number of times when they felt it necessary to exclude certain material from the final edited version in order not to offer any hostages to fortune as far as the state authorities were concerned.

For the majority of (former) citizens of the GDR who watched *Screenplay*, the disclosures such as those described above probably came as no great surprise. They were, after all, aware of the extent to which the Party was able to bring influence to bear on virtually every aspect of GDR life. Nevertheless, even the most sceptically minded East German viewer may still have been slightly taken aback by some of *Screenplay*'s revelations. One such *post factum* disclosure concerns the role played by Walter Hübner, the father of Marieluise, one of the Golzow protagonists. Even from the brief contributions he is allowed to make in the pre-*Wende* films, it would have been evident to most GDR viewers that Herr Hübner was a man whose views on life and politics clearly ran counter to received (Party) wisdom. Herr Hübner is a man of strong beliefs, but rather than place his faith in the teaching of the Socialist Unity Party he has always preferred to remain faithful to the teaching of the Protestant Church. Walter Hübner's religious beliefs, together with the fact that he is, by temperament, a somewhat cantankerous character, created a series of problems for Junge in many of the pre-*Wende* Golzow films. (It should be remembered that in the GDR the holding and expression of Christian beliefs was actively discouraged; see Molloy, 2009: 159–80). At Marieluise's wedding reception Junge filmed the father expounding on the relevance of Christ's Sermon on the Mount to present-day life in the GDR, but in the Golzow film chronicling the wedding most of Walter Hübner's remarks have been excised. In an extended sequence in *Screenplay* in which the issue of censorship is openly discussed, Junge shows us previously unscreened footage from 1984 in which the filmmaker (out of frame) is heard talking to Herr Hübner about the latter's dissatisfaction at having been silenced in this way. In the course of this interview, Walter explains why he considers it so important that he be allowed to express his dissenting views on government policies. As he goes on to explain in the interview, some fifty years previously, during the period of the Third Reich, he had chosen to remain silent, even though he could see that the country was heading for disaster. Ever since then, he had considered it his duty to express his feelings on key issues of the day, even when he knew that this would bring him into conflict with the current political leadership.[28]

So resolutely does Junge pursue his task of 'putting the record straight' in *Screenplay* that it makes for a viewing experience that some in the audience have found challenging, to say the least. Nevertheless, the film still provides some very telling insights, not only into the particular difficulties experienced by East German documentarists but also into the making of longitudinal work more generally. In the case of *Screenplay* one of the filmmakers' principal aims was to reflect on what it had been possible to produce under the prevailing conditions and to show how those conditions had determined what could and could not be revealed. In a not dissimilar way – though nothing like to the same extent – each successive update of a long doc allows for some modification and reworking of the stories and material that have so far been presented. As long as they remain in production, all long docs can properly be regarded '*in statu nascendi*'. But just like a living organism, so with a long doc the potential for its future growth will always be, in some measure, determined by all that has gone before.

Encouraging self-reflectiveness

As well as providing updates on the transition of the Golzower to the new, post-*Wende* world, *Screenplay* also contains a series of reflections on the business of filmmaking.[29] The primary means by which *Screenplay* invites the spectator to take up a critically reflective stance is through the film's narrational commentary. As well as providing the usual contextualising information about when and where certain scenes were filmed and details about the progress of individual protagonists, the commentary also aims to get the viewer to consider possible alternative ways in which the material could have been presented. This is in stark contrast to all the earlier Golzow films, which were typified by their expository, supremely confident mode of address. In *Screenplay* the narrator (Junge himself) is a far more critical, questioning presence – one who at times seems almost as much at a loss as some of his participants.[30]

This revised narrational stance is also discernible in the frequent use of intertitles in this film. Besides acting as an aid to audience orientation, intertitles are another means by which the filmmakers seek to enter into a kind of dialogue with their audience about the making of the films and the special conditions under which they were produced, chronicling a particular set of historical events. Thus, while many of the intertitles in *Screenplay* refer to key events in contemporary German history – for example, '3rd October 1991: First Anniversary of German unity'– there are just as many that draw attention to the process of filmmaking itself. Almost one-third of the way into the film, for instance, there is a title 'Looking back on opportunities to end the chronicle' that introduces a longish sequence in which the filmmakers talk about the number of occasions when it seemed likely that the project would be halted.

The biographical turn

Though the *Wende* and all that it brought constitutes the most decisive turning-point in the history of the Golzow cycle, it could be argued that an equally important event in the development of the project had been the production, a decade earlier, of *Biographies* (1980/81). It was the success of this film that prompted the Junges to consider a new strategy for the future of the Golzow project. The specific proposal that they put to the state authorities for consideration was that, over the next two decades, they would produce a series of feature-length biographical accounts of 'each of the central heroes' (Junge, 2004: 90). The filmmakers would commit themselves to providing regular updates and the project would be finally brought to a conclusion in 1999, the year that would mark the fiftieth anniversary of the GDR.[31]

Though the Junges' vision of a millennial leave-taking celebration proved to be precipitate, they were more accurate in their assessment of the new, portrait-centred focus that the project would henceforth assume. With the possible exception of *Screenplay*, all the Golzow films the Junges produced in the post-*Wende* period are biographical in their approach. From 1994 till the end of the project in 2007, the Junges completed eight feature-length biographies of Golzow protagonists, whilst the long multi-part final film *And If*

They Haven't Passed Away, They'll Still Be Alive Today (2006/7) is also made up of a series of individual portraits.

All in all, the films that make up the final, post-*Wende* phase of the Golzow cycle provide plentiful evidence of the benefits to be gained from being able to take the long view. Having seen how the protagonists have grown up in, and been integrated into, a particular social system, we now witness them having to adapt to a style and a way of life founded on wholly different principles. It is because we have become so intimately acquainted with the lives of the protagonists *before* the *Wende* that we are better able to understand and empathise with their reactions to a chain of events for which they are, in some cases, emotionally and psychologically ill prepared. In the film *The Life of Jürgen from Golzow* (1994), for instance, we witness how Jürgen, one of the Junges' most loyal subjects over the years, attempts to come to terms with his new life in the FRG. Jürgen has had a chequered career. In the GDR he eventually found work as a painter and decorator, but before then he had spent time in the East German military. There always appears to be a slight fragility in his temperament – and this is also reflected in the struggle he has had with alcohol at one stage of his life. Having come to know him as a mild-mannered, somewhat diffident young man, viewers of *The Life of Jürgen from Golzow* will be struck by Jürgen's apparent heightened level of self-awareness and ability to articulate his thoughts in ways that they may not have anticipated. Subjects' ability to reflect in a highly articulate manner on their past or present lives is a recurrent feature in long docs. In Jürgen's case, his new-found expressive ability may also be bound up with his urgently felt need to give vent to the anger he feels about some of the manifest injustices that he thinks have resulted from the introduction of new economic policies and production practices following re-unification.

In presenting their accounts of subjects' lives after the *Wende*, the Junges are careful not to be at all judgmental about how successful or otherwise their protagonists have been in adapting to the new world in which they find themselves (see Kersten, 2006). Viewers are largely left to draw their own conclusions on this matter. The one question, however, that is implicitly posed in almost all the post-*Wende* Golzow films is to what extent their subjects' experiences as GDR citizens, the jobs they have held and the organisations they have belonged to, have helped or hindered them as they seek to adjust to the new socio-economic realities. In the case of those subjects who were Party members or who were otherwise openly supportive of the socialist system, one might imagine that the *Wende* would have a deeply unsettling, if not traumatising impact. I would like therefore to briefly consider how the later Golzow films treat two of these former 'believers' and what this tells us about the problems of longer-term participation in these longitudinal projects. The participants in question are Ilona Müller and Winfried Jerchel. Ilona had worked as a Party functionary and had also been a member of the Free German Youth under the old regime. Winfried had also been a committed Party member.[32]

The case of Ilona

Although Ilona was one of the original Golzow children, she cannot really be thought of as a central protagonist, since as early as 1983 she had decided to sever her active involvement with the project. She is, however, in one of several subjects with whom the Junges reacquaint us in their final Golzow film *And If They Haven't Passed Away, They'll Still Be Alive Today* (2006/7). One can only assume, therefore, that one of the filmmakers' calculations in re-introducing Ilona in this way may have been to encourage audience speculation about how someone who had formerly worked as a Party functionary will have adapted to life in the new Germany. In the case of Ilona there was at the time of her withdrawal from the project some speculation about whether she was finding it difficult to reconcile her further participation in the project with her membership of the Party (Lemke, 2006:1) The more likely explanation, however, is that her decision to withdraw had less to do with her being identified as a Party functionary and more to do with her natural diffidence. As with several other long doc subjects, then, it was Ilona's antipathy to having her life regularly exposed to this form of intrusiveness that proved to be the tipping point so far as any more active participation was concerned.[33]

The problems that the Junges encountered when re-introducing the 'character' of Ilona in the final film are not dissimilar to those faced by Apted when he has had to remind viewers about subjects such as Charles who have now parted company with the programme.[34] There must always be certain doubts in a filmmaker's mind about the wisdom of re-introducing a subject who has withdrawn from the project. Long stay viewers may still have vivid memories of the person in question, but those in the audience who have joined the series at a much later stage will inevitably be left wondering why such attention is meted out to a character who, in one sense, is long departed.

The case of Winfried Jerchel

When re-introducing Ilona in the final film of the Golzow series, the filmmakers actually have to work quite hard to re-activate her as a Golzow subject whom viewers had effectively lost sight of more than two decades previously. Winfried Jerchel, on the other hand, who appears alongside Ilona in the final Golzow film, has been a fully participating member of the Golzow cast right from the earliest days. It is for this reason that the Junges have seen fit to devote one whole part of their last film to reprising Winfried's life. The very fact that the reprise is almost two hours in length makes for an extensive, wide-ranging account that has some of the qualities of a 'stand-alone' biopic. In many ways, however, the expansive-ness of the treatment is justified in the light of what the filmmakers are attempting to show with respect to the many continuities and discontinuities that can be traced within an individual's life.[35]

In presenting Winfried's story in *And If They Haven't Passed Away*, the Junges follow what could be said to have become standard long doc practice in skewing the narrative very much towards the present. Thus, even though we are offered regular reminders of Winfried's childhood days (including his propensity for fiddling around with bits of electrical equipment), the perspective from which the story of his life is presented is that of post-*Wende* Germany. Winfried's reflections on post-*Wende* developments and his recollections of earlier times in the East are of particular significance in that they reflect the experiences that thousands of East Germans must have gone through after the demise of the GDR. Already as a young man he had acquired the set of life-skills necessary to survive in a society where personal freedoms were quite severely curtailed. From his late teens onwards Winfried, of all the Golzower, comes to exem-plify that typical combination of caution and wariness that char-acterized the attitude to life of many GDR citizens. As he himself admits: 'I learned early on that you have to move around cautiously in this life.' (Rother, 2006) In GDR times Winfried was an elec-tronics engineer who was also a Party member and a former brigade commander at the factory where he worked. Whether Winfried's membership of the Party results from deeply held conviction or from political expediency is never made entirely clear in any of the Golzow films. The most one can say is that, even after the collapse of communism, Winfried was not one of those who immediately disavowed his former beliefs in order to make matters easier for himself in the newfound social order.

Of all the Golzow subjects, Winfried is the one who appears have been able to effect an almost effortless transition to life in the post-*Wende* world. He has simply focused all his energies on what the new market-oriented situation demands of him. After the fall of the Wall, it is not long before Winfried uproots himself from the GDR and moves to Augsburg in West Germany with the intention of starting a new life there. Having married a woman of some means, his material future seems to be assured. Though initially – like so many GDR citizens after the *Wende* – Winfried fails to find a job, he is in no way disheartened by this temporary setback.[36] He soon discovers ways of making himself employable again and ultimately proves himself just as capable of making his way in the West as he had done in the East. Some critics have linked this ability to adapt to new situations with the hard apprenticeship that individuals like Winfried had served in the East. Others have taken the view, however, that this adaptability is not so much the result of being socialised within a particular political system but has its origins in a deeply rooted human ability to adjust to changing situations. As one German critic has commented:

> Times change, but human beings remain as they have always been. Even the most authoritarian system can never totally subjugate the in-dividual. Human beings always retain at least some capacity to make their own decisions and to act in ways they think fit.' (Rother, 2006)

Finding an ending

In Winfried Junge's straight-to-camera statement in *Screenplay*, where he considers the consequences that German re-unifica-tion might have for the people of Golzow, he also reflects on what it might mean for his own long doc project (see pp. 161–2). At the end of this statement, he bravely asserts that 'This is the first day of filming in the Federal Republic of Germany', but there is still suffi-cient note of equivocation in his voice to suggest to the audience that this could well mark the end of the road for the Golzow chronicle. This sense of an ending being nigh is, if anything, reinforced by later sequences of *Screenplay* that are distinctly valedictory in tone. In one scene entitled 'We have arrived: a possible ending to the film', for instance, there are shots of the current generation of Golzow children playing in a sandpit, whilst Junge is heard in voice-over asking himself whether – even if he were given the opportunity – he would have the courage to start such a project again. He even wonders whether there was certain hubris in undertaking such a venture in the first place. The valedictory note becomes even more pronounced in the sequence that concludes *Screenplay* in which a contemplative Winfried Junge is filmed sitting at his editing desk amidst all his archived Golzow material. The sequence ends with Junge soberly informing us about the winding-up of DEFA and the plans to convert the building that once housed the DEFA documentary division into a contemporary media centre.

If the final sequence of *Screenplay* contains the strong suggestion that this could be the end of the line for the Golzow series, the film also alerts us to various other occasions when the project could have ended.[37] In a segment of the film entitled 'Looking back on opportunities to end the chronicle' the Junges identify some possible leave-taking points one of which would have been in 1969, at the time that *When one is 14* was being made, where the filmmakers felt that 'unreasonable' demands were being made by the state authorities concerning what aspects of GDR life could and could not be shown. Another potential exit point was in August 1985 when the Junges also felt that the conditions under which they were being required to operate were making it virtually impossible for them to continue.[38]

With the benefit of hindsight we now know that the Golzow project not only survived the end of the GDR and the winding-up of DEFA, it also continued well into the new millennium. That the project lasted this long is not just a tribute to the Junges' tenacity. It is also connected with the fact that, from the 1980s onwards, the Golzow films began to attract the attention of a wider audience than those living in, or who had at one time been citizens of, the GDR. There had always been those who were convinced that the Golzow films would end as soon as the GDR ended, since Junge and his team were considered to be so dependent on the patronage provided by the Party bosses. This conveniently overlooks the fact, however, that the Golzow chronicle was not regarded by those who held high office in the Party as the type of film that could be relied on for educational or consciousness-raising purposes. As Junge has observed: 'We had to fight for the project, for every film again and again, it was never entirely officially established in the GDR' (Junge, 2008: 13)

That the Golzow project was able to continue as long as it did, then, is probably therefore in large part attributable to the fact that audiences have been able to relate to those aspects of the work that are, for want of a better phrase, of more universal appeal. Individual biographies are traced over a sufficiently long period of time to allow viewers to feel a degree of empathic involvement in the lives of subjects. For German audiences in both East and West, but particularly those belonging to the generation that lived through the Cold War period, the experiences of the Golzower are bound to carry a special resonance. They bring to mind memories of mutual suspicion and enmity between implacably opposed states. Those, on the other hand, who come to the Golzow films without the burden of such memories, will most likely have a very different response. Whilst acknowledging that the Golzow series is first and foremost a study of lives lived under oppressive political conditions, the latter-day audience will, arguably, be disposed to see the more universal relevance of the experiences that the Junges have chronicled. For instance, following the *Wende*, several of the Golzow subjects found themselves having to abandon the areas in East Germany where they had spent their formative years, in the search of new job opportunities in the West. In the case of some of the Golzower the need to uproot themselves was, of course, prompted by a very particular set of political events, but there will be many in the international audience who will be able to relate these depictions of enforced or voluntary displacement to their own experiences of having to leave their homeland in search of a better future.[39]

An extended swan-song

In 2006, almost five decades after setting out on a project which by now encompassed 19 films with a total running time of almost 43 hours, the Junges commenced the onerous task of saying their long, lingering farewell to the project that had taken up the best part of their working lives with their four-part swan song *And If They Haven't Passed Away, They'll Still Be Alive Today* (2006/7). In this final film the Junges re-introduce us to most of the 'characters' who have, at some stage, made an appearance in the course of the Golzow saga, but some of whom we have not heard of for quite some time.[40]

In attempting to devise a means to bring this epic work to a close, the Junges have opted for a narrative device that is familiar to those who have ever witnessed the closing moments (or bars) of a soap opera. It is one that allows a line to be drawn under the Golzow story and enables viewers to take their leave of a group of characters or individuals for whom they perhaps felt a considerable degree of attachment. *And If They Haven't Passed Away, They'll Still Be Alive Today* thus signals to the viewer that the end of the tale has come and that some sort of closure has been achieved, but at the same time it preserves an element of open-endedness by actively encouraging speculation about how some or all of the featured Golzower will be living out the rest of their lives.

The final sequence of the film – and therefore of the whole Golzow cycle – returns us to the spot where it all began: the kindergarten sandpit. Again we hear the sound of children singing, but this time the voices are those of the current generation of Golzow youngsters about to begin school. With this powerful reminder of once-upon-a-time-long-ago, the camera pulls away from the school and slowly withdraws. The audience is left to muse not only on the cyclical character of human life but also on the fates of the now middle-aged Golzower as they move into a still uncertain future.

The legacy?

Little could Winfried Junge have imagined when he first set out on the Golzow trail in the early 1960s that he would still be working on the project more than four and a half decades later, nor indeed that, before the project ended, the very society whose 'progress' he was documenting would itself have disappeared.[41] Now that the work has reached its conclusion, however, the question arises as to its likely legacy. Any attempt to gauge how audiences will respond to a film in the longer term is always a slightly risky venture, but in the case of *The Children of Golzow* one can predict with some confidence that critics and observers will wish to draw attention to what the Golzow films tell us about the difficulties experienced by individuals who had spent the first part of their living behind the Iron Curtain but who are now having to adjust to a new way of life in the post-communist world. Of possibly greater significance, however, are the insights that the Golzow films provide, more generally, into a country and a way of life that are rapidly disappearing into the mists of history. One might venture to suggest that it this aspect of the Golzow cycle of films that is likely to prove their lasting legacy.

For one-time citizens of the GDR – and possibly for present and future generations of Germans for whom living in a united country has become the norm – the significance of the Golzow cycle may well lie in its capacity to document some of the more mundane but nevertheless defining features of GDR life that might otherwise have been all too easily forgotten. The darker and more oppressive aspects of life lived under a one-party dictatorship have been well documented and widely discussed (see Molloy, 2009: 63–85). What we have heard much less about, however, is what life was like for the millions of ordinary people who found themselves living behind the Iron Curtain during those Cold War years and who had to seek some form of accommodation with the political regimes that held sway. The special contribution of *The Children of Golzow* is arguably that it draws attention to the everyday realities of Cold-War life in the East. In this respect, the Golzow cycle takes its place alongside an increasing corpus of work that seeks, from a post-communist perspective, to reflect or recreate that always-elusive GDR reality.[42] In some cases (as with *The Lives of Others*) there is an attempt to imaginatively recapture that reality through fictional means. With various forms of documentary work, the aim has frequently been to provide accounts of some of the darker dealings of the communist state (the activities of the Stasi and the curtailment of basic freedoms). Sometimes, however, there have been attempts – using oral history resources – to produce accounts of everyday life in the East that give a possibly more balanced picture of what living under communism actually meant in day-to-day terms. A recent BBC programme *The Lost World of Communism*, a three-part series based on the first-hand testimony of people who lived in East Germany and other Eastern Bloc states during the Cold War era, represents one such attempt. In the book published to accompany the series the producer Peter Molloy comments:

> But what was life really like for East Europeans, effectively imprisoned in the Eastern bloc? The headlines of Cold War spies and secret police surveillance, of political repression and dissident activism do not tell the whole story. After the end of the Cold War, some remembered their lives as 'perfectly ordinary', others hankered for the security and certainty of life under communism while still more missed the camaraderie or the privileges attendant on power. (Molloy, 2009:1)

The Children of Golzow – it could be argued – has also gone some way to capturing the warp and the weft of this now vanished world, thus providing a sustained and thought-provoking account of what life was like for ordinary citizens of East Germany during those times. Measured in its entirety, the Golzow cycle of films thus embody what some would see as a collective memory of a culture and a social order that did not stand the test of time. That certain memories of this lost world have been filmically enshrined in the Golzow longitudinal study could prove to be its lasting legacy.

The Children of Jordbrö

As Hartleb and the Junges have discovered, winding down a long doc is no mean undertaking. *A Pizza in Jordbrö* (1994) was intended to be the last film in a series that had run for more than two decades; and Hartleb had already begun to busy himself with other projects. In the event, however, detaching himself from the Jordbrö chronicle proved to be more difficult than he had imagined. Some ten years after completing *Pizza*, Hartleb found himself having to gear up for one more effort on the Jordbrö front. *Everyone's Fine* (2006) was, however, definitively the end of the trail as far as Hartleb was concerned. Indeed, soon after the film was premiered, he went out of his way to dispel any lingering doubts about the possible continuation of the project by making the following declaration: 'This is the end of the Jordbrö chronicle. All the existential questions have now been answered, in one way or another.' (Weman, 2006: 5)

Hartleb's original idea for *Everyone's Fine* had been to structure it in an entirely different way from any of his previous Jordbrö films. His plan had been to concentrate wholly on subjects' present-day situations. As is not infrequently the case with long docs, however, things turned out rather differently. As he began work on *Everyone's Fine*, Hartleb came under some pressure to move away from his favoured all-in-the-present concept and to return to the narrative approach he had adopted in earlier instalments, one that relied quite heavily on the interwoven flashback sequences depicting the subject's earlier days. In Hartleb's words: 'I decided to include the people who'd featured in *Pizza*. It would be a sort of follow-on from that, I thought. But I didn't want any flashbacks. I wanted a stand-alone film about their lives today' (Weman, 2006: 5), On this occasion it seems to have been some of the subjects themselves who were instrumental in causing the filmmaker to change his mind on how the narrative of *Everyone's Fine* should be organised. Possibly prompted by the knowledge that this was to be the very last Jordbrö film, subjects began to come up with their own ideas about what might or might not be included. In particular, they began remembering earlier events and conversations that Hartleb had recorded but had not yet included in any of the Jordbrö films so far produced.[43] Even though he recognised that acting on these suggestions would result in a very different sort of film from the one he had first envisaged, Hartleb duly began to delve in his archive to see whether it would be practical to realise any of the suggested ideas.[44] Once he had started down this road, it soon became clear to him that there was no turning back.

One practical consequence of having to reconceptualise the film was that *Everyone's Fine* was much longer in the making than Hartleb had intended. The whole episode brings a powerful reminder that, once long docs have acquired a certain momentum, they create very specific expectations – not only on the part of the audiences at whom they are directed but also as far as the subjects themselves are concerned. The whole episode also provides a further illustration of how long doc filmmakers always need to maintain a certain flexibility of approach as their work evolves. Or as Hartleb put it once in an interview: 'It's like that with documentaries, just like authors complain of their novels that their characters refuse to do as they're told. They [longitudinal documentaries] take on a life of their own' (Weman, 2006: 5).

A Pizza in Jordbrö and *Everyone's Fine:* companion pieces?

One other consequence of Hartleb having to revise his initial concept for *Everyone's Fine* was that it has resulted in a greater continuity between this film and the earlier works than would otherwise have been the case. The affinities between *Pizza* and *Everyone's Fine* are particularly striking to the extent that they can easily be understood as companion pieces. Both films have the same formal design features in that they both rely on the artful juxtaposition of sequences from different periods of subjects' lives. Moreover – just as we have come to expect of mature long docs – both works present the material in such a way as to encourage viewers to speculate on what forces have led to subjects developing in the way they have done. Another trait that the films share is that they focus on the distance Jordbrö subjects have travelled from their original points of departure and on the extent to which some at least have been able to put difficult pasts behind them. This, in turn, raises questions about the degree to which lives have been determined by those twin forces of nature and nurture.

Another striking feature of these two films is what one might call their typical Hartlebian tone. Already some of the earlier Jordbrö films had been marked by a certain melancholy undertow, but in *Pizza* and *Everyone's Fine* this quality becomes more pronounced as subjects look back on what they have made of their lives. Thematically, the melancholy has its roots in the films' engagement with some of the darker aspects of human existence: physical or emotional suffering, the failure to achieve one's stated goals and the many other vicissitudes of life. Yet, in spite of these sad overtones, Hartleb is careful not to allow these films to become weighed down by any ponderous solemnity. Throughout his work, indeed, but especially in these last two films, Hartleb seems to be striving to achieve a counterbalance between scenes that dwell upon individuals' experience of pain, loss and suffering and ones that focus on joy and fulfilment. There is also a conscious attempt to use humour as a leavening device in these final two films. As Hartleb – with a smile on his face – put it to me in our interview:

> Humour is an important element in my films. There are some occasions in these films when you can laugh. This is, after all, a part of life. You don't always have to take yourself too seriously. (Hartleb: 2007)

The balancing out of lighter and darker moments is especially marked in *Everyone's Fine.* Here subjects' experience of sorrow and loneliness are regularly offset by sequences that are much more life affirming in their import. Hartleb's insistence on such positive counterbalancing seems to be rooted not in any naïve belief that 'every cloud has a silver lining' but in a deeply held conviction that there is something indomitable in the human spirit that will enable most individuals to survive all that life throws at them.

Organising the narrative

In terms of how they organize their respective narratives, the last two Jordbrö films adopt the tried-and-tested subject-by-subject approach. Both films also employ the kind of narrative structuring devices that play off scenes from subjects' past and present lives, one against the other. In *Pizza*, for instance, the film starts in the present and the rest of the film is then taken up with revisitations of the past, until in the final scene viewers are once again returned to the present. The film's point of departure, in a locational sense, is the pizza restaurant that belongs to Slobodan, one of the protagonists of the Jordbrö series. At the beginning of the film Slobodan is visited by a few of the other Jordbrö participants, and this is used as a narrative springboard for a series of excursions into the lives of other subjects.

In *Pizza* Hartleb also makes extensive use of what I have referred to elsewhere as the time-shuttling device. At the very beginning of *Pizza*, for instance, viewers are re-introduced to Uffe, a subject whom long-stay Jordbrö viewers had last encountered in his mid-teens. The sequence switches us between footage of Uffe in the first year of primary school and what we assume to be contemporary shots of him filmed in the maternity wing of a hospital, anxiously awaiting news about the birth of his first child.[45] This opening sequence closes with an image of Uffe together with his wife and newborn child, but we are then swiftly transported back more than twenty years to a scene shot in 1973, in which Uffe's primary school class are filmed singing what appears to be a joyful life-affirming song. Listening more carefully to the words of the song, however, one recognises that Hartleb is attempting to convey, albeit allusively, a much more serious message. The lyrics of the song express quite strong anti-war sentiments. What viewers of this 1994 film are therefore being invited to consider is whether, in the two decades that have since elapsed, the nations of the world have got any closer to realising the dream of ever-lasting peace.[46]

Having signalled to the audience that the juxtaposition of past and present scenes is to be a principal structuring feature of the work. Hartleb then sets about the task of reacquainting us with his subjects one by one. Just as with Apted in the *Up* films, the filmmaker s favoured strategy is to introduce the subject first as a child before then moving us, incrementally, towards the present. With Urban, for instance, we first glimpse him as a small boy playing with his friends, and we also hear his mother talking about her future hope for the boy. We then are rapidly switched to the present day, where we see Urban, now a handsome young man in his late twenties, showing his wife and child round the same Jordbrö places he had known so well in his youth.

Each of the chapters in *Pizza*, then, sets itself the narrative task of tracing the progress of subjects from childhood to the present day and of providing an account of what they have achieved in both a professional and personal sense. Once the task has been completed, we move on to the journey of the next life-subject, until all the lives have been covered. When the last update has been concluded, an act of symbolic closure is contrived. As night falls and all the guests have departed, Slobodan is seen cleaning up in the pizzeria and the viewer is left to wonder whether this is just the end of another day (and another update) or whether this is the curtain coming down on the whole Jordbrö chronicle.

Narrative consolidation and extension: the case of Maria

As we have discovered with other filmmakers, the major challenge as a long doc project develops is to construct a coherent narrative from a growing number of story elements. The longer a series continues, so the task of accommodating all the biographical details becomes more challenging. In each new long doc instalment the filmmaker confronts the necessity of having to provide those reminders of the subjects' past lives (narrative consolidation) and at the same time to blend in more recently obtained material (narrative extension).[47] With each successive update, therefore, a delicate balance has to be achieved between material that has a consolidatory narrative function (the tracing over of known territory) and the story elements that open up new narrative terrain.

To illustrate how a long doc filmmaker performs what is actually quite a difficult balancing act, I have chosen to analyse in some detail the extended 'chapter' in *Pizza* devoted to the story of Maria, one of the series' protagonists. Already in the early Jordbrö films it had become clear that Maria, the little girl with football-playing aspirations, had all the qualifications to be a leading long doc character. Not only had her life begun to be marked by quite dramatic ups and downs, she had also developed that much prized ability to reflect on her life in a highly articulate manner. In *Back to Jordbrö* Maria has a longish (5-minute) sequence towards the end of the film in which she talks about her complicated family history (she and her sister have different fathers), her life as a single parent and her dream of becoming a writer.

In *Pizza* we gain further insights into Maria's persona, as Hartleb subtly juxtaposes footage of her as a seven-year-old and as a 28-

year-old. The seven-year-old Maria is asked what she wants to do when she grows up. When Hartleb asks her whether she's ever thought of such things, Maria comes up with the wonderfully child-like reply: 'No, I'm just going to be grown up.' After replaying this scene in *Pizza*, Hartleb rapidly cuts to the present day. The question he now asks of the apparently self-confident woman in her late twenties is very similar to the one he put to her when she was seven: 'Maria, 28-year-old. Where are you going?' To this Hartleb again gets a not entirely expected reply: 'To Adult Education College, if I get accepted.' At this point, however, Maria pauses and seemingly becomes aware that she is not being entirely honest with her interlocutor. Having asked Hartleb to stop filming, she explains: 'I can't do this. I don't know where I'm going, Rainer. I have no direction. I've lost the map.' Such moments as these, when a participant admits to having completely lost their way, are rare, even in long docs where subjects may be prepared to disclose more of their inner selves than in many other forms of documentary. Overall, the impression that the viewer gains of Maria in *Pizza* is of a woman, who – just like Neil in Apted's *Seven Up* series – is beginning to show certain signs of instability but who has developed a remark-able capacity for self-analysis and self-reflection.[48]

Having assumed a key role in *Pizza*, the stage was set for Maria to take on a similar starring role in Hartleb's final Jordbrö film. Just as Apted has done with Neil in the final two instalments of *Seven Up*, Hartleb devotes one of the longest sequences in *Everyone's Fine* to updating us on Maria. Just as in Neil's case, so with Maria the sequence is located at the end of the film, thereby accentu-ating the narrative significance that Hartleb attaches to it. As in the other chapters of the film, the filmmaker tellingly juxtaposes past and present in the account of Maria's life in the way the material culled from the archive or from earlier films provides a kind of running commentary on her present-day reflections. As one might have expected, Maria locates the roots of many of the problems in her life in her early childhood. Growing up in a family where patri-archal values still held sway, she felt relatively unloved as a child. Watching the film footage of herself aged seven or eight is therefore an intensely painful experience. In Maria's words: 'Those shots from my first three school years: they're so painful. I can't look at them. I look into that little person's eyes. [Pause] That little child was so bloody lonely, the whole time.'

As well as casting back to these early formative years, growing up in a family with a less than supportive father, Maria is eager to reflect on how she might have inherited or absorbed other family traits. Interviewed as a 28-year-old (for *Pizza*), she had already begun to recognise that her life was following a similar pattern to that of her mother and grandmother: 'I've followed in Granny's and Mum's footsteps. I've lived at home, had children at home, and then married – and been a single mum, just like them.'

Being able to trace the lines of continuity in successive generations appears in one respect to provide Maria with a certain solace. It demonstrates to her that: 'Women are able to live their lives independent of men'. In other ways, however, there is clear evidence that some of the early traumas are still weighing heavily upon her and proving to be psychologically disruptive. In the course of the last interview (for *Everyone's Fine*), for instance, it soon becomes clear that within the last ten years she has developed a serious gambling habit, as well having become addicted to alcohol and drugs.[49] Maria's difficulties have already impacted on how she has been able to care for her own daughter, with the consequence that Kim (now eighteen) is now beginning to feel the same sense of abandonment as Maria herself had experienced as a child.

In spite of all these vicissitudes, Maria has remained – at least in her role as a long doc subject – very clear sighted about her failings and her vulnerability. Moreover, she has – just like Neil in the *Up* films – also revealed a remarkable capacity to withstand adversity. In *Everyone's Fine* she appears to have achieved a measure of stability. She is now living in a new partnership and has a rewarding job as a teacher of immigrant children. Having experienced so many ups and downs in her life, and with her proven ability for thoughtful contemplation, Maria has acquired a pivotal role in the Jordbrö series. Towards the end of the sequence devoted to her in *Everyone's Fine*, there is a very revealing moment when she reflects not only on where she has got to in her life but also on what it has meant to be a long doc subject for all these years. Glancing at some old photos of herself, she voices the following thoughts:

> What I'm trying to learn is how to live with the person that's me – though I don't really want to be the person that's me. But I've got to understand that I'm me. I can't be anyone else, nor will I become anyone else.

Time for reflection

What Maria and other subjects have learned in the course of many years' involvement in a long doc project is that it provides them with the kind of opportunity for self-reflection that ordinarily might not have come their way. Hartleb himself is convinced that the longer his subjects were attached to the project, the more prepared most of them were to talk about areas of their lives about which, earlier, they may have wished to remain silent. Speaking of *Everyone's Fine*, for instance, and comparing it with its predecessor *A Pizza in Jordbrö*, Hartleb observes:

> The new film has more life experience, it's more serious. It has its moments of light and dark, of pain and sorrow. It's deeper, more existential if you will. There's the added dimension that ten more years have given. And the underlying question is always:'How have I become the person I am?' (Weman, 2006: 5)

While long docs may have started out as an attempt to chronicle the experiences of a particular generation, many of them have indeed – in the course of their development – transmogrified into works in which individuals seek to express, often in a disarmingly honest way, how they have become the person they are (or think they are). In the case of Maria, the search for self-identity is, as we have seen, a poignant and often painful process. Likewise with other Jordbrö subjects, being asked to review the filmic evidence of how they were at an earlier stage of their lives can frequently open old wounds. Ulric, for instance, who once seemed to be in serious danger of going off the rails, admits – just as Maria had done – that watching some of these early films is a 'scary' experience. Having gone through all manner of difficulties in his childhood and teenage years, Ulric now appears to have got his life back on track again, has got a job working in a drugs prevention unit and seems reasonably content with life. Likewise Roger, now a sports teacher in a local school, admits that seeing himself in the early Jordbrö films evokes quite sad memories, since it reminds him that his parents spent so little time with him as a child. This has, however, strengthened his resolve to achieve a better balance between life and work in his own life.

> *Time present and time past*
> *Are both perhaps present in time future,*
> *And time future contained in time past*
> T. S. Eliot: Burnt Norton

One of the central concerns of many long docs is with the role that time plays in all human affairs. Long docs encourage their viewers to speculate on the speed with which time passes and to consider how human beings spend time reflecting back on the past and peering into the future. By their very nature, long docs are concerned with tracing longer-term developments. For this reason they are particularly adept at pointing up the continuities and discontinuities of life. One of the pleasures of watching a long doc, therefore, is being able to ponder the intricate relationship between past and present events – and then, in the light of such an assessment, to reflect on possible future developments. It follows from this that all long docs – whether explicitly or implicitly – will be inviting viewers to contemplate the rapidity with which life journeys are completed. There is, in other words, a strong element of *memento mori* in these works.

Of all the filmmakers in this study, Hartleb is the one who has dwelt most consistently on time and the toll that it takes.[50] Given his desire to encourage us to believe that there is some measure of equilibrium between light and shade in human existence, Hartleb has gone to some lengths to introduce distinctly positive threads into the overall narrative weave. Especially noticeable, for instance, is his attempt to trace lines of continuity in subjects' lives and to emphasise the links that bind the generations. In *Everyone's Fine* Hartleb explores these inter-generational relationships by frequently juxtaposing shots of the subject as a child in the family environment with ones in which subjects have become parents themselves. There are, for instance, several family-gathering sequences in the film – especially those centred on the families of Petra and Thérèse – where three generations of a family are brought together in seeming harmony one with the other.[51]

Contriving an exit

The overall mood and tone of *Everyone's Fine* is one that is relatively optimistic and upbeat, in keeping with the film's title. In the case of Karina, for instance, we had already learned in *Pizza* that she was eager to start studying again and wanted to become an archeologist ('Digging in the past has always interested me.') Now in *Every-one's Fine* she is well on the way to accomplishing some of her goals. Sitting together with her mother, the two of them discuss the changing role of women in society and the newfound freedom and independence that women have discovered.

Above all, it is the solace provided by life's quieter moments that Hartleb frequently evokes in the later Jordbrö films. It is therefore wholly fitting that, at the very end of *Everyone's Fine*, he should return to the theme of continuity and rebirth. In the final sequence of the film, Slobodan is seen cradling his newborn infant and we hear him expressing his feelings of wonder at the miracle of new life. ('Such emotion, so much joy. We've really longed for this time when we have children … I don't know what words to use.') Not only has Hartleb contrived a very appropriate moment to take his leave of Jordbrö, he has also found an aptly symbolic image to reassure us that, despite the many trials and tribulations subjects have gone through, all may yet be well.

As it is the final film in the series, one of Hartleb's other aims is to provide viewers with some reassurance as to how far subjects have advanced on their respective life-journeys. Just as Apted pays particular attention to the various leave-taking moments at the end of individual chapters of the *Up* films, so Hartleb in his final Jordbrö film is at some pains to underline that most of his subjects have succeeded in weathering most of life's storms and that we can therefore take our leave of them with a reasonable degree of certainty that All Will Be Well. Above all, *Everyone's Fine* leaves us with a sense – absent in some other long docs – that most subjects have been quite content to have been involved in the Jordbrö project itself. Anneli, for instance, a woman who has had to cope with many challenges in her life, including caring for an autistic child, goes as far as to suggest that her participation in the project has assisted her in her quest to gain greater self-knowledge. In her own words: 'I can't live my life again, but it feels good going through all that [the Jordbrö films] and finding a few answers. Yet I still don't really know who I am.'

A message for the audience?

One of Hartleb's clear intentions throughout the Jordbrö series of films has not only been to get his subjects to critically reflect on their lives but also to encourage similar reflectiveness in the audience.

Hartleb is the kind of filmmaker who always wants to give his audience time to reflect on the import of what he is presenting. Accordingly, shots that portray subjects in reflective pose or silent mode are sometimes held for a considerable length of time, inviting viewers to share in a subject's pensiveness. Quite frequently, at the end of such sequences, Hartleb will stimulate further reflections by some gentle musical underscoring (primarily extracts from Beethoven's 'Moonlight Sonata' or from Chopin's piano works, especially the nocturnes). Though the music will, inevitably, influence the audience's response to what is being depicted, one never gets the sense that Hartleb is attempting to pre-empt the viewer's response. Whilst he is well aware, like any filmmaker, that he is nudging audiences towards a certain interpretation by the way he organises and presents material, his concern is, wherever possible, to allow his subjects to present their stories on their own terms.

As to what he thinks the Jordbrö films communicate, Hartleb wisely refrains from making any specific claims. In response to the question I put to him during our interview – 'Well Rainer, what do you think these films have to tell us?' – he neatly sidestepped the question by saying, 'But that's something that everybody decides for themselves!' (Hartleb, 2007). He did, however, go on to suggest that he thought that there was something very powerful and even 'magical' about the concept of more or less accidentally alighting on a group of primary school subjects and of tracking their lives in such a way as to maintain the illusion that they are for ever conjoined. The real power of a work like *The Children of Jordbrö*, however, lies in its capacity to elicit from its audience various forms of speculation on what is sometimes called the human condition. As Hartleb himself once observed: 'If there's any message in these films, it is that each moment is irretrievable' (Borchert, 1995). It is never by any direct authorial address that the audience's readiness to contemplate such deeper issues is prompted, but always by the utterances and reflections of the subjects themselves. Sometimes it is almost as if – as a result of their many years of involvement in the long doc enterprise – subjects begin to develop an uncanny sense of what will be of greatest interest to that wider audience of viewers. Early on in *Everyone's Fine*, for instance, Thérèse begins to compare her present self with the person she remembers herself to have been. She concludes:

> You're the same person deep down, but maybe you get a little wiser, a

little more relaxed perhaps. You're pretty much the same person really. [Just] a few more wrinkles.

Notes

1   It is also doubtless the case that, as filmmakers approach the end of their projects, they can afford to be a little more honest about problems they may have had with funding agencies, since they are no longer dependent on them for future support!

2   It is often the case, when long doc filmmakers discourse about their work, that they employ the image of the 'journey', not only to describe the life-journeys of the subjects themselves but also to refer to the ground covered by the project itself.

3   The films are fragmentary in a twofold sense: there are severe limitations on the amount of material that even the most tenacious filmmaker can collect, and the editing process results in a highly telescoped view of these lives. Elsewhere Winfried Junge has referred to his films as representing 'moves towards capturing what we were seeking to chronicle' (Junge, 2004: 180).

4   With soap opera, the decision to close down a show will almost always be made on commercial grounds. Soaps are especially vulnerable to termination if they do not build up a sufficient head of steam in the first year following their launch.

5   In the early years of the *Seven Up* series, after Michael Apted's move to the United States, Granada Television briefly considered switching directors for the series. Likewise Winfried Junge occasionally (but with no real conviction) spoke of the possibility of someone else taking over responsibility for *The Children of Golzow*.

6   It may not be entirely coincidental that Apted chose to undertake such a retrospective review in the *Seven Up* film made on the threshold of the new millennium. One of the original aims of the first *World in Action* film, it will be remembered, was to discover 'what kind of England we could look forward to in the year 2000'.

7   Only very occasionally has Apted strayed outside these limits and then only under the most compelling circumstances, such as when he decided to film Bruce's wedding.

8   Subjects are not always as co-operative as Apted would wish when it comes to doing the out-and-about filming. Suzy, for instance, who has always harboured certain misgivings about her involvement, has been reluctant to be filmed anywhere other than in her immediate home environment.

9   Part of Tony's story in *49 Up* was filmed in his holiday home in Spain where he and members of his family now spend a part of each year. Apted provides some telling commentary on developments in British

society by juxtaposing images of Tony and family in their Spanish villa with scenes from yesteryear depicting the East End milieu in which he was raised.

10 In the case of Bruce, there is an added motivation for including footage of him teaching in a school in Bangladesh since he has, from early on his life, always maintained he wanted to become involved in socially useful types of work.

11 Winfried Junge has suggested that some of the happiest memories he has of working on the *Children of Golzow* project were those occasions when, after many hours of work in the editing suite, he found a good solution to a particularly knotty editing problem.

12 The track is now in a dilapidated and deserted state, and thus offers an implicit commentary on the way in which the old East End has been transformed.

13 *35 Up* (initially screened on two separate evenings on the ITV channel) has a running time of just under two hours, whilst *42 Up* and *49 Up* each run to just over two hours.

14 The most memorable example of this comes in *The Children of Golzow* where, in a scene full of dramatic intensity, Jochen makes it clear beyond the shadow of a doubt that this is to be his last appearance.

15 Apted observes that the loss of Symon was a bitter blow to him, since he was, in Apted's phrase 'my sole ethnic representative'. So desperate was Apted to get Symon to agree to be interviewed that he even sent one of his other subjects (Tony) round to his house to try to persuade him – but to no avail (Apted, 1998).

16 Peter's case not only raises issues about standards of reporting in certain sections of the tabloid press; it also throws up questions relating to the responsibilities that documentary filmmakers have towards their subjects. Peter appears to harbour no feeling of resentment towards Apted; indeed the two of them have remained in contact since Peter's departure from the programme. It still leaves open, however, the question of the degree to which a filmmaker may need, on occasions, to anticipate the likely results of this particular form of media exposure.

17 There is a similar *quid pro quo* arrangement in *49 Up*, though this time John makes explicit reference to it and also talks more generally about what appearing in the programme has meant to him.

18 Relations between Apted and John have reached the point where, even when he does agree to appear, he will only do so if the series' producer Claire Lewis conducts the interview.

19 The fact that the *Up* films have enjoyed such national and international success has meant that *Seven Up* subjects have had to cope with some of the less desirable consequences of being in the public eye (especially in the period immediately prior to and following a new *Up* film). Apted and his team attempt to preserve subjects' anonymity as best they can by helping them to escape from the attention of story-hungry journalists.

20 *Seven Up* producer Claire Lewis has revealed that this is far from being a spontaneous outburst on Jackie's part. She had intimated to Lewis during the preparations for filming *49 Up* that she would, at an appropriate juncture, raise these points in the course of her interview with Apted (see Bruzzi, 2007: 108–14).

21 As one critic has remarked: 'With the collapse of the GDR and the winding down of DEFA, a significant tradition in German documentary film came to an end' (Zimmermann, 1995: 9).

22 Winfried Junge has provided a highly detailed account of this period of his career in the extended interview included in the book *Lebensläufe*, 2004: 88–90; 102–26.

23 Once again one has to note the difference between Michael Apted's and the Junges' attitude to the chronicling of contemporary events. Apted largely excludes such references, whereas the Junges are always wanting to remind viewers that life histories are being played out against, and being impacted by, such events.

24 One does well to remember in this regard, however, that producing documentaries in the West also presents its own challenges. As Barbara Junge once quipped: 'The market-place has become the new censoring authority' (Junge, 2008: 14).

25 Junge has described *Screenplay* as: 'An extended dialogue in which the filmmakers have become involved with the protagonists, with the public and with themselves about the past, present and future' (Junge, 2004: 237).

26 Seeing Junge in person for the first time in *Screenplay* also makes viewers aware of the age gap between him and his subjects. When the *Wende* came, the subjects were in their mid-thirties and Junge was already in his mid-fifties. Whilst the thought of having to relaunch his filmmaking career at this stage of his life filled him with a certain trepidation, he was optimistic that the Golzower themselves were still young enough to rebuild their lives. Or as he put it once: 'they are young enough to consider the demise of their country not as something akin to the final closing-down of a business, but more as a piece of interim stock-taking' (Junge, 2004: 115).

27 German would favour the use of the term *Abrechnung* in this context. The word conveys the sense of 'coming to terms with' past events as well as critically re-evaluating them.

28 Junge describes his sometimes difficult relationship with the 'rebellious' Herr Hübner at much greater length in the volume *Lebensläufe* (2004): 115–21.

29 Among other things, *Screenplay* provides a history of how the Golzow project originated and a detailed account of the many obstacles the team had to overcome during the making of the films.

30 Insofar as the viewer is being invited to take up a critically reflective stance vis-à-vis how material is integrated into a filmic narrative,

Screenplay puts one in mind of some of Brecht's pronouncements on the *Verfremdungseffekt* (distanciation effect) and the need to get an audience to reflect critically on the means of representation.

31 As state employees Junge and his team were especially aware of the significance accorded to state anniversaries. As early as 1966, for instance, they declared their intention to bring the Golzow project to a conclusion in 1979 to coincide with the thirtieth anniversary of the GDR.

32 After the demise of the GDR many Party members were frequently dismissed from their jobs or else experienced other forms of professional discrimination.

33 There are, for instance, some parallels between the reasons that Ilona gives for no longer wishing to be a part of the project and those given by some of Apted's subjects for their wish to withdraw.

34 Apted has opted to make only the briefest mention of Charles in the two most recent *Up* films.

35 The makers of the three-part television documentary *The Lost World of Communism* (BBC, 2009) include an extensive interview with Winfried Jerchel in which he reflects back on his GDR days. The programme also includes excerpts from the Golzow films in which Winfried appears.

36 At this point seasoned viewers of the Golzow films may well remember the occasion back in the 1970s when Winfried discoursed at some length about the dehumanising impact of unemployment in the West.

37 There was even great uncertainty at the very beginning of the project (August 1961) when Junge and his team confronted a whole series of logistical problems following the building of the Berlin Wall.

38 In a sequence that they could only include in their first post-*Wende* film (*Screenplay*) Winfried itemises a whole series of logistical, technical and economic problems that persuaded the filmmakers that now might be the right time to draw a line under the whole project.

39 Michael Apted makes a similar point when he seeks to explain that the international success of the *Seven Up* series. In his own words: 'I realised, after twenty years on the project, that what I had seen as a significant statement about the English class system was in fact a humanistic document about the real issues of life – about growing up; about coming to terms with failure, success, disappointment; about issues of family and all the things that everybody can relate to' (Apted, 1998).

40 In insisting on a last appearance of a number of these minor characters before the curtain comes down, the filmmakers run the slight risk of lessening the dramatic impact that this final film might otherwise have (see Schenk, 2006).

41 There is a particular irony in the fact that a documentary, one of whose original purposes was to record how a new generation of GDR citizens was going to contribute to the building of a truly socialist society, should, in the longer term, become a work that chronicled the decline and fall of that same society.

42 In addition to the documentary work of filmmakers such as Volker Koepp, Andreas Voigt and Helke Misselwitz (and of course that of the Junges themselves, there have also been highly acclaimed fiction films such as *Good Bye Lenin* (Wolfgang Becker, 2003), and the already mentioned *The Lives of Others* (Florian Henckel von Donnersmarck, 2005).

43 The filmmaker remembers, for instance, that Ulric had had specific suggestions to make concerning 'useable' recorded material from his childhood. Hartleb felt that, once he had acceded to Ulric's request, he was duty bound to do the same for other subjects (Hartleb, 2007).

44 Insofar as the exercise of having to revisit material from an ever-expanding archive represents an attempt to retrieve significant fragments of material, it might be claimed that there are certain parallels between the work of the long doc filmmaker and that of the archeologist.

45 This scene, evoking as it does largely positive associations, is bound to carry particular resonance for the long-term Jordbrö viewer insofar as it will be likely to trigger other memories where Uffe's life had been full of torment and uncertainty.

46 The words of the song are: 'Last night I had the strangest dream / I ever dreamed before. / I dreamed the world had all agreed to put an end to war. / I dreamed there was a mighty room / And the room was filled with men. / And the paper they were signing said: They'd never fight again. / There are not any soldiers now / And cannons are no more. / And no one knows of all those words / Like soldiers, guns or war. / And people on the streets below / Were dancing 'round and 'round / With swords and guns and uniforms / All scattered on the ground.'

47 The greater the time span, the greater the likelihood that individuals will have experienced some life-changing event, and also, if a filmmaker has developed an especially good relationship with his subjects over the years, that they will be prepared to talk about aspects of their lives about which they have hitherto kept their counsel.

48 Maria sometimes uses very striking images when expressing herself, such as in *Pizza* when she suddenly comes up with the following thought: 'I'm always looking for a hole in time – so that time will stand still. Once I succeeded.'

49 Attempting to understand where the self-destructive behaviour may have originated, Maria points the finger of blame at her biological father who, she has discovered, was also an alcoholic and drug abuser.

50 Hartleb once remarked : 'Time has been my dramaturgical guide in these films' (cited in Borchert, 1995).

51 These scenes are counterbalanced, however, by a number of cases where subjects' lives have been marred by inter-generational conflict or where children have developed a marked disrespect for the attitudes or values of their parents.

Concluding remarks

On several occasions in the course of this study I have had occasion to mention the generally high esteem in which long doc works are held by their respective audiences. Barbara and Winfried Junge in their comprehensive survey of the *Children of Golzow* project (Junge, 2004), provide one of the more detailed accounts of the reception of a long doc by reproducing a number of letters and emails sent in by viewers and a cross-section of critical reviews extracted from newspapers and magazines. These materials not only provide evidence of the generally enthusiastic response to projects of this type, they also throw light on the significance attributed to individual films when they were first released and the controversies to which they sometimes gave rise.[1] In the case of viewers' letters and emails one is struck by the frequency with which respondents apply the same frames of reference to a long doc as they as they do in their responses to soap opera. Not only are they intensely moved by what befalls individual subjects; they are also full of pleasurable anticipation of what the next chapter in the unfolding saga will bring (Junge, 2004: 259, 274, 308).

Likewise with *Seven Up*, most observers are also agreed that much of the series' enduring appeal lies in the way it succeeds in combining the attributes of a compelling social history and the more homespun qualities of a soap-like drama of everyday life. As Jonathan Freedland has written of *49 Up*:

> [The film] is a full, revealing social history. And yet that is not the source of its power. That, and its intense poignancy, comes instead from the universal human story these lives tell. To see people ageing

before our eyes, transforming from children into adolescents into adults into parents and now grandparents, is to witness the narrative of human life itself ... there is quiet, affecting beauty to all this. (Freedland, 2005a)

Learning from long docs

Long docs, as objects of study and investigation, also teach us a good deal about documentary representation in a wider sense. They provide opportunities, for instance, for a sustained engagement with a number of key issues and concerns, such as the propriety of exposing a number of individual subjects to such unremitting scrutiny over such long periods of time. Other frequently debated topics include, first, the precise nature of the insights provided by this particular form of 'incremental' documentary representation, and second, the extent to which the limitations of documentary are themselves exposed as long doc filmmakers battle to marshal ever-expanding amounts of material within the compass of a single film.[2]

As we have discovered at several points in the course of this study, long doc producers themselves have sometimes felt impelled to step back from their work to reflect critically on their filmmaking practices. It is almost as if, sooner or later, the professionally driven requirement to get their subjects to indulge in various types of retrospection eventually motivates them (the filmmakers) to engage in a similar kind of accounting exercise.[3] Most filmmakers are happy to concede that in the course of working on these projects they have learned some hard lessons from mistakes or miscalculations they had made in earlier films and that they are grateful that each new film has brought the opportunity to introduce certain course corrections.

All of the long doc filmmakers I interviewed for this project were agreed that perhaps the biggest challenge they had faced was building the kind of relationship with their subjects that resulted in their no longer feeling quite as threatened or intimidated by the filming process as they might have done. Just as in other forms of documentary work, this relationship-building involves keeping in close touch with participants at times when filming is not taking place and generally showing an interest in them as individuals rather than (or as well as) subjects of investigation. Nevertheless, there is often, as we have seen, a somewhat cat-and-mouse aspect to such relations between subject and filmmaker. Most filmmakers agree, when pressed, that they have had to devise particular strategies for getting subjects to articulate thoughts and feelings on camera. As Michael Apted has observed: 'I've learned how to press people's buttons ... You kind of know how to wind them up' (Apted, 1998).

The enduring appeal of long docs

In spite of some obvious differences between the long docs covered in this study, there are sufficient common features to enable one to make a couple of final points about the enduring appeal of such works for successive generations of viewers. Part of their appeal relates undoubtedly to a property that seems to be deeply rooted in the generic substance and growth potential of these works. As long docs develop, so each of them seems to veer away from an earlier preoccupation with society-oriented issues such as the formative influence of particular social environments and becomes, instead, far more concerned with tracking the twists and turns of individual lives. All this has implications for the pleasures and gratifications that audiences derive from long doc viewing. As is clearly evidenced by viewer responses, audiences seem to be able to develop similar bonds of identificatory attachment to long doc subjects as they do to characters in soaps. On closer examination, however, the empathic bond in soaps is of a different qualitative order from that of long docs. In the latter, viewers' response is always liable to be determined by the knowledge that these films are not wholly fictional constructs but are engaging with real lives. Accordingly, it might be claimed that long docs have greater potential for stimulating self-reflectiveness on the part of the audience than their fictional counterparts.

When all is said and done, however, the essence of long docs appeal may boil down to one particular element: their proven ability to communicate, possibly more poignantly than may other forms of film and programme making, the reality of life's ebb and flow. Bringing as they do constant reminders of the transitoriness of life, long docs will inevitably, at times, strike a distinctly melancholy, if not mournful, tone. This note of melancholy is clearly discernible in Rainer Hartleb's work, though in it viewers are made equally aware that the Jordbrö films are also giving expression to a philosophy of life in which the inevitability of decline is made the more bearable by accompanying reminders about the forces of renewal. Hartleb is clearly concerned that his films should bear testimony to this idea of counterbalancing forces in human life, but there are certain moments within the films where this idea of balance is expressed in especially eloquent terms by one of the subjects themselves. The following lines from *Everyone's Fine*, for instance, are spoken by Krisoula, the woman who spent her early years in Sweden before returning to her native Greece where she has married and is now raising a family. Caught in contemplative mood and filmed against the background of the sea, Krisoula reflects back on the previous three decades of her life. She pauses and – as if conscious of the duties imposed upon her as a long doc subject – comes out with the following thoughts:

> There we have it, Rainer. The years go by, never to return. Life flows on – and away. Yet all has gone well. I'm very content, I can't claim that I'm not, or I haven't been, very content.

Notes

1   Now that *The Children of Golzow* has finally been brought to a conclusion, it is rapidly acquiring the status of a work that provides some unique insights into the realities of East German lives. The suggestion is that, for one-time citizens of the GDR, these films bring powerful reminders – or even represent a collective memory – of how things once were (see also Molloy, 2009, especially pp. 303–6).
2   The Junges have always been aware that, in spite of the epic claims made for the larger Golzow enterprise, there is much about these films that remains fragmentary and therefore the audience will be constantly called upon to speculate and conjecture. There is also a sense in which, given the particular formal constraints of the documentary form and the limited access we are allowed to the worlds they inhabit, the subjects themselves – after we have spent many film hours in their presence – remain relatively distant and in some cases even enigmatic.
3   This will either be in the course of press or broadcast interviews or sometimes – as was the case of the Junges' *Screenplay: The Times* – in the text itself.

Bibliography

Allan, Seán, and Sandford, John (eds) (1999). *DEFA: East German Cinema, 1946–1992*, New York and Oxford: Berghahn Books.

Allen, Robert C. (1985). *Speaking of Soap Operas*, Chapel Hill and London: The University of North Carolina Press.

Apted, Michael (1998). Audio commentary by Apted on the DVD recording of *42 Up* [Disc 5 of the five-disc 'Collectors Edition' of 'The *Up* Series' produced by First Run Features].

Apted, Michael (2005). Interview with the author, 19 October (Sheffield).

Apted, Michael (2006). Interview with Elvis Mitchell. Radio programme: 'The Treatment' (KCRW), 15 November.

Apted, Michael (2007). Interview with the author, 14 March (Glasgow).

Blythe, Ronald (1969). *Akenfield: Portrait of an English Village*, London: The Penguin Press.

Borchert, Thomas (1995). 'Mein Dramaturg ist die Zeit', *Süddeutsche Zeitung*, 27 May

Borchert, Thomas (2006). 'Die Kamera als Zeitmaschine', *Stuttgarter Zeitung*, 23 September: 4.

Branigan, Edward (1992). *Narrative Comprehension and Film*, London: Routledge.

Brooks, Richard (1998). 'Seven ups and downs', *The Observer* [The Observer Review Section], 12 July: 2.

Bruzzi, Stella (2007). *Seven Up* (published in the series 'BFI TV Classics'), London: British Film Institute.

Corner, John (2009) (forthcoming). '*49 Up*: Television, "life-time" and the mediated self', in Michael Kackman et al. (eds) *Flow TV: Television in the Age of Media Convergence*, London and New York: Routledge.

Creeber, Glen (2004). *Serial Television: Big Drama on the Small Screen*, London: British Film Institute.

Cuevas, Efrén, and García, Alberto (eds) (2007). *Landscapes of the Self: The*

Cinema of Ross McElwee, Madrid: Ediciones Internacionales Universitarias.

Dovey, Jon (2000). *Freakshow: First Person Media and Factual Television*, London: Pluto Press.

Finch, John (ed.) (2003). *Granada Television: The first generation*, Manchester: Manchester University Press.

Freedland, Jonathan (2005a). 'A poignant, human drama in the era of Celebrity Shark Bait', *Guardian*, 14 September: www.guardian.co.uk/media/2005/sep/14/britishidentityandsociety.comment.

Freedland, Jonathan (2005b). 'Interview with Michael Apted' [Interviewed at the National Film Theatre, London, on 17 December 2005: www.bfi.org.uk/features/interviews/apted.html.

Geraghty, Christine (1991). *Women and Soap Opera: A Study of Prime Time Soaps*, Cambridge: Polity Press.

Goddard, Peter, Corner, John, and Richardson, Kay (2007). *Public Issue Television: World in Action, 1963–98*, Manchester: Manchester University Press.

Grele, Ronald J. (1998). 'Movement without aim: methodological and theoretical problems in oral history', in Perks and Thomson: 38–52.

Hesse, Wolfgang (1974). Erkundungen im Alltäglichen , *Film und Fernsehen*, vol. 6: 15–22.

Hartleb, Rainer (2007). Interview with the author, 26 March (Stockholm).

Hill, Annette (2007). *Restyling Factual TV: Audiences and News, Documentary and Reality Genres*, London: Routledge.

Holland, Patricia (1997). *The Television Handbook*, London and New York: Routledge.

Jeffries, Stuart (2006). 'Get real', *Guardian* (part 2), 6 July: 18.

Jones, Ian (2000). 'If I could change the world, I'd change it into a diamond'. Extended review of the *Up* series: at www.offthetellz.co.uk/page_id=1012.

Jordan, Günter, and Schenk, Ralf (eds) (1996). *Schwarzweiß und Farbe: DEFA-Dokumentarfilme 1946–92*, Potsdam and Berlin: Filmmuseum Potsdam and Jovis Verlag.

Junge, Barbara and Winfried (2004). *Lebensläufe: Die Kinder von Golzow: Bilder / Dokumente / Erinnerungen*, Marburg: Schüren Verlag.

Junge, Barbara and Winfried (2006). Interview with the author, 4 October (Berlin).

Junge, Barbara and Winfried (2008). Interview on 'The Golzow Saga', published by Progress Film as part of a press pack to coincide with the screening of the final two parts of *And If They Haven't Passed Away, They'll Still Be Alive Today* at www.progress-film.de/de/filmarchiv/film.php?id=662.

Junge, Winfried (1962). Papier und Realität , *Deutsche Filmkunst*, vol. 11: 431–41.

Kersten, Heinz (2006). 'Eine unendliche Geschichte?' *Neues Deutschland (ND)*, [Feuilleton], 11–12 February.

Kilborn, Richard (1992). *Television Soaps*, London: Batsford.

Kilborn, Richard, and Izod, John (1997). *An Introduction to Television Documentary: Confronting Reality*, Manchester: Manchester University Press.

Kilborn, Richard (1999). 'Jürgen Böttcher: A Retrospective', in Allan and Sandford: 267–82.

Kilborn, Richard (2003). *Staging the Real: Factual TV Programming in the Age of Big Brother*, Manchester: Manchester University Press.

Lemke, Grit (2006). Interview with Barbara and Winfried Junge. *Tageszeitung Junge Welt* [Weekend supplement], 11 February: 1.

Lewis, Oscar (1961). *The Children of Sánchez: Autobiography of a Mexican Family*, New York: Vintage Books.

Loizos, Peter (1993). *Innovation in Ethnographic Film: From Innocence to Self-Consciousness, 1955–85,* Manchester: Manchester University Press.

Löllhöffel, Helmut (1982). 'Ungeschminkte Selbstbildnis der DDR. "Lebensläufe" – eine Filmdokumentation über die Jugend eines Dorfes im Oderbruch', *Süddeutsche Zeitung*, 22 January.

Molloy, Peter (2009). *The Lost World of Communism: An Oral History of Daily Life Behind the Iron Curtain*, London: BBC Books.

Moran, Joe (2002). 'Childhood, Class and Memory in the *Seven Up* films', *Screen*, vol. 43, no. 4, Winter: 387–402.

Moreno, Juan (2000). 'Die letzte Klappe für Golzow', *Süddeutsche Zeitung*, 10 October.

Nichols, Bill (1991). *Representing Reality: Issues and Concepts in Documentary,* Bloomington: Indiana University Press.

Nguyen, Angelika (1997). 'Niemand weiss, was aus einem Kinde wird: "Was geht euch mein Leben an. Elke – Kind von Golzow"; "Da habt ihr mein Leben. Marieluise – Kind von Golzow" von Barbara und Winfried Junge', *Film und Fernsehen*, vol. 25, nos. 3–4: 78–81.

Perks, Robert, and Thomson, Alistair (1998). *The oral history reader.* London and New York, Routledge.

Portelli, Alessandro (1997). *The Battle of Valle Giulia: Oral History and the Art of Dialogue*, Madison: The University of Wisconsin Press.

Richter, Erika (1994). 'Persönliches und Zeitgeschichte', *Film und Fernsehen*, vol. 23: 18–21.

Richter, Erika (1996). Interview with Barbara and Winfried Junge reproduced in programme notes that accompanied screening of *The Story of Uncle Willy from Golzow* at the Berlin film festival in 1996.

Richter Rolf (1982). '*Lebensläufe* – Ein Film von Winfried Junge und Hans-Eberhard Leupold', *Weimarer Beiträge*, vol. 9: 57–60.

Rosenthal, Alan (2002). *Writing, Directing, and Producing Documentary Films and Videos*, 3rd edn, Carbondale and Edwardsville: Southern Illinois University Press.

Roth, Wilhelm (1981). 'Mit leisen Mitteln radikale Filme machen', *Spandauer Volksblatt*, 3 December: 31,

Rother, Hans-Jörg (2006). 'Deutsche Lebenswege', *Frankfurter Allgemeine Zeitung*, 13 February.

Schenk, Ralf (2006). 'Zum vorletzten Mal nach Golzow', *Berliner Zeitung* [issue 72]: 25–26 March.

Silbermann, Marc (1994). 'Post-Wall Documentaries: New Images from a New Germany?' *Cinema Journal*, 33.2 (1994: Winter): 22–41.

Singer, Bennett (1998). *42 Up*, New York: The New Press.

Singer, Bennett (1999). *7 Up*, London: William Heinemann.

Smith, Julia, and Holland, Tony (1987). *EastEnders: The Inside Story…* , London: BBC Books.

Taylor, Craig (2006). *Return to Akenfield: Portrait of an English Village in the 21st Century*, London: Granta Publications.

Vulliamy, Ed (2008). 'Studs Terkel: broadcaster, author and master chronicler of everyday life in 20th-century America', *Guardian*, 3 November: 34–5.

Weman, Mats (2006). 'Farewell to Jordbrö', *Swedish Film* [Swedish Film Institute], vol. 9: 4–5.

Winston, Brian (2007). *The 50 Greatest Documentaries*, a three-hour television programme broadcast on the More 4 channel, 14 July.

Zimmermann, Peter (ed.) (1995). *Deutschlandbilder Ost: Dokumentarfilme der DEFA von der Nachkriegszeit bis zur Wiedervereinigung*, Konstanz: Universitätsverlag Konstanz (UVK-Medien/Ölschläger).

Index

A number preceded by the letter *n* in a page reference indicates the number of a note on that page. Readers are also reminded that the sets of notes that follow each chapter contain valuable information on the production and reception of the long docs under review.